The CHURCH of BASEBALL

The CHURCH of BASEBALL

THE MAKING OF *BULL DURHAM:*
Home Runs, Bad Calls, Crazy Fights,
Big Swings, and a Hit

Ron Shelton

ALFRED A. KNOPF
New York
2022

THIS IS A BORZOI BOOK
PUBLISHED BY ALFRED A. KNOPF

Copyright © 2022 by Ron Shelton

All rights reserved. Published in the United States by Alfred A. Knopf,
a division of Penguin Random House LLC, New York, and distributed
in Canada by Penguin Random House Canada Limited, Toronto.

www.aaknopf.com

Knopf, Borzoi Books, and the colophon are registered
trademarks of Penguin Random House LLC.

Library of Congress Cataloging-in-Publication Data
Names: Shelton, Ron, 1945– author.
Title: The church of baseball : the making of Bull Durham : home
runs, bad calls, crazy fights, big swings, and a hit / Ron Shelton.
Description: First edition. | New York : Alfred A. Knopf, 2022. |
Identifiers: LCCN 2021049945 | ISBN 9780593319772 (hardcover) |
ISBN 9780593313961 (trade paperback) | ISBN 9780593319789 (ebook)
Subjects: LCSH: Shelton, Ron, 1945– | Bull Durham (Motion picture) |
Motion pictures—Production and direction—United States—History—
20th century. | Baseball films—United States—History and criticism. |
Baseball in motion pictures. | Motion picture producers and directors—
United States—Biography. | Screenwriters—United States—Biography.
Classification: LCC PN1997.B7926 S54 2022 |
DDC 791.43/72—dc23/eng/20211110
LC record available at https://lccn.loc.gov/2021049945

Jacket design and illustration by Dave Plunkert

Manufactured in the United States of America
First Edition

For Rath and Peg

Contents

Part Three: Production

Part Four: Postproduction

Introduction

Not long ago, I was in Durham, North Carolina, to honor the thirtieth anniversary of the movie *Bull Durham*. As the writer and director of the film, I was to be trotted around the new ballpark that is now the home of the AAA Durham Bulls. Every night, I had a cocktail at the beautiful hotel bar—the Bull Durham Bar, in fact, named for the movie.

I was amazed to find that many locals credited the turnaround of the city to the opening of the movie in 1988. It's true that when I scouted Durham—even before I wrote the film script—it was boarded up and in trouble. Its longtime economic engine, Big Tobacco, had ended, and there seemed to be nothing to replace it. The desperate look and feel of this southern town, with its ancient, crumbling ballpark and shuttered businesses, suggested the perfect background in which to set a story in the minor leagues where young athletes' dreams similarly crumble and are boarded up. The entire region was ultimately reinvented when the tech boom of the nineties turned the Research Triangle Park (defined by the vertices of Raleigh, Durham, and Chapel Hill—each with a major university) into a kind of Silicon Valley of the South. Nonetheless, the movie seemed to get much of the credit, whether it deserved it or not.

Being on site reminded me of when I got on the plane to go back to Durham right before filming began, having nothing but doubts. Susan Sarandon was not a bankable commodity professionally at that moment, Tim Robbins was an unknown, and Kevin Costner had just burst onto the scene. The three of them had barely met, and while it seemed there was the possibility of chemistry among them, I had no proof; it was mostly an instinct.

It wasn't until rehearsals started in Durham that I began to feel that this could be a special group. Tim brought dignity to Nuke, Kevin kept the child alive in the fading Crash Davis, and Susan grounded Annie Savoy with a nonjudgmental generosity that transcended the character's eccentricities. As actors, they liked and respected one another, and that ultimately translated into the affection they had onscreen.

But then, after shooting began, the deflating pushback started from the studio, and suddenly I was fighting with the suits to defend what seemed to not need defending, namely the performances. I was fighting for what turned out to be one of the movie's strengths, and those fights drained my energy and took time away from focusing on the filmmaking itself. I'd learn in later movies that this is part of the drill—fighting the fights that shouldn't need fighting.

John Huston once said that directing a movie is like going to war. This may be an exaggeration, but it's sure as hell a contact sport. Why that is so—and why it's always been so—is a mystery to those in the trenches. Why do those writing the checks and the producers midwifing the project always throw obstacles in the way of the creative process? I suppose it's not that complicated—the engine that drives Hollywood is the ego. The financier is determined to prove he is not just about money but has a creative bent as well. Sometimes it's just politics as usual, or the star's girlfriend once dated the financier and it ended badly, or your agent hates my lawyer—the usual stew of cheap soap opera, except in the stew, money and careers and possibly good movies are at stake. Art patrons have always wanted to be heard—Pope Julius II surely told Michelangelo he thought Adam's thighs were a little meaty, and it's well recorded that Robert Evans drove Francis Ford Coppola mad as he tried to make *The Godfather*. The sublime irony is that sometimes the pope and Robert Evans are right, though mostly they're not. The Sistine Chapel and the Paramount movie came out pretty well. The director has to listen and accept and fight back—it's a curious behavioral contortion to have all your nerve endings open for discovery while you circle the wagons to defend your vision. Sometimes it helps to have an enemy; if none exists, it's sometimes the director's job to invent one. Bogeymen, real or imagined, are handy to rally the troops against. Long ago these enemies were dubbed "the suits" and have taken on mythic status as the antagonistic *other*. There are legendary directors who invent the *other* as part of their daily bread; the oxygen they breathe is the war they imagine they're involved in.

Some famous director said that directing is "fifty percent the cast and fifty percent the script," and while that's too reductive, it's also loaded with the truth. Even John Huston similarly confessed: "I remove myself from the rigors of directing by casting the movie properly." You can't overcome a casting mistake no matter how clever the editing or, as the joke goes, how high you crank the music, but I got lucky on *Bull Durham*—a perfect cast. Screen chemistry is a mysterious thing, undefinable and unable to be conjured by the most brilliant director or reinvented in the editing room. And while it can't be explained by film science, the simple truth underlying all great onscreen chemistry is this: two characters must occupy different emotional and physical spaces. Nuke couldn't be a younger version of Crash; they had to be different physically, politically, emotionally, and come from different backgrounds, even if none of that is revealed. They had to have different comfort zones as actors. Kevin and Tim are completely different people and in real life one can't imagine them competing over the same thing. In a movie, however, it's not hard to imagine them fighting over the same woman.

I say all this because, as happy as I am with the final movie, the making of *Bull Durham* was a troubled exercise—and of course we had our own *others*—but in retrospect, several movies later, it was a pretty normal series of fights, lies, clashing egos, and bloodshed, all leading toward a funny, life-embracing movie, due in large part to the incredible cast.

Making a good and successful movie is a minor miracle every time.

So why, all these years later, write a book about the making of this particular movie? I don't actually think about the movie much but there are regular requests for interviews, the occasional university film class to teach, a retrospective—that sort of thing—and now and then an article about the movie is published and there are inevitably errors. No, Harrison Ford was not offered the part of Crash, and Cher was not given the script to play Annie. Where does this stuff come from? Maybe I can set the record straight for anyone who cares, maybe I can share with young film directors the problems a first-time director will almost certainly encounter, or maybe I could just forget the whole thing and continue to concentrate on new work in front of me, which is what I care about most these days. I've frequently been asked to write about the movie and have always demurred, but then something happened that caused me to reconsider.

In Durham for that thirtieth-anniversary bash, I did a Q and A with the fans in the ballpark prior to game time, and a married couple raised their hands with more than a question. They said they had moved to Durham because of the movie and they wanted to meet me and take a photo with their two young sons. I was happy to oblige. As I posed with this family of four, I asked the names of the boys. "Tell the man," their mother counseled. The ten-year-old smiled and said, "I'm Crash." I looked at his younger brother and said, "I'm afraid to ask." The boy looked up and said, "Yep, I'm Nuke."

I guess that's why I'm writing this book.

Part One

Development

1

Forbidden Fruit

Bible stories were a big part of my growing up. The dramatic tales of Moses parting the Red Sea and coming down from the mountain and Jesus routing the money changers in the temple and the whole fantastic narrative still live loudly in my DNA. I took the required courses on the Old and New Testaments at the evangelical college I attended, perhaps the most rigorous classes I've ever taken, but by that time I was moving away from religious dogma and discovering that the universe of the secular (a pejorative word to Baptists) was infinitely more attractive. But the Bible stories still resonate.

The tree of the knowledge of good and evil was placed in the Garden of Eden by God as the one thing forbidden to Adam and Eve. Even as a child I felt like the game was rigged. We're taught that we are created human and therefore flawed, so of course we're going to eat the apple. Growing up in a family in which movies, drink, and cursing were forbidden, it was inevitable that I'd become a moviemaker who loves his cocktails and curses like a longshoreman. Clearly, it was preordained in the Book of Genesis. My parents broke the movie rule a couple of times (the rules of forbidden behavior were dictated by my father's job at an evangelical college rather than his own private beliefs). On one occasion, he and my mother packed my brother and me in the car and drove to the drive-in theater in Ventura to see *Winchester '73*, a Western about the invention of a rifle that changed the West. Directed by Anthony Mann and starring James Stewart, the movie has become something of a classic, though

I remember little as a five-year-old other than how cold it was in the car and that we were sneaking around on God by driving to another town to watch it. That was more exciting than the movie.

Another time in Whittier, where my mother's parents lived and the rules were looser (they were English and not evangelical), we went to see *Here Come the Nelsons,* an Ozzie and Harriet feature about a girdle salesman. When you see very few movies, the details remain vivid—the climactic scene has a dozen girdles tied together between two trees across a road and the crooks escaping in a car can't break through the girdles. I loved it.

The third movie I saw was in Taft, California, a tough oil town thirty-seven miles southwest of Bakersfield. It was my father's hometown, and my brother and I were staying with my grandparents when my grandmother took us to see a movie based on a best seller about a preacher, *A Man Called Peter.* This book was wildly popular in the evangelical world and had been read by everyone in every church I attended as a kid. This was also the only time my rock-ribbed Baptist grandmother had ever been in a movie theater, though we suspected later that year she went to see *Oklahoma!* (they were from West Texas, and Oklahoma was close enough) but was afraid to confess it. So, my brother and I sat in the theater watching this weeper (the preacher dies) and when it was over we all sat for the second feature because it was unthinkable to pay for two movies and not sit through both. On came *Ma and Pa Kettle in Waikiki.* The title sequence had hula girls and my grandmother was mortified that she'd ruined us; she covered our eyes and ushered us out of the theater into the searing Taft sun. At ten years old, I had glimpsed the tree of the knowledge of good and evil and the hula girls looked pretty good, even if viewed in grainy shots of a tourist luau, circa 1955.

The illicitness of the darkened theater and a deep-red curtain drawn to reveal larger-than-life images accompanied by an orchestral score was overpowering. Even if the images were Ozzie and Harriet stretching girdles across a road and the good Reverend Peter Marshall expiring too young.

—

We didn't get a television until I was twelve, and that family purchase was triggered not by the desire to see the shows everyone was talking about—*Superman* and *Perry Mason* and *Alfred Hitchcock Presents*, among others—but because of baseball. Eddie Mathews was the star third baseman of the Milwaukee Braves but, more important, he was our hometown hero from Santa Barbara—and the Braves were in the World Series. This is more than anecdotal history; it's the first great moral crisis I saw my parents confront. The Braves were down two games to one with the critical fourth game landing on a Sunday in Milwaukee, late morning on the West Coast. The first three games we listened to on the radio. To stay alive, the Braves had to win on Sunday, but we had to be at the First Baptist Church at the same time. After Sunday school, when we trudged upstairs in our scratchy wool slacks and clip-on ties to the weekly interminable eleven o'clock service, where the Reverend Gus Gableman, the least charismatic Baptist preacher in history, would drone on in a deathless monotone, something happened as startling as the events that overtook Saul of Tarsus on the road to Damascus. My father swept us boys up and rushed us to our big dented Buick station wagon. My mother, late in pregnancy with what would be her fourth son, watched us go silently, which meant she had signed off on this intervention—her will mattered and was respected by all of us. Something was afoot.

My father raced us home nervously, saying nothing. We understood the gravity of the moment but didn't yet know the stakes. We were being taken out of church, and God could strike at any moment. The Rapture might be upon us and we knew that meant all Christians would be lifted into the clouds and the pagans would be left behind, eternally damned. But given my father's sudden apostasy, would our Buick station wagon be lifted as well, or had we forfeited a life believing in Jesus for . . . we didn't even know what. What if, God forbid, my father and mother were lifted up into the sky to meet Jesus, and my two little brothers and I, because we hadn't yet been baptized and received Gus Gableman's *warm hand of fellowship,* crashed in the driverless Buick? Maybe I could climb into the front seat and manage to slow down the car before it hit a light pole and save us from a terrible death? Maybe I'd just be postponing the inevitable because the Rapture had passed us over? Maybe a forgiving God would put skipping church on this morning in the same category of sin as seeing *Winchester '73* at the Ventura drive-in or the girdle movie with my mom's parents, who weren't even Baptists? Surely God knew we had watched *A Man Called Peter* in Taft—that must be worth something—even if we saw the hula girls in the title sequence of the second feature. These were eschatological questions my father was wrestling with, and, as the oldest son, I empathized and sweated with him. Even if I didn't know the issues, I felt them. I felt him.

My father, still silent, led us straight into the house, where a man from Ott's department store (buy local, my parents taught) was just finishing installing a television set. Surely God would strike now. But he didn't—he strung us out—and when the TV was turned on and the black-and-white image came into focus, it was—we'd completely forgotten, given the spiritual crisis—the World Series. Game Four. The installer was a man we knew; he'd had a brief minor league career that hadn't worked out and now he was making do, and he understood the moment. He just said, "Eddie—I know," as he left. We watched the game in terror, aware that Eddie was having a terrible series. But after the team tied it in the bottom of the tenth, our hometown hero hit a towering two-run homer to win the game. A great weight lifted up out of the room, my father looked around, his shoulders lightened, and we started going to church less and less.

The seed for the Church of Baseball was planted.

•   •   •

In my California childhood I was able to play all sports year-round, like most kids, but it was baseball that most captured me. My father had played in college and my mother had gone to Jackie Robinson's high school in Pasadena a couple of years after the great player, so we were fans of Robinson and the Brooklyn Dodgers. My father's name, Rathburn, was vaguely referenced as having been inspired by some far-off, never-seen-nor-heard-of Texas relative; he went by Rath. Growing up in the redneck oilfields near Bakersfield, my father's hero was, somehow, Duke Ellington. When Rev. Gableman would regularly warn the congregation about the "passions of our flesh, carrying out the desires of the body and the mind," because we were all "children of wrath" (Ephesians 2:3), I thought he was talking about me and my younger brothers. It takes a while to sort these things out. My mother was an inspiring mix of inquisitive, tough-minded, nonjudgmental, and forever forgiving. Nonetheless, she never forgave Dodgers manager Leo Durocher for switching to the Giants. Rath and Peg were a formidable team.

Beyond baseball the TV provided all the classic Westerns of the period, which we faithfully followed: *Have Gun—Will Travel, The Rifleman, Maverick,* and *Gunsmoke.* The small-screen Westerns would in time lead to the big-screen ones, and I fell in love with all of them.

In high school, I started sneaking into movies with my buddy, often not knowing or caring what was playing. We liked the challenge of getting in for free. Without my identifying it, the illicitness of watching movies remained intact—we weren't supposed to be there. But the range of movies I was sneaking in to see was a helluva lot more compelling than what I'd been exposed to as a child. Suddenly I was seeing movies over a wide range of genres—*The Hustler, Dr. No, The Man Who Shot Liberty Valance.* I wasn't a snob about my moviegoing and was happy to see an Elvis Presley movie if Ann-Margret or Stella Stevens was in it, but movies like Robert Rossen's *The Hustler* stuck with me. Still does.

My college curriculum was built around how to be done with classes by 2 p.m. so I could head to basketball practice (in the fall) and baseball practice (in the spring). A brilliant English teacher turned me on to books, and fortunately I could fit a literature major into my sports schedule. Eighteenth-century English lit first got my attention and I became a Jonathan Swift junkie for a while, then Pope, then, when Albert Finney starred in *Tom Jones* just as I was reading Henry Fielding, it was becoming obvious to me that I was getting hooked on storytelling. My father, with his West Texas background, was a born storyteller. He could spin a two-hour tale about a five-minute trip to the grocery store to pick up a quart of milk. As we stood around the kitchen, his retelling of the simplest shopping errand would include a bit of a mystery about why the car wouldn't start, and a fellow he ran into in the parking lot whose brother had survived a plane crash, and the guy who restocked the dairy section whose son was a local football star, and the clerk at the checkout stand about whom an epic tale of immigration might emerge—or just a great joke—and then the seven-minute car ride home with the inevitable flat tire because we always drove on bald tires unless we could afford recaps. Sometimes he forgot the milk. Most of his stories were about playing in a jazz band with Ray Ellis in London during the war when they were nineteen. All of his tales were full of details, sometimes more details than could be absorbed. Names, places, images, sounds—he didn't spin short stories but great rambling novels.

The novels of the great British writers led me to the Americans—Fitzgerald and Hemingway and the gang. But the first writer I flipped for was Lewis Carroll. I consumed all his nonsense verse and read everything about his strange and tortured life. But, most important, I began writing reams of my own nonsense verse. When I walked around campus reciting Carroll's "Jabberwocky"—"'Twas brillig, and the slithy toves / Did gyre and gimble in the wabe"—people just stared. I tried it with my baseball buddies as well and they cautioned, "Don't say that in public. Makes you look nuts." Around this time it was becoming clear that I was living in two different worlds—the intellectual (or at least academic) world and the sports world—but it made no sense to me that they were distinct. They were dependent, connected, they fed off each other. At least I thought so.

The good English teachers at the college had assigned Albert Camus to make sure we weren't just spoon-fed the Christian apologists J. R. R. Tolkien and C. S. Lewis. *The Stranger* and *The Myth of Sisyphus* and the prescient *The Plague* were different and didn't offer answers that evangelicals always wanted to make sure we were embracing. They called Camus an existentialist although he denied it. I read that Camus was a serious soccer player, a goalie whose passion for the game was intense and pure. Camus said he got tired of debating Roman Catholic seminary students because he wanted them to convince him that their Judeo-Christian ontology was the only path forward, but he usually ended up convincing them of his bleaker view. Besides, if I could've added a footnote to his words, I would have said that it's more life-giving to be in the midst of a game stopping shots on goal and then going out for some beers to relive the game with your colleagues. The world doesn't need more seminary students who bail out on their own convictions at the slightest challenge. Camus was an athlete—why didn't they teach that in class? And then I discovered Samuel Beckett's love of cricket. Of course. I began to think that Camus and Beckett were labeled "absurdists" not in spite of loving sports, but because of it. Sports is both absurd and ordered, and full of unknown consequences. A game means nothing and it means everything. And then I found Walt Whitman, who didn't write of soccer or cricket. He wrote of baseball and called it "our game, the American game."

Foreign films entered my life in college and some landed more than others—Fellini, Truffaut, and Kurosawa were big. I caught up on the films I'd missed and looked forward to the new ones coming out. The British directors like Lindsay Anderson, Tony Richardson, and Richard Lester (actually an export American), to name a few, captured my imagination. But it was also a time to catch up on classic American films I'd missed: the works of Billy Wilder, silent films with Keaton and Chaplin and Lloyd, and the talkies of Laurel and Hardy, which I can watch forever. Nothing about going to movies was intended as preparation for a writing career or anything to do with film. I played baseball and intended that to be my career if I possibly could make it work.

It was in college that I realized how much I didn't like most sports movies, although, upon reflection, three of the greatest of all sports movies came out at this time. More on that later. I'd played enough sports by then that I felt sports films got it all wrong. Their attempts to be inspirational felt cloying and false. When you actually play the game, there is little that is inspirational going on. It's a competition; it's physical; it's a chance to test yourself. Sports movies all seemed to be made from an outsider's point of view. They didn't want to make a movie about what was going on inside Eddie Mathews's head before he hit that home run. They wanted to avoid his serious drinking problem, his marriage struggles, even the bar fights defending his Black teammate Henry Aaron. What happens on the field is the least interesting part of the game.

Take, for instance, *The Pride of the Yankees,* the beloved 1942 film directed by Sam Wood and starring Gary Cooper as Lou Gehrig, and one of my mother's favorite movies. I hated the movie as a kid (it played on TV a lot) and I don't feel much differently now. It checks all the boxes of sentimentality and inspiration and ignores the more complex story of Gehrig's relationship to his teammates, especially Babe Ruth. But as an emotional tribute to a sports hero during the war, it made great commercial sense and was, at least, markedly better than the worst sports movie ever made about a great subject, *The Babe Ruth Story,* starring William Bendix, who, at forty-two, played young Babe Ruth in an orphanage. I didn't have the heart to ever tell my mother how I felt about her favorite movie but I recognize it was of a time and place and doesn't really count as a sports movie. It's in that other category of *films-about-people-dying-that-will-make-you-weep.* Like *A Man Called Peter.*

Shortly after graduation I was offered a contract with the Baltimore Orioles organization to play professional baseball and was immediately assigned to the lowest rung on the ladder in Bluefield, West Virginia—the Appalachian League. I was about to learn that the chasm between the intellectual and the physical was much greater than I thought. That chasm was also political and volatile and explosive. I'd embarked on a difficult and most thrilling way to make a living. I was in the deep bowels of coal country, standing under the tree of the knowledge of good and evil, staring at the apple. It was exhilarating.

2

Dalko, Altobelli, and
Number 136

I signed the minor league contract for five hundred dollars per month at 10 p.m. at LAX. It was the standard beginning wage in the late sixties, but at least there was three-dollars-a-day meal money. I was a professional baseball player and soon to learn what that meant. For starters, it meant three red-eye connecting flights on Piedmont Airlines to Bluefield, West Virginia.

I arrived at the assigned hotel in Bluefield at 7 a.m., having not slept for a second. I was greeted by men who'd lost their limbs in the coal mines and who scooted around the entrance to the West Virginian Hotel begging for anything anyone could give them. Other coal-mining lifers, withered and suffering and appearing older than their years, stood by, holding signs reading BLACK LUNG DISEASE—PLEASE HELP. The air, even at this hour, was thick and oppressive and humid in a way I'd never experienced living on the Pacific Ocean. The distance from the jewel box city of Santa Barbara to Bluefield was a lot greater than the physical miles logged.

The lobby was starting to fill with players who had filed downstairs to share cabs to the ballpark. A friendly, open-faced player came straight up to me and said, "Hi, I'm Ron Shelton. What's your name?" I figured he knew I was arriving and it was a practical joke (ballplayers are big on practical jokes—there's nothing better than setting a guy's shoe on fire or nailing his clothes to the floor) but it turned out that it really was his name. The other players said I should crash, since I'd been traveling all night, but when I found out the season started the next day, I packed into a cab with them and went straight to the ballpark.

What awaited was a revelation. There were fifty players putting on ill-fitting gray wool, major league Orioles hand-me-down uniforms in ninety-six-degree humidity. Twenty wooden stalls passed for lockers, and each stall had three big sixteen-penny nails in lieu of hooks—one for each player. Three guys were crammed into each space meant for one, but what everyone immediately understood was that even though each of us had signed a contract and found his way to Bluefield in the belief he had a job, there were only twenty-five spots on the roster. Half of the young men in the room were going to be weeded out quickly. Certainly, nobody had known I was coming, and that included Joe Altobelli, a career Triple-A player who'd had a cup of coffee in the big leagues but was now about to begin a new career as our manager.

When he asked which position I played, I looked out at where guys were taking their places in the infield, and even though I'd played four years of third base in college, I noticed that there were fewer players taking ground balls at shortstop than anywhere else. So I told him I was a shortstop. Then he asked my name and I hesitated before saying, "Wayne Shelton." I thought it would be better to have my own first name rather than be "Ron Shelton Number Two," and my middle name was Wayne. So, less than ten hours after signing a contract on the West Coast, I'd flown all night to discover I not only didn't have a job, I didn't have my own name. I thought Camus would enjoy the situation but I wasn't laughing; I was digging in for a fight.

What happened next was a combination of willfulness and great good fortune. We practiced all day and all afternoon, and as we did, other players reported to the team. As the number of players grew, the odds of making the team diminished. Everyone knew that. One guy who didn't have to worry was the number two player drafted by the Orioles, an African American kid from Austin, Texas, named Don Baylor. He was cut like a Greek god, ran like a deer, hit with power, and played with physical grace—and he was only seventeen years old.

Early that first morning Joe announced that he was not to be called "Coach"—that was a word for high school kids and *college guys*. There was something off-centered and resentful about the way he said *college guys*. Clearly, Joe wasn't someone with whom I'd be bouncing around the central idea of *Waiting for Godot*, but he was likable—even as he wielded the sword above our necks. "Call me Joe," he said, "or Skip." I whispered to a guy next to me—a guy fighting to play first base—"Did he really say *Skip*?" The aspiring first baseman knew the rules because he'd been there for two weeks and whispered back, "It's short for *skipper*. It's okay." What he didn't know was that this was his last day as a professional baseball player— Skip released him before dark. Joe also announced we would be playing a Tennessee college all-star team that very night in an exhibition game to get ready to start the season the next day. There it was again, the inflection that made *college* sound like a prison record. By now it was obvious that the next day twenty-five guys would ride a bus to Johnson City, Tennessee, to become professional baseball players for real. The rest of us? A big roster reduction would be announced after the game. Half the guys I was warming up with would be gone. Probably including me.

At six o'clock Joe excused all the players who'd arrived in the last couple of days, saying that our "opportunity would arrive." He told me I should go back to the hotel and get some rest with the other late arrivals, which meant I didn't have a chance to be on the roster for the opening game. I didn't believe that an "opportunity would arrive" to anyone who wasn't there, so I stayed in the dugout to watch the game, still in the heavy wool cast-off Orioles uniform with a spring-training number. That number—something like 136—had been taken off and replaced by the proper professional number of 22, but the wool was discolored where the high number had been, resulting in a kind of double number on my back. I was "22" but it was easy to see with the discoloration that I was also "136." Most of the players were branded in this manner, revealing that none of us were high draft picks. These sorts of put-downs and dismissals inspired me.

The ballpark was rickety and vintage, the kind I like, and located in the hills above town, but still drew a decent-size crowd, even for an exhibition game. The lights were of criminally low wattage and hadn't been cleaned in years—welcome to the low minors. Somebody could get killed here. The game unfolded badly for the Baby Birds (our nickname) and Joe paced the dugout grumbling as the "fucking college guys" were shutting us out in the top of the eighth. That's when fortune smiled on me. Our shortstop twisted his ankle and had to come out of the game. Fortune for one athlete is often misfortune for another, something ballplayers are acutely aware of. The moral question is always: Should I be rooting for the failure of the man ahead of me? The answer is, of course, yes. I could see that Joe was about to turn around and see who could replace our injured short-stop and I moved directly into his line of sight so he wouldn't have time to think about it. He pointed at me and at the vacated position at shortstop, and I was in the game. The first batter hit a screaming line drive to my right. I made a diving backhand play, short-hopping the ball, and threw the guy out. It was a very flashy play and, as ball-players know, not as hard as it looks. They're called "reaction plays" and nobody expects you to actually pull them off, so when you do, fans stand up and cheer at the unexpected wonder of it all. A squir-relly ground ball off the end of the bat at the edge of the infield grass is much harder—and looks much easier. A bit of flash caused people to ask, "Who's the new guy at shortstop?" He's number 22 and 136, that's who he is. In the bottom of the eighth inning I got lucky again. Trailing 2–0, we got the bases loaded with two outs and I came up. I hadn't slept in forty-eight hours and could hardly see the ball in the dim lights, around which thousands of moths fluttered. The first pitch was a fastball strike, which I took just to get adjusted. The second pitch was a curveball for strike two. Neither pitch was that impressive but they were difficult to pick out of the darkness. I figured my entire career could consist of this exhibition game against, God forbid, *college guys.* If this pitcher threw a nasty Koufax hook or had been holding back on some ungodly heat, a la Sudden Sam McDowell, I'd be finished. If he'd been any good he'd have thrown anything but what he did throw—cock-high, half-assed cheese with nothing on it. I tripled in three runs and we won the game. A third baseman named Ron Shelton had taken off from LAX twenty-four

hours earlier; a guy named Wayne Shelton was now starting shortstop for the Bluefield Baby Birds in the Appalachian League.

I tell this story not to chronicle my modest baseball achieve-
ments—and nobody on the planet would recall the events I've just
described—but they capture something about life in the game that
every ballplayer would acknowledge. A baseball life is fragile and
absurd. It's also wondrous and thrilling. It also produces expressions
like "cock-high, half-assed cheese," which means, of course, "weak
heat in the zone."

Two weeks later, when Joe called me into his office, I knew it
couldn't be bad news because I was hitting well and playing errorless
shortstop. He dragged deeply on a cigarette.

JOE: How'd ya like to play second base?

RON: I'm liking shortstop.

JOE: The organization just signed their number one pick out
of Long Beach, California, a kid named Bobby Grich, and
he's gonna be their shortstop of the future.

RON: Naw, Skip, he's gotta beat me out.

JOE: He's already beat you out.

RON: Why?

JOE: They gave him a lotta dough. How much they give you?

RON: What about Jimmy Murrel, our second baseman? He's
playing great.

JOE (another long drag on a Camel): Let me put it to you like
this, son—do you want to play second base or do you want
Jimmy Murrel to play second base?

RON: Skip, I love second base.

Thus I became a second baseman, and when I left Bluefield I
reclaimed my first name. (The other Ron Shelton and I were in
touch in recent years; as I write this, his son, Derek, has just become
a major league manager.) I clawed my way up the rungs of the orga-
nizational ladder to AAA, where I played in Rochester, New York, for
the Red Wings. I walked away from the game after a little more than
a year there, during the strike of 1972. The *organization* became the

formidable off-screen presence—and sometimes villain—to those of us laboring in the factory. The organization was like Rome in AD 100, when the good emperors were in charge—it was frightening but not evil to those of us in the provinces who were hoping to someday earn our way to the Eternal City of Baltimore. The Orioles organization was a brilliantly run outfit, in the midst of developing the most dominant teams in baseball for two decades. Still, to a player in the minors, the term *organization* could provoke chills—the way *college guy* could provoke disdain.

Toward that end I discovered that if I preferred reading to playing cards on long bus rides, it was better to hide my books in skin magazines so I'd appear to be one of the guys. Jim Bouton's classic *Ball Four* came out when I was in AAA and he talked about the importance of being "one of the guys" so that the organization didn't think you were an agitator or, worse, a clubhouse lawyer. College guys were always suspected troublemakers. I loved the Bouton book, though most players didn't. They saw it as a betrayal of the sanctity of the clubhouse. I saw it as humanizing all these athletes, who were much more compelling in their flaws and fears than the PR version foisted on the fans. Plus, it was funny. Because baseball players live in close quarters and travel together and play almost every day from February to October, there's little opportunity for posturing. Everyone's naked, literally as well as figuratively, and everyone's daily performance is not only reduced to statistics forever but is on display for ruthless critique by fellow comrades in arms. There's no hiding, and that seems to unleash unedited personal and often funny assaults among players that somehow bond rather than divide. In baseball terms, "to be released" was to have your contract canceled and be given the pink slip—it was over. Fear of being released was always in the air, and players in a slump would sing Engelbert Humperdinck's hit "Please Release Me": "Please release me, let me go, for I don't love you anymore." It was a way of fighting off the demons because, of course, players still loved baseball more than anything but they couldn't sing the truth—that it was baseball, or at least the organization, that had stopped loving them.

Reading, along with movie matinees, provided a sanctuary for me from the fear that drove everyone. That fear also made you more alive. One season I got hooked on Mickey Spillane and Thomas Mann. I wolfed down the eight hundred pages of *The Magic Mountain* but *Kiss Me, Deadly* was a quicker read. A player asked what *The Magic Mountain* was about and I answered, "I don't have a clue but I can't put it down." I wasn't an aspiring academic or intellectual— there's no argument about that—and I spent as much time as the other guys hanging out in bars and strip clubs. Most of my time was spent contemplating how to hit the slider or, better, to lay off it, and how to beat out the guy ahead of me and not let the guy on the rung below catch up. Beer led to Jack Daniel's led to Scotch led to . . . How could anyone play baseball and not drink?

• • •

I first heard of Steve Dalkowski while playing for the Stockton Ports against the Bakersfield Bears in Bakersfield, California. A small man was lurking in the dark near our bullpen down the right-field line. He had a flask and looked out of place. After the game he approached our manager, Joe Altobelli, who'd moved up from Bluefield as a manager. They spoke in the shadows, Joe gave him something, and the man disappeared. We asked Joe who that guy was and he explained simply, "That's the hardest thrower who ever threw a baseball. Steve Dalkowski." I didn't hear his name again till late in the season, when Dalkowski knocked on the clubhouse door after a game in Stockton, near midnight. He looked even worse and Joe talked to him awhile and again gave him some money. Joe then settled in and started telling us some of the larger-than-life stories about "Dalko," as he was affectionately called. A left-handed pitcher from Connecticut, Dalko is reputed to have thrown a ball through a wooden fence, torn off a man's ear with a fastball, terrified Ted Williams, and thrown a fastball so high and wild in Wilson, North Carolina, that it went through the welded metal backstop fencing twenty-five feet above the ground. The legends are backed by his stats, but despite his God-given talent, his demon was the bottle, and he never beat it. He never made it to the major leagues, although he got close. Two years later, Joe was my manager on the Red Wings, and he talked about Dalko again. Joe said that after nine years in the minors, when Dalkowski finally learned to control his fastball and earned a trip to AAA, the organization insisted that he be assigned Altobelli as his roommate. "They wanted me to mature him," Joe said. Or at least keep track of him. Joe said he never saw Dalkowski all year, except at the ballpark. "I roomed with his suitcase" was the line.

So much of a pro ballplayer's life is on the road that even when he's in his hometown—mine was, over the season, Bluefield, West Virginia; Stockton, California; Dallas–Fort Worth, Texas; Clearwater, Florida; and Rochester, New York—it's *not* his hometown. For the players who are married and have a child, as was my situation, the burden put on your wife and family is untenable, regardless of how game, supportive, and flexible your wife is—and my wife was. To the player, it's a great untethered adventure. To the support system, it can also be hell. A player lives in an apartment or a hotel room nine months a year, and most of the job happens at night, so killing time in the day becomes a serious focus. Soap operas filled the void for some of the guys—there was the *General Hospital* faction and the rival *As the World Turns* gang. Locker room discussions could get heated. I was part of the third group; we were for doing anything other than watching the soap operas our mothers watched. Movies were the solution.

Afternoon matinees started at one, which meant you could get a cab to the ballpark by four-thirty. An additional bonus was that the air-conditioning in movie theaters was always better than in the hotel, and in cities like Bakersfield, Fresno, Amarillo, and El Paso, the need for functioning AC was critical. Because of the meager salaries, nobody could quite afford an unshared cab ride, so I'd make sure I dragged some guys along. The ensuing discussions about the quality of the movie we'd just seen were without nuance. Reactions were binary—"The movie was a piece of crap and I hated it" or "Great fuckin' flick." Thumbs-up or thumbs-down and no discussion in between. Never was heard "I need some time to sit with this awhile" or "I have complicated and perhaps contradictory feelings about this that I need to sort out." I'm still trying to figure out what Ingmar

Bergman movies were about, except *Hour of the Wolf;* that was about insomnia, which I had.

In El Paso I took some teammates to see an early Brian De Palma movie, *Hi, Mom!,* in which there's a sequence with Black Panther–type radicals. The players hated the movie, hated everything about the Black radicals, and didn't want to talk about it. I tried to engage. Bad idea. "It's a movie," I said. The response was basically, "I don't care if it's a movie, I don't like those Black motherfuckers." There was a literalness to the way ballplayers watched movies, as if everything happening onscreen was actually occurring in front of their eyes. I wished I could watch movies like that, but I was always trying to figure out what was going on as well as why and how.

There's a kind of film education in going indiscriminately to movies, whatever the rating, whatever the reviews. *Rio Lobo* to Russ Meyer to Alain Resnais, they were all a way to get from one o'clock in the afternoon to the ballpark. Settling into a cool, dark theater was already a reward. I had no expectations. I was a generous audience.

• • •

In Little Rock, Arkansas, a heavy thunderstorm hit while we were playing cards at three in the morning. We dreamed the storm would last all night and the next day and cause the field to be flooded and the game to be rained out. In the Texas League, there were very few days without a scheduled game; the season felt endless. We begged for days off but they never came. Out of that desperation we determined that while the tarp covering the infield had probably already been laid down by the ground crew in anticipation of this storm, that tarp could be removed. If it was, the field would flood—and we'd have a night to ourselves. So four of us got a cab and headed to the ballpark at 4 a.m., then convinced the frightened cabbie to wait for us while we climbed the fence of the ballpark as the rain poured down. We discovered what any *college guy* should have known (and at least two of us in the cab were *college guys*): there's a reason a ground crew has twenty men or a motor to remove a tarp from a field—it's heavy as hell. We couldn't budge it and had to abort our mission. We did manage to take the small tarp off the batter's box, for reasons I can't fathom to this day, rendering that critical part of the diamond almost unplayable. Escaping the ballpark was harder than breaking in, however, and one of our star pitchers, whose name was Dizzy, cut his hand climbing back over the fence. The cabbie hadn't waited for us, and we were left to walk the four miles back to the hotel as the rain grew heavier. That night I went 0 for 4—standing in the mud at home plate, unable to gain footing—and Dizzy went on the disabled list for two months. He told Joe that he had cut his finger on a can of beer.

That road trip to Little Rock provided a Road to Damascus event for me. *The Wild Bunch* was playing across the street from our hotel and I came out of the theater a changed young man. Sam Peckinpah's masterpiece hit me differently than other movies had, although I wasn't quite sure why. It was visually gorgeous but also so much more. Layers kept peeling like an onion and I wanted to know more about these characters and the story and the filmmaking. I saw *The Wild Bunch* all four days we were in Little Rock. Why did I care about these killers, led by William Holden, who were being chased by another gang of killers, led by Robert Ryan? That was exactly what Peckinpah wanted me to do—care about them. The story seemed to be about chaos, but it really was about order. It was violent, male, ruthless, but it was being observed by innocent women and children. Hired guns and murderers filled every frame, but it took place in a moral universe—or at least a universe searching for a center. As a story, it kept unfolding and evolving and the moral choices kept shifting, light kept being shined on them in different ways. I wanted to know more about it. About movies.

I walked away from baseball when spring training was canceled due to the first baseball strike in history, in 1972, though I still had a Triple-A contract. The fight was over pensions and arbitration, and there were rumors that the entire season would be canceled as well, and though ultimately the schedule was only shortened, the players' union was emboldended by its success. I was married, with a three-year-old daughter, and it was time to leave. I was twenty-six. I thought I was old.

Do I have regrets? Unlike Edith Piaf, I have plenty. Baseball is a game of regrets. Once we were playing in El Paso in the Texas League at the old Dudley Dome ballpark, which balls flew out of—it was a hitter's paradise. It was also the best road trip of the year because after the game, the five-dollar-a-day AA meal money went a magnificently long way after a short walk across the bridge into Ciudad Juárez, Mexico. I led off the game, and the catcher on the El Paso Sun Kings (an Angels farm team at the time) said as I stepped in, "Curveball. And it's really lousy." I didn't believe him. Then the guy threw what was indeed the *lousiest* curveball I'd ever seen. It just hung up there like a full moon on a string. A big, fat piñata. I could've tattooed it. I didn't swing. I should've believed the catcher, even if he was on the other team. This was the minors—the guys on the other team were, like you, fighting the same *other*. And the catcher, who seemed as dismayed at my nonresponse as I was, said, "Last time I ever give you a pitch." I should have swung.

Just before deciding to walk away from the game, I got a call from somebody in the Orioles organization saying I'd been traded to Detroit and that I was going to be assigned to their AAA team, the Toledo Mud Hens. I debated hard whether to continue—the Tigers weren't loaded like the Orioles; you never know what might happen. Except maybe you do. But I regret not playing another year. I could've been a Mud Hen.

Wait till next year, we were taught. You went 0 for 4 last night— tonight you'll go 4 for 4. Except you won't. Bart Giamatti said it's a game designed to break your heart.

3

Lysistrata in the
Minor Leagues

Cut to fifteen years later.

I'd painted houses, dug ditches for a landscaping company, substitute-taught in two states, applied for a job on the graveyard shift at 7-Eleven (was turned down), gone to graduate school in Arizona (not in English lit), published a couple of short stories in obscure literary journals, and somehow landed on my feet as a screenwriter with a couple of actual credits. What I had not done in all those years was watch baseball. I read the box scores to follow my friends from the minors who'd gone on to play in the major leagues, but I never watched a game on television, even the World Series. It was not a conscious decision. I was just done with the game. I went home to visit family in my hometown and was walking down the main drag, State Street, when a guy I barely knew named Milton, who owned the jewelry store, saw me and popped outside to say, with grave disappointment, "Jeez, Shelton, I thought you were the one guy around here since Eddie Mathews who was going all the way." What can you say besides, "Sorry to disappoint you, Milton"? It was clear that not only could you not go home again, you couldn't even go home the first time.

I was living in an apartment in Los Angeles on the road to divorce. My older daughter was in college, the younger in high school and staying with me on weekends. It was not the *best of times,* which happened to be the name of my second flop as a movie writer. Marriage counseling that evolved into divorce counseling had made clear how

brutal the baseball years were on a partnership, and everyone was trying to move on, whatever that meant.

I don't know if there were screenwriting classes or books on the
subject back then, but I learned to write scripts by incessantly going
to movies and trying to figure out how they were constructed. During
my off hours from the various jobs over the years, I'd written scripts
and had enough self-critical facility to burn them all. I wrote a dreadful novel, which also found the flames. The first script I wrote and
torched was about my favorite professional wrestler, "Classy" Freddie
Blassie, who had flowing platinum hair and was the villain everyone
loved to hate. He used to crunch the TV announcer's glasses on camera and create havoc everywhere. Fans at the Olympic Auditorium
in downtown L.A. ripped the backs off their seats to throw at him
in the ring. He was venal and fabulous. When I saw a reference in
a newspaper article to a tulip-growing festival in which the winning
tulip breeder was the team of Mr. and Mrs. Fred Blassie ("he of wrestling fame"), I figured I had something. The villain who grows prize
tulips sounded like a movie idea to me. It wasn't. I finished writing
it, which is half the battle, and as the flames consumed Mr. Blassie
and his tulips, I came to the conclusion that it really wasn't an idea
for a movie—it was an idea for a character. There was no formidable
obstacle or conflict to overcome. I also learned that it's easier and a
helluva lot more fun to write villains, which several years later served
me in the film *Under Fire;* the detestable Nicaraguan dictator Anas-
tasio Somoza and especially the CIA operative Marcel Jazy, played
by the great Jean-Louis Trintignant, had all the best lines. The rest of
the good speeches I gave to a journalist played by Gene Hackman, a
character who was based on my father and was no villain at all.

Somewhere between "Classy" Freddie Blassie and working with
Hackman and Trintignant, I wrote a not very good script about professional baseball. It was titled *A Player to Be Named Later* and was
about a pitcher, a catcher, and a woman. It contained the seeds of
what would become *Bull Durham,* but far from the flower. I was
not precious about showing it to anyone who'd read it, and somehow it got into the hands of a wonderful literary film agent named

Geoff Sanford. We became friends, colleagues, and co-conspirators for many years. My new agent got it to producer Ed Pressman, a true original and quite un-Hollywood character with a serious film résumé. Ed was quiet and soft-spoken, had gone to both Stanford and the London School of Economics, and came from the Pressman Toy family in New York. It was said that he invented Tri-Ominos, whatever that was. Ed bought the script for ten grand. I could stop painting houses and call myself a professional writer.

The problem was that Ed's cash flow wasn't so good and he couldn't actually pay me, so my agent negotiated a deal where I'd be his story editor for three hundred dollars a week. This was a great job for me but it also reflected everything that was wrong with Hollywood. On what basis should the writer of the unmakable *Classy Freddie Blassie Story* be given the authority to pass judgment on other writers' works? Not so lucky for the poor writers submitting screenplays in good faith to Pressman's company, but it was a crash course in script reading and writing for me.

Ten scripts a week were put on my desk. By the following Monday I had to deliver "coverage" to Ed's desk. This is the term for a one-page summary of the plotline and characters, written by a "reader" (someone usually young and cheap, or in this case, me) so that the producer or studio executive doesn't have to actually read the script. The coverage also includes a paragraph that recommends the script as a potential movie to be made, or buries it with a thumbs-down. This low-level reader has the power of an emperor in the Colosseum.

The compelling thing I quickly learned was that good writing separated itself from bad on the opening page. The good scripts were so stunningly different from the others that after studying them, I found my own writing improved practically overnight. I couldn't recommend whether a screenplay should be made into a movie—that was way above my pay grade (but then again, everything was above my pay grade)—but I could sure as hell say, "This is a damn good piece of writing. Read it." Sometimes they did, sometimes they didn't.

One script that floated out of the stack on my desk and was so clearly superior to the rest was by a little-known writer, Oliver Stone. It was called *Platoon*. Ed owned it and was trying to get it made by a studio. Everyone passed. I couldn't believe it. Ed also owned *Conan the Barbarian,* which studios were fighting over. Ed had a great eye for material and was responsible for Terrence Malick's first movie, *Badlands,* so he obviously read more than the coverage. A couple of years later, Ed's option ran out on *Platoon* and it got made by one of the studios he had tried to sell it to. It won Best Picture and Best Director, as well as a couple of other Oscars, and earned, in today's dollars, around $400 million.

On one occasion, however, Ed did not read a submission. On a Friday, he handed me a script and said that the writer/director, a talented woman from Kentucky, was coming into town to have lunch with him on Monday to discuss this new project. She had some heat because she was coming off an indie film that had been well received. Ed said he would also read the script on the weekend but asked for some special coverage, maybe a bit more detail than normal, which could serve as his notes. The script was set in the world of blue-blood Kentucky money and the debutante subculture that was part of a long tradition—a world I didn't even know existed.

At nine o'clock on Monday morning, I put two pages of coverage on his desk. He arrived at ten and asked if I could edit down what I'd written. I promptly did. At eleven he wanted it shorter yet. Again, I shortened it. The entire coverage and recommendation section was now half a page. At twelve-twenty, just before the lady writer/director arrived, Ed clearly hadn't gotten around to reading any of this (much less the script) and asked simply, "Can you give it all to me in three sentences?" I retreated to my office and quickly turned the whole thing into three sentences. Moments later, this very nice woman arrived, fresh from the plane, anxious to know Ed's response to the script. Ed asked me to accompany them to lunch. He hadn't read the three sentences, either.

As we walked to the Warner Bros. commissary, the following conversation took place:

LADY WRITER/DIRECTOR: I can't wait any longer—what did you think of my script?
ED: We love it!

LADY WRITER/DIRECTOR: I'm thrilled. I'm just curious: What do you think it's about, thematically?

ED: Ron's better than me at summarizing these things—Ron, what do you think this script is about?

RON: Well, it's a real *coming of age* story, I feel.

LADY WRITER/DIRECTOR: Oh, no! I was so afraid that's how it would be interpreted.

ED (staring daggers at me): Ron, how could you say that? (To lady writer/director) What do you think it's about, thematically?

LADY WRITER/DIRECTOR: I see it as a *rite of passage* story.

ED: Precisely! Just what I was going to say!

I didn't say another word through lunch. The whole time Ed was discussing a script he hadn't read and knew nothing about, I was thinking, What's the difference between a *coming of age* story and a *rite of passage* story? All through lunch, the lady writer/director looked down on me from a great height.

One more Ed Pressman story, and it should be understood that Ed is one of the good guys trying to make movies about human behavior, not loss leaders for theme parks.

I wanted to make a movie about Jerry Lee Lewis and especially the background of God and the Church versus the "devil's music," his cousin Jimmy Swaggart, the whole thing. Ed indulged me and arranged for me to hang out with Lewis a bit, not only at the Palomino Club in L.A., but on a trip to Nashville. Hanging out with Jerry Lee Lewis can shorten your life, but I escaped and wrote a treatment, and Ed set out to get a meeting for us to pitch it to Don Simpson at Paramount. The late Don Simpson was one of the town's hottest producers, who eventually burned himself out, but if Don liked a project, it got made. Simpson was fully immersed in the sex, drugs, and rock-and-roll culture of the day, which seemed to make him a perfect candidate for a movie about the tempestuous Lewis. It took months for Ed to get a meeting.

On the big day, Simpson sat us on a couch far from where he sat in his massive Paramount office. We had thirty minutes, during the first twenty-five of which he recounted his various sexual exploits in explicit detail. It was fascinating and embarrassing, but what I cared most about was that the time allotted for my Jerry Lee Lewis pitch was getting shorter. Finally, with five minutes left:

DON SIMPSON: Okay, your dime. Go.

RON: Jerry . . . Lee—

DON SIMPSON (interrupting): If you say "Lewis," this meeting is over.

RON: Schwartz. He's a butcher in Philly. It's a butcher story . . .

ED: Ron's lying. It's not about a butcher. It's about the musician.

RON: Of course it's about Jerry Lee Lewis—

DON SIMPSON: Rock is over. It's New Wave now. It's Floyd Mutrux. Bring me Floyd Mutrux.

RON: I don't know Floyd Mutrux. I don't even know who he is.

DON SIMPSON: Okay, you're down to two minutes. Got anything else?

ED: Yes we do.

RON (whispering to Ed): We do?

ED (to Simpson): You know who Raggedy Ann is?

DON SIMPSON: Yeah, 'course I do. Why?

ED: Well, we have Raggedy Andy.

DON SIMPSON: I like it. Tell me more!

ED: Ron's the better storyteller. Ron, tell him the story of Raggedy Andy.

RON: It'll take too long. We're outta time.

DON SIMPSON: Dreyfuss could do it. Or Wilder! I'll set another meeting!

ED: Let's do it.

On the elevator down:

RON: What the hell is Raggedy Andy?

ED: I had to say something. Maybe you can figure it out for our next meeting with Don.

There was no next meeting with Don and I left Pressman soon after, when I began finding writing work. But the lessons I learned in those few months were invaluable. A script has to cut through a mountain of bullshit just to get on the stack on someone's desk, and then it has to be good enough to float out from the pile and get people to notice. The first line matters. The first description of place matters. It has to attract producers, studios, money, actors. It has to be different.

Don't write about Raggedy Andy. Write something you know, the oldest piece of advice in the business.

• • •

Under Fire was a political movie about the Nicaraguan revolution and the challenge of the press to stay neutral when a clear-cut moral right-and-wrong decision unfolds in front of them. Is it possible to tell the story without taking sides? And does it matter? Those were the key questions to be answered. I traveled around Nicaragua with director Roger Spottiswoode, along with photojournalist Matthew Naythons and international correspondent Rod Nordland (both of whom had covered the war in person), researching the story before writing.

We shot *Under Fire* for Orion Pictures in southern Mexico, and Spottiswoode generously brought me into the middle of the production, entrusting me to direct the second unit. The first unit director of photography was the great John Alcott, who had shot *Barry Lyndon, A Clockwork Orange,* and *The Shining* for Stanley Kubrick. I had to report at 5:30 every morning to the camera truck on location to request specific lenses I wanted to use that day, and justify why I needed each piece of equipment. When film dailies were projected every night at the hotel, Alcott and his ace British crew barely paid attention to their own brilliant footage, but when the second unit's work came up onscreen, John sat up in his chair and watched like a hawk, ready to critique every frame of our footage. The whole experience of production, from prep through post, became my film school. At the end of the shoot, Alcott offered that if I ever directed a movie, he'd love to shoot it. I took serious note of that offer and hoped someday to take advantage of his genius.

In the city of León we were told about a local teenage pitcher (baseball is big in Nicaragua) who was recruited by the Sandinistas to "pitch" hand grenades into the church tower that Somoza's La Guardia military was using as a perch for their snipers. The local kid threw enough strikes to kill the snipers. I loved the story for obvious reasons, and the incident became a scene in the movie—a scene that some critics called "too Hollywood."

My experience on two movies made clear that not only did I like crew members and the whole process, start to finish, I also liked actors and was comfortable talking with them—something, apparently, many directors are not. The whole process felt athletic—the enormous amount of preparation, all for a tiny amount of playing time. For all the time spent prepping to film a movie, in actuality it is very few minutes each day that film is actually rolling through the cameras. As for the actors? Who wouldn't want to hear their thoughts on a scene or a line? We know where the buck stops, but the process is dynamic and not autocratic, even if the structure is militaristic.

Both *Under Fire* and *The Best of Times* (also directed by Spottiswoode, and starring Robin Williams and Kurt Russell, about an ex–high school football player trying to replay his great high school failure and finally turn it into a moment of glory) were domestic box office failures. *Under Fire,* however, found an audience in Europe and screened to an enthusiastic crowd at the Venice Film Festival. Methinks they thought it was somehow Marxist because it was antifascist. It wasn't, but nobody asked, and the standing ovation was nice. Pauline Kael loved it in *The New Yorker.* Vincent Canby hated it in *The New York Times.* I'd been cheered and I'd been booed. These things were old hat to me. Try going into the corner bar by Silver Stadium in Rochester after you've booted a ball to cost the Red Wings a game.

Based on my track record of never having written a financially successful movie, buoyed by generally polarized critical response to what I'd done already, and determined not to paint houses again, I declared I was ready to direct. A ghostly silence followed my declaration. I understood that I'd have to write a script that I would direct, whatever it was, but I'd heard plenty of horror stories in which a writer/would-be director got a script sold and cast, only to be bought out by the studio who wanted a trusted director with a résumé.

There was no protecting yourself from that, but it led to the now-obvious recognition that if I wrote about a subject so specific to my experiences, at least it could not be argued that some other director knew more than I did about my world. So, what did I know? Writing another political movie now was a career ender, and I barely had a career to end. What else? House painting was a nonstarter as a movie idea. Substitute teaching was a horror show and I didn't like horror shows. Marriage? Apparently, I didn't know much about that, either. So . . . here I was again. Baseball. Minor league baseball. I bleated my announcement to the world, and it was greeted by more silence and a yawn.

Except from Thom Mount, producer, former president of Universal Pictures, onetime "baby mogul" (a term used for a number of youthful studio heads who emerged in the seventies and eighties)—and part owner of some minor league baseball teams. His head of development, Charles Hirschhorn, called me once a week for a few months to say, "We're interested in your minor league baseball idea. Let's set up a meeting." After being dogged with calls from Hirschhorn, and dead calm silence from everyone else in town, I set a meeting with Mount.

Only then did it occur to me that I didn't have a clue what the story was. But at least I had a meeting set with a producer who had a legit résumé and, more important, who might actually know what the minor leagues smelled like. Appropriately enough for the subject at hand, these meetings are called "pitches," and I was about to pitch something amorphous and incomplete at best. Yes, it was based on my life, but one's life is not a story until it's got a structural narrative.

The first key question: How could I know what the story was that I was pitching when I hadn't written it yet? This was a problem then and it remains a problem all these years and scripts and movies later. The process of writing is also one of discovery. Do I really want to know what it's about on page one or would I (and ultimately the reader/viewer) be better served with discoveries along the way—mine and theirs? I'm of the school of E. L. Doctorow, who said, "Writing is like driving at night in the fog. You can only see as far as your headlights, but you can make the whole trip that way." At the same time, it's not an unreasonable request by the financier to ask what the hell they're buying. To this day, if I want to be paid rather than write on spec, I'll often write half the script just to figure out how to pitch it. Sometimes I'll just write the whole script and skip the pitching process. That's always my preference because when you opt for a payday, the payer owns your work forever, and even if they don't like it, it's almost impossible to get it back. The upside of writing on spec is that you own your script, even if nobody wants it. I've got a few of those on my shelves, too.

So I had a meeting but I didn't have a story. What I did have was three characters who had been living in my head for all the years since I left baseball. Each was a composite, an archetype, and if I was lucky, an original at the same time. I figured that if the tale was about a ménage à trois, it wouldn't come across as a baseball story. I determined that if the woman was sleeping with one of them but the other one was the right guy, well, you didn't have to understand the infield-fly rule to connect with the drama. If it sounds calculated, it was. Out of nowhere came the idea that the woman might withhold her sexual powers in order to effect an outcome—and suddenly it seemed like a hook I could pitch. I was unaware if there were any contemporary versions out there of Aristophanes's classic Greek play *Lysistrata,* though I assumed there were, but surely none involved baseball. It was a timeless conceit and seemed like, if nothing else, it might make a good pitch. "*Lysistrata* in the minor leagues." That was all I had when I went to see Thom Mount.

My brain was swimming as I crossed the parking lot to his office on Canon Drive. I'd read somewhere that Orson Welles and his Mercury Theatre players never knew what story they'd be pitching their bosses until time had run out and they were crossing the parking lot to make their pitch and had to come up with something or they'd be fired. I remembered that they identified themselves as "last-minute inspirationists" and I found that quite romantic until I was actually crossing the parking lot with nothing more than a lifetime batting average a touch over .260 and a vague reference to Aristophanes.

As I approached the office, Charles Hirschhorn was exiting. The head of development, it should be understood, would normally be present at any pitch meeting to discuss a possible new project, especially in my case, as he was the one who had been calling me for weeks to set up the meeting.

"Where are you going?" I asked.

"I quit," he said. "I can't work for Thom Mount. Good luck."

Unsure of how Hirschhorn's exit might affect the meeting, I marched in and pitched what little I had. Thom Mount greeted me warmly and seemed to like the five-word pitch. Then he asked, understandably, "Do you have any more to the story?" I did. Kind of. I told him there was a pitcher and a catcher and a woman, and she's sleeping with the wrong one. Then, remembering that my wife had always encouraged me to write a baseball story from the woman's point of view, I added, "And the woman tells the story." He bought it. It would never happen today. He knew *Lysistrata* and he knew the infield-fly rule—that's a small group to find in Hollywood—and he owned a piece of the Durham Bulls baseball team in the Carolina League. He also had a production deal at Columbia Pictures on the Warner Bros. lot. Crossing the parking lot back to my car, I had sold a movie.

But I still didn't have a story. I had baseball and Aristophanes and a scale deal (the lowest allowable fee) to write and direct. To protect myself I insisted on a clause in the contract that said I couldn't be fired till after one week of shooting. I was gambling that everyone would love what I was doing, so replacing me wouldn't even be considered. Besides, I was cheap. An established, famous director was not. But I still had to figure out what I'd just sold.

My first concern was that I'd lost touch with professional baseball and recognized that the big money now available to major league players had made them distant and aloof and entitled. Sportswriter friends commented on how arduous it had become to communicate with major league baseball players, and they always added, "Ballplayers used to be the most available and engaging of all the athletes. Now they're jerks." Now they had agents and PR people and go-betweens and fat contracts. The major leagues looked and felt corporate in a new way I'd not experienced. I wondered if the minor leagues were the same, and worried that I'd pitched a story set in a world that was no longer compelling. I had to go back and hang around the minors to see if they, too, had changed.

I flew to Raleigh-Durham to spend a couple of weeks driving around the Carolina League and Sally (South Atlantic League) towns. The first time I walked through the tunnel into the rickety and wondrous old Durham Athletic Park, I felt a familiar rush: nothing had changed. It wasn't exactly nostalgia—I'm not sentimental that way—but it felt like there was actually a time warp going on. Fans, kids, cheap food, pretty girls, players who chatted with fans during the game, the leisurely pace of it all, accompanied by a tinny Hammond B3 organ. Though I'd never played in the Carolina League, it might as well have been Stockton or Bluefield or Shreveport or any of those places I'd unpacked my bags. Looking around, it was obvious—there were no agents or PR guys or handlers and certainly no fat contracts. Players weren't entitled, they were desperate.

I wandered down to hang out behind the bullpen. It was the minors, so nobody cared. Security was lax, the players were close enough to touch. I overheard them talking about their stats, about their fears they were going to be released if they didn't start producing soon, about their girlfriends back home, about the blonde sitting behind the first-base dugout and did anybody know her? And if they did know her, did she have a girlfriend? Just fragments of conversation is all I heard and all I needed. The meal money was running out—Class A pro-baseball players now received five dollars a day for food—and halfway through a road trip everyone was borrowing from the clubhouse boy. Nothing had changed in the minor leagues.

I picked up a Carolina League record book and browsed through it, comforted by thousands of names and numbers. There was a life and story behind every one. Who hit the most home runs in 1955? Who threw the most strikeouts in 1932? Most of this, fewest of that, and occasionally the name of someone would pop up who would later become a star player, maybe even a Hall of Famer. Willie McCovey played in the Carolina League, and Joe Morgan, and Rod Carew and Satchel Paige and . . .

I checked out who had hit the most doubles every year because I identified with doubles—I led the California League once in doubles (co-led, actually, but who remembers, besides me?). A number jumped off the page—some guy hit fifty doubles in 1948; that's a ton of doubles, a lot more than I hit—and the name of the player jumped off the page as well: Lawrence "Crash" Davis. That was the best baseball-player nickname I'd ever heard: "Crash." That immediately became the name of a character I hadn't yet invented. I decided he had to be the catcher (even if the real Crash Davis was a second baseman—like me). I figured Lawrence "Crash" Davis was probably dead and long gone and I wouldn't need permission or clearance, so I started to feel comfortable knowing I had one of my principal characters, even if it was just a name. Names matter. Crash Davis felt like someone I knew, someone I could write. He felt a little like me.

In a rented car, I drove around the league to other baseball towns and found more of the same. I just showed up, bought a general admission ticket, which was usually around five bucks, and wandered. The towns and the ballparks blurred together, although each place had its particular local flavor. While I was far from a gourmand and not remotely a vegetarian, it didn't take long to realize that raw vegetables in the South were considered exotic, foreign, and possibly part of a Yankee conspiracy. I craved a simple salad and calculated that in Columbia, the South Carolina state capital, there was surely a market demand for greens on the menu by out-of-state visitors there on official business. I chose the Radisson Hotel near the state capitol building to settle into for a few days. I was happy; Columbia also had a Mets single-A farm team.

I sat down to dinner in the hotel dining room and was greeted by a large-framed, open-faced, sweet young man who was fresh out of waiter training school. Before I could order a cocktail and ask if they had salads on their menu, he lit up the room and said, "Hi there. My name's Ebby Calvin LaRoosh, but you can call me Nuke." I asked him to stop and say that again, slowly. He repeated it. "May

I ask how you spell 'Nuke'?" I asked. In my mind there was only one Newk, the great Dodgers pitcher in the fifties, Don Newcombe, but I wanted to check. He thought about it for a few seconds and with utter guilessness said, "Y'know, nobody's ever asked me how to spell it before." I had my pitcher.

The salad was forgettable but I scribbled down his name on a cocktail napkin, immediately changing "LaRoosh" to "LaLoosh" to distinguish it from Lyndon LaRouche, the strange, cultlike leader of a Marxist movement of the time. I may not have had a story but I had a battery—a pitcher and a catcher—and they even had good, solid baseball names.

It's often the case that I need to hear a character speak—in my own head—before I can learn who they are. With Crash it would become his entrance line: "I am the player to be named later." That was significant because the "player to be named later" is always a "throw-in" to a trade. It means, as an athlete, you're dispensable, interchangeable, just another guy to fill out a roster. Nobody would willingly embrace the term—but Crash does just that. I wrote it that way to suggest he's smart enough to see some humor in the self-effacing irony. There is nothing self-effacing about Ebby Calvin "Nuke" LaLoosh. His opening line is, "Hey, Skip, you think I need a nickname? All the great ones have nicknames."* It's equally telling that he delivers the line with his pants around his ankles. The dynamic between Crash and Nuke is set in motion.

But who's the woman? She's going to tell the story, after all, and I didn't have her voice yet. I needed to hear her speak. I drove to Asheville (home of the single-A Tourists ball club) to see the "oldest wooden ballpark in America," as it was billed. Asheville is also the home of Thomas Wolfe but more compelling was that the road went past the site of Black Mountain College, long since closed, but onetime home to Hall of Fame immortals in the creative arts: Wal-

---

* Throughout this book there will be quotes from the original script, which may vary from what's in the film. The differences come from changes made on the day of shooting.

ter Gropius, Elaine and Willem de Kooning, Robert Motherwell, Merce Cunningham, John Cage, Robert Rauschenberg, Buckminster Fuller. All were teachers or students on a bus-league route in the Carolina League. Wandering on back roads whenever possible on the three-and-a-half-hour drive, I tried dictating the voice of the woman into a micro-disc recorder that I always carried. I began:

> I believe in the Church of Baseball . . .

A few miles later:

> I've worshipped all the major religions and most of the minor ones. I've worshipped Buddha, Allah, Vishnu, Siva, trees, mushrooms, and Isadora Duncan. I know things. . . .

A picture started to form that maybe this woman was a composite of many friends from the sixties who had gone on self-described spiritual quests launched by the madness of the times and now, twenty years later, had landed in another new place. I'd never been on a spiritual quest. I was too busy trying to figure out how to make a living. Now I wondered, If this woman *knows things,* what does she know? I drove for a while and then dictated some more:

> For instance, there are 108 beads in a Catholic rosary and there are 108 stitches in a baseball. When I learned that, I gave Jesus a chance. But it just didn't work out between us. The Lord laid too much guilt on me. I prefer metaphysics to theology. You see, there's no guilt in baseball and it's never boring . . .

For starters, I was wrong about the Catholic rosary, which can have any number of beads, but Buddhist prayer beads do have 108, so the idea still worked. I didn't learn that till ten years later. The other idea in the evolving monologue was that Annie wasn't judgmental.

She'd try things, even Jesus, and the parting was always amicable and open-ended. The big lie in the monologue thus far was that baseball is never boring. You ever watch your kid in a 23–16 Little League game with thirty walks and twenty errors? Nonetheless, whoever this woman was, I was starting to listen to her more than dictating to her.

> . . . which makes it like sex. There's never been a ballplayer slept with me who didn't have the best year of his career. . . .

Probably not true, but do we care?

> Making love is like hitting a baseball. You gotta relax and concentrate. Besides, I'd never sleep with a player hitting under .250 . . . not unless he had a lot of RBIs and was a great glove man up the middle. . . .

Was the "glove man up the middle" line too much of a joke? Or could the line be shaded as a throwaway aside? Not sure, I kept it.

> A woman's got to have standards.

Then I launched into a sustained piece of the monologue that wouldn't make the final cut, though sometimes I think some of it should have survived.

> The young players start off full of enthusiasm and energy but they don't realize that come July and August, when the weather is hot, it's hard to perform at your peak level. . . . The veterans pace themselves better. They finish stronger. They're great in September. While I don't believe a woman needs a man to be fulfilled, I do confess an interest in finding the ultimate guy—he'd have that youthful exuberance but the veteran's sense of timing. . . .

Maybe it's too obvious. Onward.

> You see, there's a certain amount of life wisdom I give
> these boys. I can expand their minds. . . . Sometimes
> when I get a ballplayer alone I'll just read Emily Dickin-
> son or Walt Whitman to him, and the guys are so sweet,
> they always stay and listen. Of course, a guy will listen
> to anything if he thinks it's foreplay. . . .

And then a line that I thought could get me in trouble—

> I make them feel confident and they make me feel safe
> and pretty.

But turning around now. She's talking, I'm listening.

> 'Course what I give them lasts a lifetime, what they give
> me lasts 142 games. . . .

Is she complaining? Or just reporting—

> Sometimes it seems like a bad trade. But bad trades are
> part of baseball. Who can forget Frank Robinson for
> Milt Pappas, for God's sake?

Okay, she's just being philosophical. She's planting the idea that
the tradeoffs in her life might not be even. We're just hearing it in a
new context. What bothered me in the line was the Robinson-for-
Pappas trade because Milt Pappas was a helluva pitcher who won
209 games in his career and was pitching well after the trade, and
then hurt his arm. This woman, whoever she was, shouldn't be seen
as denigrating Milt Pappas. Ten years after the movie came out I was
in a Greek restaurant in Chicago and the owner said, "There's somebody I want you to meet," and he took me to a booth to meet the
real-life Milt Pappas, who by this time had been long retired. Pappas
wouldn't shake my hand and was still pissed off at being presented

as the bad side of a trade. Didn't I know how many games he'd won? He'd struck out over 1,700, been a three-time All-Star, and was in the Baltimore Orioles Hall of Fame. How dare I? All I could think of was to say I was sorry and that the monologue should have said, "Bad trades are part of baseball. Who can forget Lou Brock for Ernie Broglio, for God's sake?" Except in recent years I met Ernie Broglio and he, too, is a helluva guy.

> It's a long season and you've gotta trust it. I've tried 'em all, I really have, and the only church that truly feeds the soul day in and day out is the Church of Baseball.

She was done talking to me, at least for the moment. I stuck the recorder in my pocket and drove until I found McCormick Field, the old wooden ballpark, where Babe Ruth, Ty Cobb, and Jackie Robinson all once played.

• • •

Back in Durham, the season was winding down. In the late-afternoon sun, the Durham Bulls were going through warm-ups and batting practice. I wandered down to the field just to enjoy the familiar rituals of taking endless ground balls and shagging flies when you weren't taking your cuts. An older man in an Atlanta Braves uniform, who had been at the cage, counseling young players, ambled back to the dugout, where he unbuttoned his jersey, took off his hat, and lit a cigarette. He was balding and his face sweated heavily. The cigarette seemed to relax him. He looked familiar and I stared until I finally had to ask a young player who the old guy in the dugout was. "That's Eddie Mathews," the player said. "Ever heard of him?" The image of the aging Mathews sitting there stopped me in my tracks. I'd never met him but he still occupied a place in my private mythology—in the lexicon of Cooperstown, he was an *immortal.* Couldn't the Braves organization have found a better job for him than minor league roving batting instructor? Wasn't there a cushy job somewhere with a house on a golf course and a guaranteed fat salary? It was upsetting.

I started to go over and introduce myself but what would I say? "You were my childhood hero" might make him feel old. "I played in the minors. . . ." Big deal. "I'm making a movie"—you think I care? "We both went to Santa Barbara High school and I won the Eddie Mathews bat my junior year for having the highest batting average on the team, and not only do I still have the bat, it sits in a corner of my bedroom as a weapon in case any intruders come in the middle of the night."

I left him alone.

4

Edith Piaf and the
Texas Playboys

(Act One)

I returned to Los Angeles, stuck the recorder in a drawer, and forgot
about it for a while. The deal with Thom Mount had to be papered,
and even though it would be a boilerplate scale contract, somehow
lawyers would figure out how to drag it out—they were getting paid
by the hour. Besides, I had something else to work on. Before the trip
to Durham, I'd been asked to write a treatment and script for a feature
film to star Richard Pryor and John Cleese. I couldn't imagine two
more diverse comic sensibilities, which is what made it a compelling
challenge. Each was brilliant and iconic, and my inchoate theories
of screen chemistry could be put to the test. I don't remember what
storyline I came up with, but after a couple of weeks of thrashing
about I got a call from the studio to inform me they couldn't make
the deals with Pryor and Cleese, so the whole thing was dropped. I
never got paid because my deal was never finished before it fell apart.
This is standard operating procedure, however, and caused no alarm.
I only wish I could have seen Pryor and Cleese onscreen together.

My other deal, this baseball thing, was a much simpler matter,
however, so I pulled out the recorder and began typing the woman's
monologue.

First the woman needed a name, and "Annie" seemed a good place
to start. Baseball groupies have traditionally been called "Annies"—a
name that feels warm and unthreatening and almost pastoral. Rock-
and-roll groupies, with their spiked hair and tattoos and leather gear,

wouldn't be called Annie. A baseball Annie could be someone you'd bring home. I typed in "Annie" and then saw a matchbook cover on my desk that said SAVOY, so that became her name. Savoy was a dive bar in Hollywood but it conjured up big-city sophistication—maybe the Savoy Ballroom on Lenox Avenue in New York, or maybe Paris—but it was a good balance for the girl-next-door-ness of my Annie.

Now that she had a name, she needed her music. While writing, I often play music that suggests a mood or tonal landscape. It can never be thematically specific but should be somehow reflective of the character—maybe it's just music the character might play. From the outset with Annie, it was go down either the Patsy Cline road or the Edith Piaf road. I chose Piaf because it seemed a less obvious choice for a woman in the South, though she probably played Patsy Cline in her car. Plus, though I hadn't met Annie yet, I did have all that stuff about regret and rose-colored glasses.

As I typed in the monologue with no particular idea where it would lead, it felt right that if Annie was going to be our guide, she might as well lead us from the outset. She would not just be a narrator with a point of view, she would physically take us to the ballpark and into the world. She puts on makeup while we get a view of where she lives—the bedroom is revealed right away without lingering on it—and she's out the door, through the neighborhoods of Durham, to the ballpark. She finishes what she has to say and enters the park.

I was immediately nervous about the monologue. Was it too literary? Too arch? Trying too hard to be poetic? After Buddha, Vishnu, Allah, trees, mushrooms, and Isadora Duncan, not to mention the soul, the Church, Jesus, Walt Whitman, and Milt Pappas, I was certain we'd gone far enough down that path for now. The story needed an antidote to Isadora Duncan. Max Patkin was waiting on the bench.

Deemed the "Clown Prince of Baseball" (but not the first), Patkin was a fixture in the minor leagues for forty years, staging pregame baseball-related clown routines and even interrupting the game in progress. He was allowed to coach first base for a couple of innings—surely no other sport allowed the promotional entertainer to do anything like that. He always made me laugh, although I was in the minority among players, who thought his act stale and old-fashioned. I used to sit in the dugout before the game to watch his routine while most of the players stayed in the locker room. Over the course of a season, Patkin and his act crossed a team's path a couple of times, once at home, once on the road. He was a big attraction, even though his act consisted mostly of throwing dirt on himself and spraying water from his mouth into the air and following players around, mimicking them.

One night after a game in Amarillo I ended up sitting at the bar with him for a couple of beers. He had a long, sad, classic clown story—he had been a minor league pitcher until Joe DiMaggio hit a home run off him in a wartime exhibition game. The homer traveled so far Patkin chased Joe around the bases, throwing his glove and kicking dirt on the Yankee Clipper. He said it was the most applause he ever got, so he soon quit baseball and became a clown.

He was also a ballroom-dancing champion, a rubber-limbed physical comic, a man with a new career on the rise as an entertainer. Then his wife ran off with another woman and broke his heart, so Max spent the rest of his life on the road in the minors. "Never missed a date in forty-one years" was his rap, although he took the bus from town to town or hitchhiked with scouts or umpires or anybody he could find. I loved Max and figured he might be the antidote to Annie's speech (although Isadora Duncan and Emily Dickinson would have loved him). So, when Annie finishes her monologue with the final words "the Church of Baseball," she enters the ballpark and it's Max Patkin who awaits, with his ancient, ritualistic vaudeville act, grinding his hips, spewing spittle, bending like a pretzel—giving his all to another performance in front of a small crowd. The music that accompanied the act was Bill Haley's iconic "Rock Around the Clock," which Haley let him use without charge. It seemed the story I'd sold must be under way because I was on page three.

A screenplay is like sheet music with one great exception. At best, a screenplay will get played only one time, but music can be reinterpreted forever. If a scene from a movie script is played too broadly or too introspectively or too self-consciously funny or . . . or . . . it can change the entire tone and intention the writer was striving for in the screenplay. If writing for another director, or on a "hired gun" assignment, I invariably put more parenthetical clues at how something (a line, an exchange, an entire scene) is intended to be played. The director may ignore it, but he does so at the risk of changing the tone of the entire movie. This is not to say that sometimes the director's fresh take on the material won't turn out to be a revelation, and produce a more compelling version of the script than what the writer had in his head. While working in isolation, the writer is likely envisioning a movie that will never get made. I walked out of showings of two movies that I'd written but did not direct and, to this day, have not watched the second half of either. At the same time, Roger Spottiswoode elevated my script of *Under Fire.* If, early in my career, I wrote something that I planned to direct, I tended to shy away from excessive parenthetical clues, which seemed to be both insulting to the reader and an admission that if the text needed explaining, there must be something lacking in it. Many battles wiser, I tend to err on the side of clarity (an admonition I preach when I teach an occasional writing workshop). The audience for a screenplay, after all, is varied in the extreme. Actors are the main people I'm trying to get a script to, but often the road to an actor is an obstacle course of land mines called agents, managers, financiers, producers, producer-girlfriends/boyfriends-trying-to-break-into-the-business, middlemen, and an endless cabal of unnamed studio executives. Clarity matters.

After the first day of writing *Bull Durham,* I had a title sequence plus two more characters with great names lurking offstage, waiting for their entrances. There was still no outline, so I determined to get all the people onstage and see how they interacted, in the hopes that would give me a structure, a story, a theme, anything to cling to.

The one thing I believed in then (and now) about screenplay structure was that it must have three acts. Act Two should be as long, more or less, as Acts One and Three put together. The first-act curtain must raise the stakes, and the second-act curtain must raise them higher. As for what page number on which various plot points must land (as the books preach), I'm not a fundamentalist. Three acts are the posts and lintel that hold up the building, and a story can only be cantilevered so far off the post before gravity takes over. Nonetheless, rules are meant to be bent and broken. I knew from my previous efforts that second acts were the tough part of any story because they had to keep upping the consequences of choices the characters made until the story reached a more heightened dramatic place than it was in an hour earlier. Years later I was walking a Writers Guild picket line around the Fox studio lot when I saw a striking writer with a sign that read: I HAVE A GREAT THIRD ACT—TALK TO ME. What I wanted to say was, "If you have a great second act, then the third act writes itself." Wisely, I shut up. Structurally, certain "moves" the script makes become like load-bearing walls in a building. As the narrative shifts and adds weight, the scenes and character development have to be strong enough to carry the growing weight. If the turns in a screenplay are earned, the building grows effortlessly and can take a number of shapes. If not, it crashes under its own weight—the load-bearing walls weren't there. If offered a script to rewrite, the first thing I look to see is if the load-bearing walls are in the right places. If they aren't, it's not fixable. I was very conscious of building to a load-bearing wall at the end of Act One.

In case Max Patkin hadn't shifted the tone enough away from the cosmic spiritual journey of Annie Savoy, I figured introducing Ebby Calvin "Nuke" LaLoosh with his pants around his ankles might finish the job. My intention was also to give him and his girlfriend du jour, Millie, a certain innocence. Millie's presence in the clubhouse is owed to her father having given the electronic scoreboard to the team. Ebby Calvin LaLoosh (not yet "Nuke" in the film) is introduced in flagrante, but it's critical to any screenplay that we connect with the protagonists, even if we don't particularly like them. Empathy matters more than sympathy, and so what Ebby Calvin says as he's caught having sex in the clubhouse before his professional debut matters a great deal. It's important that he be blissfully oblivious, naïve, even sweet—as he is not only having sex but unembarrassed by being caught. This is one of Nuke's gifts, I would discover along the way: that he had an obliviousness that shielded him from criticism. Did players really have sex in the clubhouse? I never saw it, but everyone had a story; in some ballparks the bullpen provided the space for illicit rendezvous. It didn't seem like a very romantic spot to me, but nobody confused what was occurring with romance. It was, after all, the sixties and seventies when I played, even if the movie is set twenty years later. Jim Bouton was asked by a skeptical interviewer when the movie came out, "Did that sort of stuff really happen?" to which he responded, "Oh, yeah, all the time." Mickey Mantle himself, when asked by the Yankees to describe his fondest memory in old Yankee Stadium, wrote a now-infamous letter describing a bullpen blow job in some detail. The Yankees chose not to publish it on their "Old Timers' Recollections" page (or whatever it was called), but the letter was leaked anyway. So young Ebby Calvin caught with his ass showing in Durham Athletic Park seemed innocent enough.

After his entrance, the story needed to see Ebby Calvin in baseball action immediately. It was easy enough shorthand to have him throw his professional debut pitch into the broadcasting booth (shades of Steve Dalkowski). A simple physical action in a movie can replace pages of dialogue and do it better than words can. We immediately see that LaLoosh is a gloriously undisciplined physical specimen, exactly the kind of guy Annie might be looking for each year.

We also see it through the eyes of Annie, who's mentoring the free-spirited young Millie. Why does the story need Millie? In practical terms, she gives Annie someone to talk to, but it also allows the woman revealed in flagrante delicto to emerge as a character with her own voice and point of view. When Millie appeared on the page and started to speak, she was familiar to me but I didn't know where she came from. I knew that if I kept listening to her, I might remember more about who she is, or was, or if I ever knew her at all.

• • •

It was time for Crash Davis to make an entrance. I imagined him as a character from a Western and even started to think of the movie as a Western. Crash was a hired gun who went from town to town ply-ing his trade in a consummately professional manner. The hired gun archetype fills the screen in Peckinpah's *The Wild Bunch,* John Sturges's *The Magnificent Seven* (based on Kurosawa's *Seven Samurai*), Richard Brooks's *The Professionals,* and scores of other Westerns. He's a character whose past might be unknown, whose home is the next place he lands, and who collects his paycheck and moves on. In the narrative tradition, there might be an unexpected connection with a local woman, who touches him and whom he touches, and it seems for a moment that they will end up together, but they can't; he will move on to the next job, town, gunfight—although there might and probably should be a kiss. John Ford's great tale of the gunfight at the O.K. Corral, *My Darling Clementine,* is a classic example. Henry Fonda, as he rides away at the end, gets off his horse to kiss Cathy Downs (Clementine) and then shakes her hand, as she waits on the edge of town. (Darryl Zanuck, the head of Fox Studios, and Ford famously fought over the ending. Ford wanted only a handshake; the studio added the kiss. Curiously, it's a most satisfying compromise to me, although lovers of the film still fight over it.) Though the kiss lingers, in our minds, he rides on.

In Crash's entrance scene, he reports for duty to two veteran baseball lifers, Skip Riggins and Larry Hockett, the pitching coach, men who reflect precisely what he doesn't want to become, someone toiling anonymously in the far reaches of lower professional baseball holding out hope (probably false) that someday the big leagues will come calling. It was important to establish Crash's character quickly because we'd already met the other protagonists and it was time to see how they interacted.

Besides, this was probably the movie star's part, and you can't leave the star offstage for long. To start the scene and set up Crash's entrance, I buried some exposition with Skip and Larry reviewing Ebby Calvin's mind-bending debut. Eighteen strikeouts—new league record. Eighteen walks—new league record. Hit the mascot, the sportswriters, and so forth. All the numbers were inspired by the statistics of Steve Dalkowski, but from a storytelling point of view, they reveal what happened in the game without having to show much of it. They also create a light moment that is a slight misdirection to Crash's imminent entrance, with his gravitas and existential crisis. But if it's not funny, it doesn't work, and at the heart of it, it's expositional.

Screenplay exposition—that is, the dissemination to the reader (or audience) of critical background information needed to serve the story—is often not given the attention it demands. I work hard to bury the exposition in drama or humor or anything that doesn't feel expositional. In *Cobb*, a later movie about the last days of the tyrannical genius baseball player Ty Cobb, there's an early scene in which he violently throws a collection of pill bottles across the kitchen. With each toss, he identifies the drug he's about to shatter against a wall. It's terrifying, it's entertaining, and when he's flung the last bottle, we know he's dying. Nothing had to be said about it. In *Under Fire*, Nick Nolte plays Russell Price, an adventure-seeking photojournalist who lands in Nicaragua during the revolution of 1979, where he runs into a colleague, a veteran, old-school journalist, Alex Grazier, played by Gene Hackman. Filling in Price, much less the audience, on the history of American political interference in Central America, not to mention the various warring factions of the left, right, and center of that country, was a daunting task I gave to Grazier. Upon Price's arrival, he and Grazier have a beer in a local restaurant and Price wants to know which beer to drink. Grazier recommends one beer over another because of the political affiliation of each. Quickly the cause of the Sandinista rebels and the intransigent evil of the Somoza regime is revealed in simplistic terms through the choice of beer. Later, the story can elaborate, but the audience has a foothold. In *Bull Durham* I was sure that very little exposition would be necessary because most of the audience would be dropped into a world they knew nothing about, a world without conventional villains or even conventional goals, other than to survive. But they knew baseball.

Like most athletes, Crash remembers the tiniest details of the games he's played, including not only the pitch and the count on which he homered off Larry many years ago, but also that he hit the ball over a tire ad billboard that earned him a free wheel alignment. Crash's dry sense of humor leavens his pride and quiet but righteous anger—he won a free wheel alignment; he likes that. Larry tells us he tried quitting baseball once and ended up selling Lady Kenmore washing machines at Sears, Roebuck and that it was "nasty, nasty work," which is his way of telling us he can never quit the game. If it means being a pitching coach in the Carolina League, so be it. I worked at a Sears in Spokane, Washington, in the off-season once, and though I didn't sell Lady Kenmores, I did come to work at 6 a.m. every day to make Christmas bells to decorate the appliance department. It was nasty, nasty work.

The entire scene is also expositional without appearing to be. We learn quickly why Crash is there and why he doesn't want to be; we also get the key information about Nuke. The tiny exchange between Crash and Larry about a home run hit long ago tells us how long these men have been fighting the battle and how vivid each memory is.

Crash's mission is laid out for him by Skip and Larry, an experience that is so humiliating Crash can only lash out. His job? To "mature the kid" and mentor him so the organization has a better chance to realize their investment in him as a first-round draft pick. Crash's interpretation of the assignment is the correct one—namely, that the organization has no further belief in him as a player. He still has a dream of getting back to the big leagues, but it appears he's alone in that belief. It's clear that the organization senses he might be *management material,* and Crash could acknowledge that the powers-that-be are offering him a new chapter in his baseball life, but he knows what they're really saying is that he can become Skip or Larry whenever he's ready. He's not ready; his angry response reveals that the fire still burns: "So my Triple-A contract gets bought out so I can hold the flavor-of-the-month's dick in the bus leagues? Fuck this fucking game. I fucking quit." But Skip and Larry and the whole damn organization know he can't quit. He slams the door to leave and they wait patiently, knowing the door will open in a matter of seconds and he'll ask for the only information that matters to him: "Who we play tomorrow?"

Steve Dalkowski had, at last, been handed to a more capable Joe Altobelli in the hopes that the veteran could mature the kid.

•   •   •

After just one scene, we know a lot about Crash. He's got a sense of irony or he wouldn't have introduced himself as "the player to be named later"; he's simmering with rage that, after all his years of battling to get to the big leagues, he's still stuck in the hinterland; and he's unable to give up something he loves so much. The third thing might be the most important.

Crash Davis loves something more than it loves him back. The external force of opposition is the "organization" that has determined it's too late for him to have what he's been working for. But the internal force of opposition—do I still have it and does anyone care?—is stronger because it's something he might be able to act upon. He doesn't know that yet, and certainly I didn't. I was just writing a story to see where it took me.

Crash Davis is a cowboy, so after writing his entrance scene I settled on Bob Wills and the Texas Playboys for his music. The music pre-dates the time of the story by fifty years but I was into western swing at the time and my father's Texas side of the family used to play Spade Cooley at the house in Taft, so I went with it. I knew that Texas swing wouldn't be right for a soundtrack (should the movie ever get made), but I also sensed that Piaf and Bill Haley might work well together. Ebby Calvin didn't need music. Whatever was loud and girls danced to was fine with him.

Screenplays don't have much time to put all the forces of opposition and attraction together. Now that the three protagonists had made their entrances, it was time to have them meet. I've always liked the term *watering hole* for a neighborhood bar where familiar faces gather to howl at the moon or hook up or just plain drink. Wildebeests and gazelles gathering at a pond on the savanna seemed a decent image for a bunch of ballplayers looking for a place to forget about their slumps or rising ERA, and maybe get lucky with a local college girl. There was no model for such a place in my years in baseball, but as a narrative conceit it served the story. The bar (later called Mitch's Tavern after the actual location in Raleigh) became a set piece that functioned like a piece of proscenium theater. Annie sits with Max Patkin, old friends (another conceit that strains credulity). Ebby Calvin dances out of control with any girl in sight; and Crash drinks alone. It might as well be onstage.

The beats are linear. Crash sends a drink to Annie, forcing Max to introduce them. Max drops the line about Crash "I actually saw him read a book without pictures once." This gets Annie's attention; she's already noticed that Crash is not only great-looking, but he's her age. And now he reads books? She asks Crash to dance, he says he doesn't dance, and she just says, "How embarrassing." When a character says, "I don't dance" it should be clear to the writer that before the story's over, he'd better be dancing. Ebby Calvin comes over, introduces himself, and asks Annie to dance. Crash stands up, gets between them, and says, "She's dancing with me."

Scenes in a screenplay need a turn, a moment when the scene suddenly isn't about what it was about up until that moment. A scene shouldn't be about the same thing at its end as it was at the beginning. The scenes we remember in movies are those that turn and sometimes turn more than once and keep revealing themselves. Now that the three protagonists are meeting, and the alpha males are sniffing it all out, we're set up for a turn. Ebby Calvin challenges Crash to "step outside and party," and Crash, rather than act in the mature way he seems set up to do, accepts the challenge with a shrug. Annie is momentarily disappointed in Crash, but privately might be a little turned on by the two men being willing to fight over who gets to dance with her.

This whole dancing thing gets personal for me. I can't dance, never could, am bewildered by it and in awe of everyone who can. The only thing that frightens me more than dancing is flying in small planes. Growing up in the Baptist Church, where dancing was forbidden, had little to do with it. Dancing wasn't discouraged in my family, nor was it taught. The Church believed that dancing, to borrow from a phrase taught in Catholic schools, "might lead to the occasion of sin." First you dance, then you have sex—a clear linear projection. If that was true, then we all would dance all the time. I suspect I just wasn't musical enough. There's an old joke that only Baptists understand: "Why don't Baptists fuck standing up? Because someone might think they're dancing."

When Crash says he doesn't dance, it could be me. When he's willing to fight, it could also be me. These aren't character strengths, but this guy, inside my head, is quickly becoming personal. Outside the bar, the scene takes its second turn. Ebby Calvin wants fisticuffs, but Crash is too smart and too seasoned for that. He quickly sizes up his rival, who happens to also be his student, and makes a fool of him. When Ebby Calvin charges Crash and is decked with a short left hook, the turn is still coming. Crash then offers Ebby Calvin a hand to pull him up off the ground, and introduces himself as "your new catcher."

The final turn in the scene comes when Ebby Calvin smiles, pats Crash on the back, seems genuinely excited to meet him, and turns to the other players to proudly introduce "my new catcher." That's the turn that completes the scene.

Back in Mitch's Tavern, at Annie's table, she's glad they've settled this and invites them to her house. Ebby Calvin is put off, Crash is fascinated, presumably because if it comes to another mano a mano with the kid, the kid doesn't have a chance. They follow Annie to her house, which feels like a turn but is only a feint.

At this point in the writing I'm trying to remember what the hell I sold to Thom Mount and recalled that, after "*Lysistrata* in the minor leagues," I pitched that there is a woman, and two players, and she's sleeping with the wrong one. If she is sleeping with the right one, there's no story. The scene begins with Annie Savoy putting a vinyl record on a phonograph (no tape cassettes for her), and Ebby Calvin and possibly even Crash Davis are introduced to Edith Piaf. *Non, rien de rien / Non, je ne regrette rien / Ni le bien qu'on m'a fait / Ni le mal* . . . The music I played in my apartment served the moment, the dramatic setup, and Annie.

Annie's in complete charge at the top of the scene. She lays out her ground rules: she'll choose her lover for the season and identifies Ebby Calvin and Crash as the two best prospects so far. Crash wants none of her schemata, though it's clear he wants her. There's a little badinage, driven by her. Crash is irritated by the whole thing (he's also intrigued). Ebby Calvin doesn't have a clue. Annie's not used to a ballplayer not being dazzled by her. She throws out pheromones and ants building cathedrals and quantum physics, but Crash isn't buying any of it. He rises to leave, and tells her: "I don't believe in quantum physics when it comes to matters of the heart." This clearly isn't your normal ballplayer in the Carolina League, and she parries with a challenge: "What do you believe in?"

I figured it was time for a speech to land a movie star. Movie stars need to read great lines in a script so they can tell themselves only a movie star can deliver such lines. I needed something a bit over the top, quotable, and unforgettable. It was okay if it was excessive—I could fix it later, maybe even in the editing room if, God willing, I ever got there. And so, as fast as I could type, I wrote:

```
                  CRASH
      I believe in the soul, the cock, the pussy,
      the small of a woman's back, the hangin'
      curveball, high fiber, good Scotch, that
      the novels of Thomas Pynchon are self-
      indulgent, overrated crap. . . . I believe
      that Lee Harvey Oswald acted alone, I
      believe there should be a constitutional
      amendment outlawing Astroturf and the
      designated hitter. I believe in the "sweet
      spot," soft-core pornography, opening your
      presents Christmas morning rather than
      Christmas Eve, and I believe in long,
      slow, deep, soft, wet kisses that last for
      three days. Good night.
```

First of all, Pynchon is not overrated. For a brief moment, I thought it might be something Crash and Annie could argue over and that they might switch sides at the end of the story, each persuaded by the other as their resistance toward the other weakened. I never developed that further, however, determining it would occupy too much space. How Pynchon turned into Sontag is for a later chapter. I am not a conspiracy theorist and do believe that Oswald acted alone and it's been nearly proven in later books by Gerald Posner, Vincent Bugliosi, and Larry Sabato. Mostly I included the Oswald reference as a way to get under the skin of all my JFK-assassination-conspiracy friends, but also because it was an unpopular position when I wrote the script, long before the anti-conspiracy books were written.

Crash Davis should have some contrarian positions—it was good for his character. Good Scotch? Yes, but uncommon for a minor leaguer who'd be happy for cheap beer or whatever's in the well. The small of a woman's back? Yes. The constitutional amendment? Yes. But the speech is intended to get Annie's attention while making Crash hard to characterize. Is it a bit arch? Maybe. Is it self-conscious? Maybe. Is it believable? Not really. Is Crash playing games with her? Yes, because she's playing games with him. But still, it feels too writerly, a speech that calls too much attention to itself. It does, in the end, however, seem to do what it was intended to do.

When Crash finishes his speech and bids "good night" (in a gentlemanly way), Annie's only response is "Oh, my." She wants to find out more about this man but he's gone into the night, and he's gone because he doesn't buy into her rules. Her system has failed her, and his pride has failed him.

"Oh my" was the signature phrase of sports broadcasting legend Dick Enberg, and now it belonged to Annie. By her own rules, Annie now was left with the wrong guy, although in most seasons Ebby Calvin would be a perfect student for her life wisdom and particular brand of training. He was big, strong, sweet, lovable, and open-minded. Most seasons, however, Crash Davis didn't show up in Durham. Having no regrets, or at least trying not to, Annie embraces Ebby Calvin as fully as she's capable. On their first night together she teaches him how to undress, ties him to the bed, and reads Walt Whitman to him.

The story starts with Annie applying makeup as she's about to head to the ballpark. A few hours later we're back in her bedroom. When the night is over we know that Annie wants Crash and Crash wants Annie—and she's in bed with the wrong guy, who happens to be their mutual student. In the last line of the evening, she introduces Ebby Calvin LaLoosh to Walt Whitman: "Limitless limpid jets of love hot and enormous, quivering jelly of love, white-blow and delirious juice . . ."

To end the night, the script plays it off LaLoosh:

```
CLOSE ON EBBY'S FACE—Intrigued, aroused,
frightened.
```

The end of the night is also the end of Act One. It's taken place in about five hours. There's almost no baseball in it. It felt like a load-bearing wall was in place.

5

It Don't Get No
Better Than This

(Act Two, Part One)

I was on page twenty-seven and needed a title. The contract called it *Untitled Minor League Baseball Project*, which makes for a lousy shorthand. I liked titles like Wim Wenders's *The Goalie's Anxiety at the Penalty Kick* and Tony Richardson's *The Loneliness of the Long Distance Runner*—they had sports themes, evoked an emotional world, and were true to the material. They were also terrific movies. They also wouldn't do shit business in America's mall-complex theaters. In the same mode, I liked *A Player to Be Named Later* for the script, but ultimately thought it was too obscure, and maybe a touch European and angst-ridden.

I had Max Patkin, who lived in King of Prussia, Pennsylvania, and guys named Crash and Nuke and a guy dressed like a bull, and there was a beautiful woman telling the story—it needed a title that was short and maybe slightly rural and one you could remember. The South was still full of old, decaying barns covered with painted signs advertising tobacco no longer produced. Bull Durham and Mail Pouch were the most common, but the signs were faded and peeled and the barns gradually collapsed as the tobacco industry diminished. I called it *Bull Durham* as a working title, and it never changed. It might have been Thom Mount's idea—I don't remember—but I put it on the title page and it just kind of stayed there.

My private rule as a writer is not to commit to a certain amount of pages a day, but to commit to a certain amount of time every day.

There's no waiting for the muse, and although there's a lot of truth to what Hemingway allegedly mandated—"Write drunk, edit sober"—if 9 a.m. is your writing time, then that's a challenging proposition. And 9 a.m. is my time. I try to walk away in the afternoon.

When I wrote *Bull Durham,* I committed to being at a pickup basketball game at three every day, so that became the pattern. It was a good one because I would physically burn off the chair-sitting stress plus get into a lot of head-clearing arguments. It also led to my coming up with the idea for *White Men Can't Jump,* but that's another story. I have a private rule that writer's block cannot be acknowledged. When I'm stuck, I keep writing even if it all hits the trash can for a while. I write to make discoveries, not to connect the dots, and so I felt after ending Act One with Walt Whitman, I needed some baseball. That tended to serve the writing throughout—sometimes it just felt like it was time to play ball.

One goal in telling this story was to tell it from an athlete's point of view. In this case, as the woman was telling the story, I had to make sure that every baseball scene turned the tropes upside down and allowed the players' view of the game to emerge. That raised a question: What is a player actually thinking about when he's in the middle of a game and not supposed to be thinking? It was easy to give Skip the line that every ballplayer at any level has heard his entire life, "Don't think—it can only hurt the ball club." In service of that notion, my screensaver says, DON'T THINK—JUST WRITE.

I launched in and set up the locker room with a new character, another member of the team, Jimmy, announcing prayer meeting, for which he's roundly booed. There were no locker room prayer sessions when I played, and players didn't point to the sky and, presumably, God, when they crossed home plate after going deep, like they do now. In recent years, it sometimes seems the "athletes of faith" outnumber everyone else, and I can't remember the last boxer who didn't thank God after a fight. But I wanted Jimmy to be an open-faced, nonjudgmental kid, and I had in mind he would be given a special reward for that, although that probably meant he wasn't, in a strict sense, an evangelical.

Nuke enters, looking beat up from his night with Annie, and

Larry is elated, because if Nuke is Annie's choice for the season, it practically guarantees he'll have a good year. Larry doesn't pay attention to Nuke's declaration that there wasn't any sex, only a poetry all-nighter, and then Nuke declares that hearing poetry all night is "more tiring than fucking." He wrestles with "limpid jets of love" and turns to Crash for help, but Crash lectures him about the fungus on his shower shoes. The intention here is to put all these ideas into a very short scene so that Walt Whitman can live in the same space as shower shoes with fungus. Since I'm in Act Two, it's too late to set the tone—but it's important to let the reader/audience know that this story probably isn't going to end with a grand-slam home run in the bottom of the ninth at the end of Act Three.

There's a serious point that Crash's speech makes:

```
CRASH
You'll never get to the Bigs with fungus
on your shower shoes. Think classy and
you'll be classy. If you win twenty in the
Show you can let the fungus grow back on
your shower shoes and the press'll think
you're colorful. Until you win twenty in
the Show, however, it means you're a slob.
```

Superior athletes are cut a lot of slack by management and media. If Ty Cobb hit .267 lifetime he'd have been in jail. Instead, he hit .367 and was in the first group inducted into the Hall of Fame. Appalling behavior is explained away and forgiven endlessly—if you're a winner. Even Crash is saying that's the way of the world— but lectures to Nuke that until he's a winner, he hasn't earned the right to behave a certain way. I also wanted to use the term *shower shoes* because I'd never heard it before the minor leagues. They were basically flip-flops but *shower shoes* sounded classier to me.

On page twenty-nine Crash comes to the plate and launches the second act, and this scene has to accomplish a number of things. I wanted to get inside Crash's head now and hear his internal monologue while he's trying to hit. Every ballplayer has one—even Ted

Williams, the most intellectually analytical of all the great hitters—and most players carry on a battle between both sides of the brain. On one hand, hitting a baseball is reactive—see the ball, hit the ball—and on the other it's a complex analysis of what a particular pitcher throws in a given situation, what pitches you have trouble with that he throws, how to recognize different pitches as they leave his hand, his tendencies, your tendencies, your track record against this pitcher if there is one. . . . It's endless.

And then there's everything else that crowds into your head. A batter knows his statistics to four decimal places as the game unfolds. If a hitter is on a 1-for-6 streak (and struggling), he knows as he races to first that if the ground ball he just hit up the middle goes through, he's now 2 for 7, which is .2857, which rounds off to .286, which is a very good batting average, all else being equal. He also knows, as he approaches first, that if that terrific Dominican shortstop makes the play and nips him at first, he's now 1 for 7 in his last two games and that works out to .143, which will get him back on Piedmont Airlines in a hurry. Such is the life of a hitter—or at least the mortal ones, the group I'm familiar with. If that ground ball up the middle goes through, the beer tastes better and the woman in the bar after the game might be interested. In any case, she'll certainly look better.

But other things spin in the batter's head. Life, death, finances, marriage, girlfriends, family . . . When I played you could add Vietnam to that list. For a player who isn't white, the list is inevitably longer. It's impossible to always make yourself mentally quiet at the plate, although that's the requirement. Relax and concentrate—here comes a ninety-five-mile-an-hour cutter.

Annie has lived in Crash's head since the previous night when he made his "I believe in . . ." speech, something he may be regretting. Now she's sitting in the first-base box seat watching him, after spending the night with Ebby Calvin, whom she has rechristened "Nuke." That's a lot to deal with when the pitcher's throwing cheese.

I asked a lot of hitters what they thought about at the plate and the answers ranged from "nothing" to "pussy." Hmm. I would suggest there's another camp, the group of hitters who are *thinking too much*—Crash would be in that group. So, he's looking for a high fastball and talks himself into being ready for it and then realizes he's already too analytical—and the pitcher hasn't thrown a pitch yet. The immortal Henry Aaron said that he always guessed what pitch would be thrown, that it was impossible to be ready for everything. I wish I'd read that advice while I still played; it would have been a lot easier to guess than to try to emulate Ted Williams's scientific analysis. Then again, Williams also believed in "guess hitting," though his guesses were intellectually superior. Crash is caught in the same dilemma and, trapped by his own intelligence (unable to "see the ball, hit the ball"), he swings at a bad pitch and tries to analyze his way out of it until suddenly he's down two strikes and Annie pops into his head. He needs to step out of the box and clear his head.

```
CRASH STEPS OUT OF THE BOX—Motions to the batboy
for the pine tar rag. The boy brings it over.
Crash reapplies it to his bat.

                    BAT BOY
     Get a hit, Crash.


                    CRASH
     Shut up.
```

Simply put, the throw-in with the batboy was my answer to all the stories and movies in which Babe Ruth (or surrogates thereof) visited the dying kid in the hospital and asked what the kid wanted and the kid always wanted the Babe to hit a home run for him. And the next day the Babe always hit the home run—and then the kid would throw away his crutches and joyfully run around the hospital. It was all reminiscent of a faith-healing service in a big tent.

Even as a kid I knew that the faith healing on TV was just a show, like professional wrestling, but it was confusing. If Jesus was "the way, the truth, and the life," were we supposed to accept these televised faith healings as miracles, comparable to Jesus himself raising Lazarus from the dead? Not to mention, if he turned water into wine, why weren't Baptists allowed to drink? Why was it grape juice rather than wine being passed around with broken saltine crackers for monthly communion?

These were easily corrected tenets of the faith—wine versus Welch's (not to mention squaring up a saltine cracker with the body of Christ)—but this faith-healing thing was a real stickler.

The dramatic falsehood that suggests the Babe or his wannabes could hit a home run on command is an upsetting lie to a kid who knows that if you could hit a home run whenever you wanted, you would never do anything else. Besides, Babe Ruth also struck out 1,330 times in his career. What does the poor boy with crutches think when he's listening to the game on the radio the next day and the Babe whiffs?

Back to Crash's "shut up": there's nothing more irritating than a sweet, open-faced, good-hearted kid wanting to be friendly when you're chasing an 0 for 4. Crash strikes out, of course—he has to—and when he gets back to the dugout there's a note from Annie waiting; she thinks she's identified his mechanical problem. She knows baseball, but she probably already knows that she's about to become his *real* problem. She might also suspect that *he* is about to become *her* real problem.

Millie is reintroduced in the process when she reads to Annie Crash's note in response: " 'I want to make love to you.' " If it seems a little early to baldly state Crash's want, it's because it's a new want for him—he didn't anticipate finding anything in Durham that he might care about, much less want—and besides, we're on page thirty-two by now.

Crash and Annie meet in a batter's cage to begin the courtship, even though she's committed to Nuke, which she articulates:

```
                      ANNIE
     Despite my love of metaphysics and my
     rejection of most Judeo-Christian ethics,
     I am, within the framework of a baseball
     season, monogamous.
```

She lays out her rules. Clean, clear, specific. It's too late for Crash because her rules say it is, and the idea is planted that she has quickly painted herself into a corner of her own making. Crash keeps pushing—"Your place or mine"—even though he has no interest in competing with Nuke. But there are two revelations in the scene that, if the intention works, reveal one thing that neither realized until this moment.

                    ANNIE
You had your chance the other night.

                    CRASH
What'd you see in that guy—he's a young,
wild, dim pretty boy.

                    ANNIE
Young men are uncomplicated.
     (Crash mutters)
And he's not dim. He's just inexperienced.
My job is to give him life wisdom and help
him make it to the major leagues.

                    CRASH
That's my job, too.

They are joined at the hip by the thing keeping them apart— Ebby Calvin "Nuke" LaLoosh. And therein lies the rub of why they might be perfect for each other. Crash is too professional to abandon his assignment "to mature the kid," and Annie is too committed to her course as mentor of *life wisdom,* whatever that is. This is one of those things that takes on greater importance when it emerges in the writing than it would have if outlined. Hearing Crash and Annie talk makes it immediately clear that while they're stuck with this problem, it will also keep them connected. They may be frustrated, but they're also intrigued . . . by each other and by Nuke.

The second revelation in the scene is that Annie discovers Crash is on course to become the greatest home-run hitter in the history of the minor leagues. She's thrilled. He calls it a "dubious honor" and insists it means nothing to him, asking her not to mention it to anyone. It becomes their secret.

I had no knowledge of anybody keeping minor league home-run records, and 246 dingers (the number Annie references) seemed unobtainable, so I just tossed it in. Since then I've learned that a man named Buzz Arlett has been called the greatest minor league player in history and hit well over 400 home runs in the Babe Ruth era. He turned down major league offers because he made more money in the minors. Recently, Mike Hessman claimed the minor league record when he hit his 433rd homer. Unlike Crash's desire for silence, this was a much-publicized event and took place in the Toledo Mud Hens ballpark, where I once played as a visiting Red Wing. I hit exactly no home runs in Toledo. So, Mike Hessman doubled the record Crash Davis was trying to reach. It doesn't matter.

As they take turns hitting pitches from a machine, Crash makes an aggressive play for Annie:

                    CRASH
    Fact is you're afraid of meeting a guy
    like me 'cause it might be real so you
    sabotage it with some crap about a young
    boy you can boss around—

It's hardly a romantic come-on, and she roundly bats it away with the same ease with which she's hitting a baseball in the cage:

                    ANNIE
    Oh, Crash, you do make speeches.

As originally constructed, the scene wasn't yet over. I added a sequence wherein a Little League team arrives next to the cage for a baseball birthday party, then Nuke shows up in his Porsche looking for Annie and challenges Crash: "What're you doing here? Stealing my girl?" But Crash just steers Nuke to the birthday party to sign autographs. Later, in rehearsals, I cut out the entire Little League/ Nuke sequence. It was clear that the scene was over with "Oh, Crash, you do make speeches."

Nonetheless, I didn't have a clue how I was going to shoot a scene while the principals hit baseballs coming from a machine.

• • •

Early in Act Two, we're back in Annie's bedroom. Nuke and Annie are under the covers thrashing around. There's nothing embarrassing here, except in the drama. Annie calls Nuke "Crash," and Nuke calls her on her revealing gaffe.

> NUKE
> You said, "Crash."

> ANNIE
> Would you rather me be making love to *him*
> using *your* name, or making love to *you*
> using *his* name?

It's a convincing argument, and Nuke wisely accepts it.

If this were a Western and Crash the hired gun wandering from town to town to ply his trade, he could not have a past. Nuke, however, brings his past with him. It's all he has, and when he calls his father to share that "these hitters are better than the ones in high school," he ends up asking for his mother, who might be more understanding. Nuke calls from a pay phone in front of the world, hoping his father won't come to visit until he's pitching better. Crash would never call home in public, and we're not even sure there's a home to call. Regardless, the short scene in which Nuke calls home didn't make the final cut.

• • •

Annie's teaching methods for Nuke are beginning to reveal themselves; it's time for Crash to show his own m.o. with a guy he can't tolerate. But first, it felt like it was time for a scene about the background and color and flavor of minor league baseball—a scene that gives secondary characters a moment to breathe. First drafts of screenplays should be full of things to cut out, and I'd had enough experience by then watching two of my scripts made into movies to know that it wasn't possible to predict what would survive the cut, even if I would be the one doing the cutting.

In that spirit, there's a short scene set in the bullpen before a game as a promotion unfolds in front of us. These kinds of sequences have to be constructed in a way so they can be lifted out of the narrative without hurting the flow. That way, when the studio comes with knives because you're behind schedule, the director can always magnanimously sacrifice one of these mini-scenes at the budget altar.

The script suggests a hot-air balloon dropping cash on the field as two hundred Little Leaguers charge out to chase the paper money floating in the breeze. It was later changed when we discovered there were no hot-air balloons in Durham, but the cash drop wound up staying. My affection for minor league promotions is well documented and, unlike most players, who stayed in the clubhouse till the promotions were over, I was always in the dugout eating them up. There was a vaudevillian-road-show-of-desperate-to-fill-the-ballpark quality to these promotions; they separated the minors from the corporate cool of the big leagues.

My favorite minor league promotion was *Big Valley* Night in Stockton, California, when I played for the Ports. *The Big Valley* was a hit TV show in the late sixties, set in a mega-ranch in Stockton a hundred years earlier. The big star was Barbara Stanwyck, whom I would later be smitten with when I discovered *The Lady Eve* and *Double Indemnity* and all her other films. It was big news at that time that such a legend would do television. The male stars included a young, blond, athletic-looking actor named Lee Majors, who reeked of All-American-ness, and his swarthy counterpart, Peter Breck. Our general manager had the inspired idea to bring Majors and Breck to the ballpark to wear old-fashioned period baseball uniforms and stage a reading of "Casey at the Bat" before the game. Ernest Thayer's famous poem (the only one he wrote) was first published in the *San Francisco Examiner* in 1888 and, as its popularity grew over time, two cities in the country claimed to be the model for "Mudville," the team Casey plays for and lets down. Stockton, California, is on the delta and claims it is indeed Mudville, but so does Holliston, Massachusetts, making its claim because Thayer was a philosophy major at Harvard and surely spent more time there than in California. Thayer, once the editor of the *Harvard Lampoon,* never settled the issue and lived out a long, full life in, of all places, Santa Barbara, California.

Big Valley Night was hugely promoted with the cooperation of Twentieth Century–Fox, which produced the show. The team owner (who owned a bread company, as I recall) was thrilled when the game sold out days before the event. On the night of the big promotion, however, with ten thousand people in the stands (the only full house of the season), the limo bringing Majors and Breck arrived at the clubhouse, where the two actors could put on their nineteenth-century uniforms and rehearse a reading of the poem: one of them was to be the pitcher, the other was to act out the part of mighty Casey as he strikes out. But Lee Majors didn't show up and Peter Breck was smashed, so deeply in the cups that the players had to drag him into the clubhouse and lay him down on his back, burying his forehead with ice wrapped in towels. Our general manager was an angry wreck while, outside the clubhouse, the crowd was chanting for the stars. It was decided if we could get the uniform on Breck, we could prop him up somehow and parade him around in short center and have him wave. Or something. Clearly, he couldn't be Casey at the bat.

But what to do about the missing Lee Majors? Perhaps this was a sign that I would someday make a better living in the theatrical arts, but I noticed that the new player who had just arrived—nobody even knew his name—was about six feet one and had that blond All-American thing that Majors had.

"How 'bout the new guy pretends he's Lee Majors?" I offered.

"Impossible. That'd be deceitful. No way," the GM responded.

The players all looked around, and maybe it was Ralph Manfredi, the third baseman (and a pal), who said, "Hell, he looks just like him." Somebody else thought the new guy looked *better* than Lee Majors. The clubhouse quickly decided this was an inspired idea and the GM, his hands tied, kept staring at the new guy until finally he barked, "Put on the damn uniform and don't get too close to the crowd or they'll see you're a fake."

We dragged Breck out to the field and posted a player on either side so he wouldn't fall over, and our faux Lee Majors was such a hit that he got closer and closer to the crowd and finally started signing autographs. *Big Valley* Night was the most successful promotion by the Stockton Ports in a decade.

Another great Stockton Ports promotion was called Used Car Night, in which the lucky ticket holder would win a "pretty decent used car that runs." The winning ticket stub was held by a five-year-old Mexican American boy who had apparently found his way to Billy Hebert Field without an adult. When we left the ballpark after midnight, the GM and the little boy were still standing on the infield, stadium lights still on, with a 1955 two-tone Ford station wagon.

So, our Cash Drop Night, even with a small budget, seemed quite doable.

As the cash drop played out, a short bullpen scene created an opportunity to introduce two new players in three-quarters of a page, keeping it all shorthand. Secondary characters must be created as if they each have their own story to tell, only there's no time to do anything more than sketch them out. The sketched strokes matter and the characters have to be created in haiku, lest they don't make the cut. There is a tendency for many writers to fall in love with their secondary characters because they don't have to carry the weight of the drama. I continually remind myself that I can't spend too much time with the pizza delivery guy's problems, even if I care about them.

While these characters illuminate the main story and add to it, they don't have to develop, grow, change, or even surprise—but they're critical to the whole. The Latino player, José, is introduced rubbing a chicken-bone cross on his bat. Another player, Bobby, is deep in a slump and wants some of the magic but is cautioned that it only works "if you believe in voodoo." I had some concern that the only Latino player in the story would be into voodoo—was that a cliché?—but at the same time I was aware of the reaction that many American players had when they played in the Caribbean and experienced the so-called black arts and its impact on baseball.

Latino culture was not as big a part of professional baseball when I played as it is now, and there was an exotic fascination (often along with racism) associated with Caribbean play. Players brought back stories of chicken-bone crosses placed at bases (usually second base, for some reason) and the need to occasionally counter a pregame curse by cutting off the head of a live chicken. These stories were recalled with respect and even fear. This stuff was real.

Dave Leonhard, a teammate at Rochester and former pitcher for Baltimore (and at the time the only major leaguer to graduate from Johns Hopkins), pitched in Puerto Rico one winter and wrote a piece for *The Baltimore Sun* that recounted incidents he experienced that only could be explained by some magical or spiritual force. Ironically and sadly, the article was perceived as pejorative by the Puerto Rican press and he was banned from playing there again, although his intention in the article was the opposite. I provoked stories out of him whenever I could about this wondrous world, and have never forgotten that each Caribbean team had to carry a witch doctor, who was also a player, on the roster. A switch-hitting utility infielder who was also a witch doctor was much sought after and worth building a roster around. So, José survived the cut because every team needs a witch doctor.

• • •

Nuke makes his first appearance on the mound with Crash behind the plate on page forty. A page number is basically a reminder that something should be happening by now. Page thirty means that if you were watching in a theater, you'd be approximately forty minutes into the movie, including the titles.

Crash approaches the mound to talk to Nuke.

```
CRASH
Don't try to strike everybody out.
Strikeouts are boring. They're fascist.
Throw some ground balls—it's more
democratic.
```

The lines are a direct steal from Bill "Spaceman" Lee, former Red Sox star and one of the game's great iconoclasts. When I met Lee years later, I asked permission to use his line (which I'd done ten years earlier). He granted it; socialist that he is, he didn't feel that he owned it. I thought Lee was the kind of guy Crash would get along with, not because they would share political ideologies (though they would have argued about them over good Scotch, which they would also argue about) but because they'd respect an informed *other* opinion and neither was, in the end, an ideologue.

The turn in the scene happens not when Crash tells the batter what pitch is coming, but when Crash then tells Nuke that he told the batter, which leaves no doubt about which man is in charge. A couple of years after the movie came out, I ran into Joe Garagiola and Johnny Bench, who were having lunch near my office at Raleigh Studios, where they were shooting a commercial. Garagiola said he didn't like my movie because a catcher would never give away a pitch. Bench said, "The hell he wouldn't! I did it all the time."

In 1969 our Stockton team won the league championship. In the middle of the season, however, we went into a team-wide hitting slump. The cause of this slump, we were convinced, was simple. Our bat order from Louisville Slugger hadn't arrived, so our bats were broken and taped up and we were picking up cheap bats, nothing of professional quality, from the local sporting goods store. We complained, we moaned, we struggled at the plate. In a movie, this is where the grizzled old baseball coach sits the young players down and says, "I'm sick and tired of hearing all this pissing and moaning. You got to understand somethin'. It don't get no better than this." He'd be right, of course.

Our bat order finally arrived in several cardboard boxes. We smelled the wood like it was luxurious Spanish cedar even though it was merely northern white ash covered in shellac. The new bats were rubbed and caressed in front of our lockers before the game. Our hitting slump was about to end. Except that very night, with our fresh-from-Louisville bats, some guy with an ERA around 7.00 threw a perfect game at us. We totally whiffed. After the game, in the showers, silent and humiliated, we watched as our old manager (and one of my favorite managers ever), baseball lifer Billy Werle, stood stark naked in his shower shoes and dumped the entire bat order into the shower, where they then lay, soaking in the water. "New bat order, my fucking ass!" he screamed. We stood as naked children, afraid to move.

But there's something else I remember about this scene. Billy Werle was one of those guys with giant nuts that seemed to hang nearly to the floor. We all stared at that, awestruck, even as we were supposed to be focusing on our wet bats. And when he finally retreated to his tiny office and we scrambled to retrieve and dry off our beloved, hitless bats, someone said, "Did you see those nuts? That's major league."

That's why Skip throws the bats into the shower in the script.

• • •

Another reason I resist detailed outlines before beginning to write is that they don't allow for dramatic sequences to appear just because they feel right. Scenes that make no sense in a linear construct, that seem to come out of nowhere, and yet are the perfect tonal shift as the story unfolds, cannot be imagined beforehand. At least that's how I function. So after the bats were thrown into the shower, I felt the story needed a moment to ground the fun these men are having as they hang on, desperately trying to sustain a man's career playing a boys' game. Most minor leaguers live with the ever-present fear that being released is just a slump away. On my third day in Bluefield, a note was fixed to the sixteen-penny nail in my locker, but not *my* nail. It read, "Skip wants to see you in his office." One of the players who shared my locker went to see Altobelli, believing he'd made the team—but no, he'd been released. Shaken, he packed his bag and left. Players at nearby lockers looked at one another in shock and someone said, "That's fucking terrible—can you believe it?" Another guy, a catcher, whose clothes hung on the second nail in our shared locker said, "It's you or him. Why you crying?" I got the lesson. Two weeks later, the catcher was gone, too.

A second memorable release happened in spring training the next year. A pitcher from Puerto Rico, Israel Torres, came out of one of the manager's offices, sat on a stool, and started bawling. I knew enough Spanish to know he was saying, over and over, "I can't go home. I can't go home. . . ." He went home.

But the most stunning release happened in Stockton, two years later. A young left-handed pitcher named Rich showed up in spring training, having been traded to the Baltimore Orioles organization from another team. Left-handed pitchers are always sought after, and he had been assigned to the Ports team. He pitched out of the bullpen and got everybody out with a good curve and an effective enough fastball he could spot. At the halfway point of the season, which we won (seasons in the minors are divided into two halves, with a playoff between winners of each half), this guy had an ERA of 0.00, which is not only unheard of, it's merely *perfect.* He had a wife and a baby and lived in the apartment complex with all the players, and one day he came staggering outside, shaken, and announced that he'd been released. The reason, he said, was that there'd been a mistake and Baltimore had traded for the wrong guy. They had wanted another player with a similar name and hadn't realized the error until the season was half over. It seemed not to matter that, wrong guy or not, he'd gotten everyone out. His career ended with a perfect earned run average. As he packed his bags and family to drive back home, he just kept muttering, "I'm the wrong guy?" I always wondered what happened to the right guy. And how he could be better than perfect.

INT. INSIDE SKIP'S OFFICE—NIGHT
Skip and Larry open a couple of beers.

THE DOOR OPENS—BOBBY ENTERS wearing only a towel.

```
                        BOBBY
        You wanted to see me?


                        SKIP
        Yeah, Bobby, shut the door. This is the
        toughest job a manager has . . . but . . .
        the organization has decided to make a
        change. . . .


                        BOBBY
        Skip, I know I'm in a slump but I hit the
        ball hard today, right at 'em. A couple
        flares drop in and I'm back in the groove!
```

The nearly naked twenty-five-year-old man pleads helplessly—his career is over.

It was an easy scene to write because three short speeches say it all. I was just thinking of Israel's lament, "I can't go home, I can't go home," and Rich's cosmic question, "I'm the wrong guy?"

• • •

You are never home in the minor leagues. It's a constant road trip because even your "hometown" isn't your hometown, it's just another apartment, another short-term lease where you're guaranteed to forfeit the lease-cancellation deposit. If that apartment is occupied by four single players, it's a lock that the damage deposit will also be forfeited. A player lives in an apartment for several months, April to September, bookended by spring training and possibly the playoffs, if he lasts the full season. Plus there's all the time spent on the road during the season. And then, perhaps, winter ball in Florida (I played in Clearwater) or Arizona or the Caribbean or Mexico or Venezuela. This is tricky enough if you're single. If you're married, it's impossible.

My script needed a road trip. The narrative problem was that it took the spine of the story away from the character at the center, Annie Savoy. It's her story, at the end of the day, and now the two men she's involved with (one physically, one emotionally) are about to go away for a while. The storytelling trick was to keep her at the heart of the tale even when she's not in it.

To honor the obligations set up in Act One, I also needed to keep her alive as a mentor to Nuke. The road trip gave Crash a chance to do his own mentoring without Annie's strong voice interfering. Crash and Annie share a teaching philosophy, synergistic but not exactly in sync on the details. And she's the only one having sex with Nuke. The solution was for Annie to send a part of herself along for the ride—in this case her garter, which she tells Nuke to wear: It will "dangle off your thighs and buns in such a wonderful way that you'll start seeing things differently." The garter keeps Annie at the center of the story while she's offstage. It also gives Nuke a lot to think about.

I wrote a page of Annie's voiceover as she philosophizes about the nature of ballplayers going on road trips. The intention was for her to represent the women's Greek chorus (wives and girlfriends) worrying about the fidelity of their men while off to war. I wrote it. I never used it. It was a bad idea because it raised questions that had nothing to do with the story. Did Penelope ask questions about Odysseus? Maybe, but Homer doesn't tell us. And my script wasn't about Odysseus going off to fight the Trojan Wars for ten years and spending another ten years getting home to Penelope. I was merely dealing with a fourteen-day road trip to Winston-Salem and Fayette-ville with two guys named Crash and Nuke. I wrote the voiceover, I cut the voiceover.

Instructively, I was informed by the use of voiceover at the spine of Billy Wilder and I. A. L. Diamond's script for *The Apartment*. The narrator was C. C. "Bud" Baxter, played by Jack Lemmon, and his voice added an empathic neurosis to a story that somehow folds romantic comedy into acidic social criticism. It's dark, and it's light, and the narrator reveals enough of himself to connect the two disparate tonal strands by adding a third—his own voice—that lets us know more about him than Wilder and Diamond let you see in the onscreen drama.

The other use of voiceover that sticks with me is at the heart of Terrence Malick's first movie, *Badlands*. Sissy Spacek, playing the erstwhile girlfriend of serial killer Kit Carruthers (Martin Sheen), based on Charles Starkweather, narrates a different movie than the one we're watching. *Badlands,* produced by my former boss Ed Pressman, shows a beautiful use of voiceover as an *unreliable* narrator. In *Bull Durham,* the intention of Annie's voiceover was to have a *reliable* narrator, who, at first, shares more than she intends, and then winds up not giving a damn about what she has shared.

By page fifty, not much had happened yet in the script, which seemed like a problem. I imagined a road trip sequence that was a short film unto itself, packed with all the fun and absurdity of the baseball life that could be squeezed into fifteen pages. This was not a great idea. Basically, what it provided was a healthy page count destined for the cutting-room floor. The only things that mattered for the story were that Nuke, while contemplating the garter, begins to listen to Crash, and that his downward spiral be dramatically solidified so it will render him at the mercy of his mentors.

The road trip begins with Nuke playing the guitar badly and butchering the lyrics to "Try a Little Tenderness." He begins, off-key, with "Oh she may get woolly, women do get woolly, because of all the stress. . . ." This is a particular issue with me, as I can't always tell if a singer is on pitch and if the chord changes are correct (I'm not a musician, though I'm surrounded by them), but I do pay attention to the words. Crash interrupts angrily (he, too, thinks the words matter) and admonishes Nuke because he respects neither the game nor himself (nor the lyrics). Nuke tries to dismiss Crash.

NUKE
I ain't pissing nothing away. I got a
Porsche already. A 944 with AC and a
quadraphonic Blaupunkt.

```
                    CRASH
You don't need a quadraphonic Blaupunkt—you
need a curveball. In the Show, everybody
can hit the fastball.


                    NUKE
How would you know? You been in the majors?


                    CRASH
I was in the Show for twenty-one days
once. It was the greatest twenty-one days
of my life, and you can't piss on that.
You never touch your luggage in the Show—
somebody else handles your bags. They got
white balls for batting practice. The
ballparks are like cathedrals, the hotels
all have room service, the women have
long legs and brains. It's a smorgasbord,
boys. . . .
```

The perception of Crash changes instantly. He has credentials that none of them can imagine—even Nuke is impressed. In terms of revealing character, the speech is intended to suggest gravitas and modulate Crash's slightly delusional desire to get to the big leagues at his advancing age. He's been there, however briefly, so maybe his dream of getting back isn't completely mad, though it's receding into the distance every day. He's in Durham, in low Class A ball, he's getting older, and he knows there are probably four catchers with futures between him and the Show. Still, he's been to the promised land. After a scuffle caused by Crash calling Nuke "meat" but mostly caused by Crash allowing his simmering rage to boil over, Nuke settles down and asks for help.

```
                    NUKE
Teach me how to throw a breaking ball.
```

Two things for baseball people: Would a young player be drafted number one if he didn't have a breaking ball? Back then, yes—it happened all the time if the kid brought serious cheese. And *meat*? For decades ballplayers called each other "meat" as a kind of substitute for "meathead," though it was a vaguely affectionate sign that you were one of the guys.

To keep the story moving and the audience tracking the season, the road trip is narrated by the announcer, Teddy, who re-creates the broadcasts in a tiny studio using recorded crowd noise and a flimsy sound effect of ball hitting bat, because it's too expensive to send him on the road. This is, of course, based on the Major League Baseball broadcast re-creations that were common well into the 1950s, and were a staple of college football broadcasts as well. Did they happen in the minor leagues? I didn't know, but it worked for the story and that's all that mattered.

Meanwhile, our Durham Bulls are struggling on the road. Things begin to look up when they get off the team bus at the next cheap motel just as another bus is unloading, this one full of mostly nubile young females in the "Fantasy on Ice" troupe, some minor league equivalent of the Ice Capades, which my aunt John used to take us to at the old Pan-Pacific Auditorium. (Aunt John was one of six aunts from Texas who resettled in the Central Valley of California. She chose Bakersfield, which was the most like Texas. The aunts all had boys' names because when my great-grandmother Gertrude was pregnant with each of them, there was much prayer that a son would be born to work on the hardscrabble farm. In each case, a daughter arrived, but the male names survived. That's another movie.)

Remember my failed attempt to get a day off by removing a tarp in Little Rock? It felt right that the young sirens in the traveling ice-skating show would be the motivation for players to want a rain-out, and that Crash would provide the veteran's wisdom on how to achieve it. I even had a player contemplate, "A night off with the ice skaters might get us back on track." Such is the desperation of a player in a slump.

The script then spent too much time with our Bulls players chas-

ing the women around the hotel, and being chased, in a kind of
bawdy farce that only gets them in further trouble with the manager
and coaches. It had little to do with the three lead characters and the
too-slowly-unfolding dynamic among them, but it looked good on
paper and we eventually shot it. And cut it. The biggest loss was a
speech that Skip gets to make to the ice skaters when they're caught
with the players just before the bacchanalia begins.

                    SKIP
Who are you?

               ICE SKATER #1
We're ice skaters. Can we go now?

                    SKIP
No. I want you to hear my philosophy.
It'll do you some good.
     (beat)
Here it is. This is a simple game. You
throw the ball, you hit the ball, you
catch the ball. You got that?

               ICE SKATER #1
Yes.

                    SKIP
Are you lovely creatures aware that you
are about to compromise yourselves with a
buncha bums who are—
     (to Larry)
—what are we?

                   LARRY
Eight and twenty-four.

                        SKIP
Eight and twenty-four! How'd we ever win
eight games?

                        LARRY
It's a miracle.

   I liked Skip being paternal with the young women, and he makes
a big, tough, threatening speech that puts the players on notice.

                        SKIP
Look, guys—I'm a man. I got needs, too. I
understand this party, but . . . sex is
the one thing you can get further behind
in and catch up on faster than anything I
know. There's a baseball lesson in there
somewhere. Where's Crash?

                        NUKE
He can't make it.

                        SKIP
Aw, Christ, he don't have to come. He's
hitting .350.

                        PLAYER
Don't you think that's a double standard—
we're here and he ain't?

                        SKIP
I believe in a double standard for guys
hitting .350. Look, men, you got a choice.
You wanta be roasting your nuts off welding
Midas Mufflers onto exhaust pipes up the
assholes of Cadillacs . . . or do you
wanta be sitting in the Caddy while some

```
other guy's crawling around in a monkey
suit with a blowtorch?
    (beat)
There's only two places you can be in
life—in the Caddy or under it. These are
the best years of your lives—these are the
glamour days! It don't get any better than
this.
    (threatens)
But if this club don't start winning soon,
there's gonna be changes made.
```

The road trip had one other story point that didn't survive, and for good reason. Max Patkin, who would live a dozen years after the making of *Bull Durham,* dies in the script. It's an off-screen death in an automobile accident, and it presented the opportunity to stage a ballpark funeral. Like the ice skaters, it had nothing to do with the spine of the story and was doomed from the start—though it was shot.

As the road trip concludes, we know two things: Nuke is pitching so poorly that, out of desperation, he's starting to listen to Crash. We also learn from Teddy the broadcaster, "This is the most wretched road trip I've seen in twenty years and possibly the worst Durham team in half a century." The sequence concludes with Nuke's dream of pitching near naked—in a garter and jockstrap—in front of a crowd of jeering fans. When he wakes up with a jolt, he's on the bus sitting next to Crash, who understands the fear and comforts Nuke. The road trip is over, though it took the cutting room to sort through what mattered.

If page count matters, I was roughly halfway through the script and hadn't gotten to the hook of the idea that I had sold the script on—*Lysistrata* in the minor leagues.

6

Aristophanes and the
Bermuda Triangle

(Act Two, Part Two)

I have a private theory about screenwriting: if I'm not suicidal by page sixty-five, I'm doing something wrong. The midpoint is where it's easy to start repeating yourself. You write a scene that works in Act One, then there's a tendency to keep writing variations on that scene forever—or at least during the whole second act. But in Act Two, the stakes have to keep being raised and characters have to keep making choices that have an impact. This can be subtle—bodies don't have to fall out of closets—but stakes still need to be raised. Though structure is famously critical in screenplays, sometimes it's just intuition that needs to be trusted. If the story feels slow to the writer, it's glacial to the reader. And if it's glacial to the reader, the movie doesn't get made—unless a movie star coming off a megahit is attached.

I hadn't figured out how to get to the premise of the story I'd pitched, but it was obvious I couldn't wait much longer. The idea of withholding sexual favors to achieve an endgame is a small idea in the script, but it does raise the stakes. And it felt like an idea that might continue to pay off. A season in the Carolina League is Annie's Peloponnesian War, only if it's not taken too seriously.

Nuke is exhausted when he returns from his disastrous road trip. He can't get anybody out, the team's on a losing streak, nothing in his world is going as he expected it would—his dreams have turned to nightmares. At least he's got Annie's warm bed to look forward to. She picks him up at the ballpark in her vintage 544 Volvo and takes him home to her backyard for a pitching lesson that focuses on the mental approach rather than the physical. (I always designate the make and model of any important car in the script and the 544 was a family favorite that got handed down until it was beat to hell.)

Sports psychology was just being recognized as a legitimate field of study in the late eighties, which makes Annie prescient, although sleeping with the client is probably not in the manual. Millie waits in the backyard in full catcher's gear over a sundress (like the car, the dress is scripted), while Annie steers Nuke to a pitcher's mound that's been there awhile—clearly he's not the first pitcher she's schooled. When she suggests that he breathe through his eyes "like the lava lizards of the Galápagos Islands" and offers that the parietal eye is part of Fernando Valenzuela's no-look windup, Nuke is tied into knots. When she touches his crotch with her glove to explain how the chakras connect, he's a mess—but he's getting looser and, as sports psychologists in generations to come will tell us, he's getting "out of his own head."

Nuke tries to assimilate this mad assortment of instructions and delivers another pitch, which goes ten feet over Millie's head and through a window. Annie's delighted because Nuke was free and unbound in the delivery, even if the results were disastrous. For me, throwing the ball through the window was important to the scene because it's a kind of pratfall that can balance Annie's headiness. I was unaware at the time of Preston Sturges's rules of comedy. Although some of the specifics are dated, the final and most important rule still holds:

1—A pretty girl is better than an ugly one.
2—A leg is better than an arm.
3—A bedroom is better than a living room.
4—An arrival is better than a departure.
5—A birth is better than a death.
6—A chase is better than a chat.
7—A dog is better than a landscape.
8—A kitten is better than a dog.
9—A baby is better than a kitten.
10—A kiss is better than a baby.
11—A pratfall is better than anything.

Throwing a ball through a window doesn't fit the primary definition of a pratfall (a "fall on your buttocks"), but it's low, physical, and unsophisticated. Nuke's had enough of Annie's worldview and picks her up to carry her into the house.

> NUKE
>
> I give up. Let's go inside, make love, and fall asleep till it's time to go to the ballpark.

> ANNIE
>
> Or . . . we could just take that sexual energy and save it for a few hours and rechannel it into your pitching tonight. You're a powerful young thing, Ebby Calvin. . . .

> NUKE
>
> I can't keep up with you. First you say sex is gonna make me a better pitcher—now *no* sex is gonna do it?

> ANNIE
>
> It's all the same thing—there's an energy cycle that runs like a river. . . .

Finally, the writer gets to the point. As scripted, the scene then wanders down an unnecessary side path that didn't stand a chance of survival in the final film: Nuke spots Max Patkin's ashes sitting in a small urn on a table in Annie's gazebo. The scene turns to a discussion of life and death. Who cares? The answer is no one.

Knowing when to get in and out of a scene is a separate discipline, and when I began screenwriting I was still thinking more like a writer of fiction than of movies. As a result there was a tendency to let scenes go on too long and to serve the minor characters rather than the star parts. It's easy to fall in love with the secondary characters—the coaches, the girlfriends or boyfriends, the announcer—because they don't have to carry the burden of forward movement. They're easy to write, they're fun, they fill up and sell the world you're trying to evoke, but they're low-risk. *Bull Durham* was full of secondary characters who had their own stories. In the original screenplay, for instance, Deke's wife had a number of small scenes that revealed the precarious and unrewarding job of being a player's wife, always worried about how her man is doing, with no time for herself.

Nuke, now removed from Annie's bed for the moment, tries on the garter in the clubhouse, where he's met with derision and cheap gay jokes from his teammates—all except Crash, who knows this is Annie's idea and thinks it might be a good one. Crash, ever the mentor, even adjusts the garter on Nuke with the line "The rose goes in the front, big guy." It's not a line in the script but it's a great line and came out of rehearsal, probably from Costner, as we played with the scene. As the scene was written, an argument among the players ensues about whether God is male or female but it felt dated even as I wrote it and it fell away quickly. When there's a line like "The rose goes in the front, big guy," it's time to get the hell out of the scene.

Which led to the ballpark funeral of Max Patkin. It involved a church gospel group and a soloist singing the old warhorse hymn "In the Garden," which opens with "I come to the garden alone, while the dew is still on the roses" and is as familiar to any aging Baptist as "Jesus Loves Me." I thought the ballpark was a perfect garden for the song, and as players from both teams lined the field, in the background, Larry the pitching coach filled a rosin bag with Max's ashes, as was Max's wish. It was a lovely scene, beautifully backlit. It didn't survive. For years I kept putting that hymn into scripts hoping it would make the final cut. It never did.

• • •

The biggest mistake a sports movie can make is to have too much sports in it.

A movie can't compete with television showing sports action, but it can and must reveal all the moments that television can't touch.

The baseball sequences in the script are about character more than plot, and not because there isn't a plot (or much of one, anyway). They need to be funny or flip the tropes or shine light on the clichés from new angles. A televised sporting event may have fifteen to twenty cameras—I have one or two. The trick is to put my one camera where none of the twenty TV cameras can go.

The road leads back to Sam Peckinpah again. In reference to his Westerns, he said: "I love clichés because clichés establish an immediate connection with the audience. Clichés reside in the collective unconscious. And what is a film? A film is just a collection of clichés. The work of the director is to love the cliché, adopt the cliché, and then work against it. You have to remake the cliché in a way that nobody has ever made it before. That is the work of the director." Peckinpah knew it was also the work of the writer.

The cliché of an amulet that a character might wear as he goes to war is flipped. The amulet is a garter, and Nuke finally begins wearing it, with Crash's blessing (most of the time he agrees with Annie's tactics). Nuke begins pitching better because he's not thinking about pitching; he's thinking about Annie. Crash, by contrast, has sometimes struggled at the plate because he, too, is thinking about Annie—although for him it's a more serious contemplation. Nuke quickly accepts—again, thanks to Crash's and Annie's counsel—that "It don't make me queer, right?" which is a step out of the ignorance with which he landed in the story. Nuke finally has a good inning, but Crash won't let him enjoy it.

                         NUKE
        I was great, eh?

                         CRASH
        Your fastball was up and your curveball
        was hanging—in the Show they woulda ripped
        you.

                         NUKE
        Can't you let me enjoy the moment?

CRASH
The moment's over.

Crash won't give Nuke a pat on the back because Nuke doesn't deserve one. He's pitched one good inning by page seventy-seven! As Crash heads to the plate, he announces to the team that if the pitcher throws him a breaking ball, he'll take him downtown—one of the many terms in the baseball vernacular for *home run.* The pitcher throws him a curve and Crash promptly hits it over the fence, which earns him even more respect from these doomed minor leaguers. Crash, although he's always just barely concealing his simmering rage at his assignment with Durham, can't help but do his job. He's a professional, which Nuke is not. At least not yet.

BACK TO THE FIELD—Nuke's next pitch.

THE NEXT BATTER POPS UP—Crash circles into foul ground to make the catch, whipping the ball around the infield.

It's a meaningless moment in the story—a pop-up in foul territory—but it was important to fill the story with such meaningless moments of action that I hoped would add up to a meaningful evocation of the game. A scripted foul pop-up to the catcher, later a scripted broken-bat pop-up to the second baseman, or a routine double play disconnected from the central narrative all were intended to paint a picture of the game as players saw it, not as fans remember it. In the dramatic terms of watching a baseball game, these moments are boring. As a player, the *boring* moments are fully engaging—you better catch the damn pop-up in foul territory or you're back on a bus headed home.

At last, the story is moving forward—and I'm worried that it's still too slow. Nuke is starting to pitch better, but not as well as he thinks. A pitcher who hasn't won a game can't be guilty of hubris, though Nuke has his version. Crash calls for a pitch and Nuke shakes him off, thinking he knows better than his mentor. Nuke refuses to throw the pitch Crash calls for, so, once again, Crash tells the batter what pitch is coming. For Crash, it's not a matter of giving up a possible home run that could lose the game; it's a matter of pride, of fulfilling his mandate to teach Nuke everything he knows.

The first lesson to a young pitcher is to shut up and listen to the catcher. It's the whole reason Crash is in Durham. I still wonder why the catcher in El Paso gave me the sign on the first pitch of that game in the Texas League, which seems like a hundred years ago. It also seems like yesterday because I haven't forgiven myself for not swinging. The scene is not about Crash giving away pitches—that's old news.

The scene is about *him telling* Nuke that he's giving pitches away. It implies that he'll keep doing it until Nuke does exactly what he's told. Nuke gets the message clearly. Also, he's wearing the garter, so he's getting the message from Annie as well. Both of his teachers are finally getting through to him, even if they're still not having any success getting through to each other.

Crash tells Nuke to hit the bull mascot with a pitch—and he does. Another pratfall. But Nuke has yet to fully absorb his lesson; he now shakes off another pitch. Crash clues in the batter, who immediately hits a long home run. In the movie, the ball hits the bull sign—there is no bull sign in the script. I added that later, on location during prep.

> NUKE
>
> You told him I was throwing the deuce, right?

> CRASH
>
> Yeah, he really crushed that dinger, didn't he?

Nuke, at last, gets it. Crash is the boss *on* the field and Annie rules *off* it. He also decides that maybe there's something to this sexual-abstinence thing and now agrees with Annie that they shouldn't have sex until he loses.

I was deep into Act Two and there was still no plot, in any conventional sense. Worst of all, I needed a montage to move the story forward. Montage in a narrative film does one of two things: it moves the story forward in an elegant way that can't otherwise be achieved economically; or it's an editing-room trick to cover a multitude of filmmaking and storytelling miscalculations. The latter isn't what Sergei Eisenstein or D. W. Griffith had in mind. For a montage to work, it needs to be designed into the script and generate forward narrative movement; it's critical that things have to be different at the end of it than they were at the beginning. So, over various images of the road trip:

                    ANNIE (VOICEOVER)
        Nuke was so encouraged that he took a vow
        to not have sex until they lost. . . . I
        figured Nuke would win a couple, then lose,
        and things would get back to normal. . . .
        But it didn't happen like that.
                  (beat)
        And for one extraordinary June and July,
        the Durham Bulls began playing baseball
        with joy and verve and poetry. . . . The
        two sides of my own brain were all jumbled
        up and cross-wired. . . . While one side
        was being neglected, the other was in
        paradise watching our Bulls play like big
        leaguers.
                  (beat)
        We swept a four-game series with Kingston,
        two games at Winston-Salem, and kicked the
        holy shit out of Greensboro in a three-
        game series. . . . Crash, who kept hitting
        dingers, was approaching the minor league
        record . . . though I told nobody.
                  (beat)
        After sweeping a July 4 doubleheader, the
        Durham Bulls were tied for first. . . .

At this point the montage images of the guys on the road give way to Annie at her shrine, alone in her house—the first time in the sequence we've seen Annie, though she's been talking throughout.

                    ANNIE (VOICEOVER)
        But beautiful as the winning streak was, I
        was getting damn lonely. . . . Something
        had to be done. I needed a man.

End of montage. And now Annie recognizes that her life construct—a young player for the season and off he goes, full of life wisdom—isn't making sense anymore. Maybe it never did. Annie doesn't *need* a man (she told us that in the opening monologue), but she *wants* a man. And she now knows that what she doesn't want or need any more is a *boy*—Nuke.

• • •

In 1970, I was playing in the Texas League. Sometime in mid-June I was hitting over .320 and sailing along, waiting to be called up to Rochester in the higher-level International League. I went into a massive slump—something like 0 for 30—before blooping in a flare. Magically the slump was over, but the call-up didn't happen and I didn't get back to Rochester till the following year. When the slump ended and I had a multiple-hit game, I was invited to be the guest on the radio broadcaster's postgame show.

Don't forget that, at that time, nearly 350,000 U.S. soldiers were in Vietnam and they were coming home in body bags. I'd lost friends. Everyone had. But in the bubble of playing professional baseball, it was as if none of that was going on. Players were afraid to talk about it, although everyone held their breath when the annual birthday-lottery draft happened. My brother's birthday came up as number one and he immediately enrolled at the University of Montana in Missoula to be close to the Canadian border in case there was a knock at his door. It seemed like an appropriate subject for a radio interview—I mean, what else was there?

The interview started out fine. "Yeah, I think I'm outta the slump and the team is starting to pull together" kind of stuff. Hell, we were ten games under .500 and there was racial tension in the clubhouse, not to mention unhappy players who weren't getting the playing time they thought they deserved. Joe Altobelli, once again my manager, was calmly trying to hold things together. The local press was all over us, and we deserved it. But now I had a mic. It was my turn. The broadcaster kept the conversation fairly banal, or at least he tried. Until finally, "You're from California. Tell us a little about that . . ." or something like that, and I started to ramble: "Yes, I'm from California, a state that has lost more young men than any other state in this ill-conceived adventure in neocolonialism in Indochina. . . ." I wanted to bury the hawkish argument of the domino theory and give a short primer on the corruption of the Nguyen Cao Ky regime. I didn't get as far as I wanted because at some point I could see how the poor broadcaster was not only appalled but frightened. I felt bad. It wasn't the time for such a speech. The broadcaster and I managed to steer the discussion back to an upcoming series against Shreveport, and when he said, "Thank you," we were both relieved.

Before I left, off mic, he said, "Next time, just talk about your hobbies." I wasn't sure what hobbies he meant—a *hobby* always suggested model airplanes or beadwork. "Hobbies?" I asked. He offered hopefully, "Do you like to hunt or fish?" In truth I'd never done either, but I said, "I do now."

A few weeks later I was again the guest on the postgame radio show. I must have had a helluva game because I know they were loath to invite me again. But I was prepared. This time, I went on and on about my off-season deep-sea-fishing adventures and how much I was looking forward to another winter chasing marlin and the "big ones." The broadcaster wisely didn't ask what the "big ones" were, and was a happy man when I finished. He knew I was lying. It didn't matter.

The best postgame moment I can ever remember was when I heard Leon Roberts, an outfielder for the Seattle Mariners, on the car radio in the late seventies. He was asked about a slump the team had been in and he responded: "Well, that's what happens when you have erotic pitching, erotic fielding, and erotic hitting."

On the next road trip, Nuke is now desperate for everything Crash can teach him.

                    NUKE
        I love winning, Crash, you hear me? I love
        it. Teach me everything.

                    CRASH
        It's time you started working on your
        interviews.

                    NUKE
        What do I gotta do?

                    CRASH
        Learn your clichés. Study them. Know them.
        They're your friends. Write this down.
              (beat)
        "We gotta play them one day at a time."

                    NUKE
        Boring.

                    CRASH
        Of course. That's the point.
              (beat)
        "I'm just happy to be here and hope I can
        help the ball club."

                    NUKE
        Jesus.

```
                    CRASH
Write, write—"I just wanta give it my best
shot and, good Lord willing, things'll
work out."


                    NUKE
"Good Lord willing, things'll work out."
```

At this point we're having a good time in the scene and it could write itself for twenty pages, but there's not actually any story development here. Nuke has been listening to his mentor for a while now—the scene needs to turn or the humor isn't earned. When a scene is working, the writer isn't dictating—he's reporting what he's hearing his characters say. Scenes turn because they have a life of their own and the writer is discovering what's been set in motion as it evolves. So, when Crash asks the simple question "So, how's Annie?" I knew the rest of the script would write itself. Nuke is increasingly less enamored of Annie than he is of his ERA. Crash is still falling in love with her.

```
                    NUKE
She's getting steamed 'cause I'm still
rechanneling my sexual energy. . . . Maybe
I should cave in and sleep with her once
just to calm her down. What'ya think?


                    CRASH
You outta your mind? If you give in now,
you might start losing.
    (beat)
Never fuck with a winning streak.
```

Nuke nods seriously, listening to the master.

This is a moment that would never show up in an outline and would mean nothing in a pitch to a studio exec. Studio executive: "That's it? That's the big turn? *Never fuck with a winning streak?*"

But given the intimate scale of this particular drama, it is a big turn. Crash realizes he can now keep Nuke out of the bed of the woman he's smitten with by supporting her very own instructions. Annie's teaching lesson to Nuke is collapsing on her. And it's why detailed story outlines always miss the very thing the story is about, because the writer can't know it until he discovers it. Otherwise, it's just connecting the dots.

● ● ●

Much has happened in a few pages, thanks to Annie's omniscient voiceover and Crash teaching Nuke on the bus. Nuke is now fully committed to not sleeping with Annie—and that's a lit fuse waiting to blow up when the road trip ends. Even Millie and Jimmy might be having sex; they pair off when he offers to give her his Christian testimony. So when Nuke shows up at Annie's house, she's Circe on steroids.

She tries to seduce Nuke. He refuses. We're living in a different dramatic universe than that of a few minutes (a few pages) ago. Nuke quotes Crash:

```
                    NUKE
Crash once called a woman's . . . uh . . .
pussy—y'know how the hair kinda makes a
"V" shape?


                    ANNIE
Yes I do. . . .


                    NUKE
Well—he calls it the Bermuda Triangle. He
said a man can get lost in there and never
be heard from again.


                    ANNIE
What a nasty thing to say.
```

                         NUKE
He didn't mean it nasty. He said that
gettin' lost and disappearing from the
face of the earth was sometimes a good
thing to do—especially like that.
     (beat)
But he also says that there's a time for
discipline and I think this is one of
those. . . .

                        ANNIE
Crash is a very smart man. . . .

Annie has now praised Crash's wisdom. In the scene prior, Crash praised Annie's wisdom. In story terms, they're both on the same side of the issue—for different reasons, of course—but emotionally and romantically they're clearly desperate for each other. Their egos and pride are what's keeping them apart. They actually haven't spoken to each other for forty-five pages—almost an hour of movie time. It was time to put them together to see what might happen.

As Annie's failure to seduce Nuke draws to a close, she challenges him by going against everything she's been preaching:

                        ANNIE
Nuke! You got things all wrong! There's
no relation between sex and baseball. Ask
Crash.

                        NUKE
I did.

                        ANNIE
What'd he say?

                 NUKE
He said if I gave in to you I'd start
losing again.

                 ANNIE
He did?

                 NUKE
I'll be back when we lose.

Annie, knowing she's about to be hoisted by her own petard, blown up by a bomb of her own making (emotionally, at least, and hopefully with some humor), charges out to find and confront Crash. I'd been waiting to write this scene for weeks. It's charged because they are so deeply attracted to each other but have kept getting in their own way. Crash is living alone in a kind of boardinghouse, not interested in hanging out with the younger players. He takes solace in being alone—this is the gunfighter in his off hours. And into this scene bursts Annie, full of fire. . . .

And I wrote a lousy scene.

And kept writing it.

And writing it.

It became the only scene that I later wrote dozens of versions of as we were shooting the movie. Usually when a scene isn't working, it is the wrong scene. Good scenes write themselves. But this was the right scene in the right place—it just wasn't working.

Annie and Crash needed to collide. So why was it bad? It was overwritten, over-speechified, tried too hard to be sexy or, a big mistake, too sexual (big difference), and said things that didn't need saying and didn't say things that needed saying. It's the kind of scene in which the writer has to be careful not to try to overachieve. The scene was in trouble from the beginning and took a long time to sort itself out. It didn't really come together till the morning it was shot. More on this later.

The scene, though a disaster in its early iterations, strangely did have a perfect finish.

                    ANNIE
This is the weirdest season I ever saw—the
Durham Bulls can't lose and I can't get
laid!

                    CRASH
        (softly)
You okay?

                    ANNIE
        (shakily)
I need a drink.

The most important scene in the movie is triggered by Annie's line "I need a drink"—and we return to Mitch's Tavern, where Annie, Crash, and Nuke all met. I confess that I love a bar at nighttime—even the worst of them are soothing in some ways (maybe it's just the booze)—but in the daytime a bar is bright and grotesque and unsettling.

Which is why Annie and Crash go straight to the tavern, empty of customers and too exposed in the daytime. And Crash asks the question I thought the audience might be asking:

                    CRASH
    Why baseball?

Annie's monologue is launched. Two and a half pages, Crash just listens, openly, sympathetically, as Annie shares with him her secrets. It was everyone's favorite scene in the script.

I later cut it out. A whole chapter about the bloodletting will come later.

                      • • •

Back to baseball and the meeting at the mound. This scene exists to flip the trope that deeply serious life-and-death strategic baseball questions are being discussed when players, coaches, and the manager all meet on the bump. We've been seeing all along that the catcher's relationship to the pitcher might not quite be what we thought.

Goose Gossage, whom I met years later, told me that Thurman Munson sometimes would visit the mound to say: "Who signed you? You might have the worst stuff of any pitcher I've ever caught. It's embarrassing wearing the same uniform with you. If you're traded, which is likely, what team would you like to go to?" and the like. (The words are mine, the tone and intention were Munson's, as related by Gossage.) Munson's irreverence and gallows humor always relaxed Gossage, which was what the great catchers want to do. The Goose thought that Munson could have beaten the shit out of anyone on the team, and that informed every word he uttered. Crash is intended to have the same gravitas, albeit at a minor league level.

I remember trudging to the mound in Stockton once after another one of our pitchers got hammered and was taken out of the game. As we prepared to give encouragement to the new guy heading in from the bullpen, Manfredi (third baseman, drinking buddy, college guy), said, "Damn, I wish I could hit against *our* pitchers. I'd hit .400 and be in Double A."

If Crash is the gunslinger without a past, Nuke's past follows him right into the ballpark, where his father stands behind the screen at home plate with a giant camera, filming him. Even Nuke, who has the gift of not being easily embarrassed, is embarrassed. His father's appearance is throwing him off. It forces the meeting at the mound to help Nuke out of a jam.

This is the easiest kind of scene to write, and the first draft never changed, except for the last line. It also breaks my cardinal rule that a scene has to be about something. The conversation on the mound is not ostensibly about anything, certainly not anything to do with the spine of the story. On the other hand, it's about everything. It's the reason I made the movie. That's what it's about. Later I'd have to make that argument to the suits.

•   •   •

Arguing with the umpire is one of the most civilized traditions in baseball, and I cringe whenever I read that the way to speed up the game is to outlaw this ritual. The game stops. The player or, more likely, the manager charges onto the field and the dance begins. There are unwritten rules to this, of course. You can't touch the ump, spray spittle on him, reference his family, or kick dirt on his feet.

In my day, you also couldn't use the word *cocksucker*—though almost any other word was allowed. I asked a veteran player if you merely had to *say* "cocksucker" or did you have to *call the ump* a "cocksucker"? The veteran didn't know, and I never tested it. The most colorful and flamboyant umpire baiter in my era was Earl Weaver, the much admired and feared Hall of Fame manager of the Baltimore Orioles. He could turn a dispute into a one-act play, part Arthur Miller rage, part Marx Brothers.

The ritual itself—like a baseball fight—is cathartic. If a fight between players breaks out, the game stops until the fight ends. The game will continue. Life will go on. A baseball fight isn't ugly and dangerous like a hockey fight. In a baseball fight, rarely does anyone get hurt, at least intentionally. The goal is to show you're ready to fight, but not to actually fight. There's always a team rule that if a teammate gets in a fight, you are obligated to rush onto the field to back him up. So, inevitably, a beef between two guys suddenly becomes a beef among fifty guys, forty-eight of whom have no beef at all with anyone. But if you don't charge onto the field, you get fined. Worse, you get a reputation as *not one of the guys.*

I was at the plate against the San Jose Bees when, for reasons nobody had a clue about, our runner on second base started jawing with their shortstop. In seconds, they were trading punches. I looked down at the catcher and said, "I don't know about you but I'll get fined if I don't run out there." "Same with me," he said. So, we ran out to second base, found a comfortable spot in short center field, where we could flail our arms wildly and ineffectively while getting lost in the crowd. We were quickly joined by two dugouts full of players and some late-arriving bullpen pitchers. Fifty guys pretended to scuffle, all careful not to get hurt. About the only thing I remember that the other catcher said (as we faux jousted) was "Hey, where do you guys go to have fun after the game?" To which I said, "There's no fun in Stockton." Fight over, back to the plate, on with the game. There are occasional brawls in which players really do have mean intentions, but most of the time it's just good, solid theater.

Never forget that players from one team rarely hate players on another team. That's for the fans. Dodgers fans may hate the Giants and Giants fans may hate the Dodgers, but that doesn't translate into the dugout. Players are all on one side of the divide. They hate management.

THE RUNNER SLIDES—Crash blocks the plate. A cloud of dust. A close play.

THE UMPIRE SIGNALS "SAFE"—And Crash flips out. In a second he is nose to nose with the UMPIRE.

                    CRASH
        I got him on the knee!

                    UMPIRE
        You missed him!

                    CRASH
        Goddammit, Jack, he still ain't touched
        the plate.

THEIR FACES ARE INCHES APART—Screaming face-to-face.

                    UMPIRE
        Don't bump me.

                    CRASH
        It was a cocksucking call!

UMPIRE

Did you call me a cocksucker?

CRASH

No! I said it was a cocksucking call and
you can't run me for that!

UMPIRE

You missed the tag!

CRASH

You spit on me!

UMPIRE

I didn't spit on you!

CRASH

You're in the wrong business, Jack—you're
Sears, Roebuck material!

UMPIRE

You're close, Crash—you want me to run
you? I'll run you!

CRASH

You want me to call you a cocksucker?

UMPIRE

Try it. Go ahead. Call me a cocksucker!

CRASH

Beg me!

UMPIRE

Call me a cocksucker and you're outta
here!

                              CRASH
          Beg me again!

                              UMPIRE
          Call me a cocksucker and you're outta
          here!

                              CRASH
          You're a cocksucker!

                              UMPIRE
          You're outta here!

THE UMP THEATRICALLY THROWS CRASH out of the game.

Crash's anger was more about his frustrations with Annie than the fact that the ump missed the call. Also, it's intended to be funny, which modifies the rage. This is no time for a minor league Eugene O'Neill to show up. Note that Crash calls the umpire by his first name. Teams stay in the same hotels and hang out in the same bars as umpires; everyone knows everyone and tracks who's going up, who's going down—and who disappears from the traveling circus forever. Umpires, like players, are scouted every day, and they, too, are trying to move up the ladder to the Show.

In the story, *finally*, things are starting to happen quickly.

It was time to hear what Annie is thinking and feeling, beyond her role as narrator:

                      ANNIE (VOICEOVER)
          When Crash got thrown out, the game got
          out of hand. . . . José made three errors
          with his cursed mitt. . . . Nuke never
          quite got in the groove, though he didn't
          pitch bad . . . and the winning streak
          came to an end with a 3-2 loss. . . .
                    (beat)

> The good news was that a man was about to
> come calling. . . . The bad news was—it
> was the wrong guy.

And as he must, the wrong guy indeed comes calling while she plays Piaf. (Nuke knows that Annie's home because "I can hear that crazy Mexican singer in there!") Nuke has brought his father, a hearty Christian of the "Praise the Lord" school, to meet Annie.

Until this moment, it's Nuke who keeps Crash and Annie apart. Annie won't bend her rule of being monogamous within the framework of a baseball season, and Crash has stopped trying to seduce her (though he's still dreaming). In truth, they're each also afraid of fully engaging the other because they know this one is different, this might be something that doesn't end when the season ends, this might go past September.

The only way to get to the reality of their relationship is to remove Nuke from the equation, and the deus ex machina is simple—he gets called up to the major leagues. It's not unheard of for a top draft pick with a big bonus to be added to the major league roster when it expands in September, even if just to get a temporary taste of the big leagues.

As Annie sends him lovingly on his way, happy for him and relieved for herself, Nuke tells her he'll be back after the season.

ANNIE
No, honey, when you leave Durham, you
don't come back.

Nuke seeks out Crash to tell him the good news, but Crash wants none of it; the smallest version of Crash is revealed. He's jealous, although he would never admit it, and is such a boor that Nuke decks him—returning the favor with which Crash introduced himself at the beginning of the story. Crash, ever the professional, even in his moment of greatest humiliation, wants to make sure Nuke hit him with his nonpitching hand.

                        CRASH
    If you get in a fight with some drunk,
    never hit him with your pitching hand. You
    might get injured.
         (smiles)
    That's another lesson for you. Now quit
    screwing around and help me up.

    Order restored, more or less, and there's only the grace note of
their farewell to play out. Early the next morning Nuke clears out his
locker in the empty clubhouse while Crash sits and gives his last bits
of counsel. It could be a father and son, and that's how it's written.
Crash, now sober and slightly embarrassed about his behavior the
previous night, apologizes. Nuke says, "Forget it." Nuke's evolving
maturity reveals itself everywhere in the scene.
    Crash tells him, "You gotta play this game with fear and arro-
gance." (This may be the line in the script that most closely captures
how I look at the world.) And Nuke shows he gets it by turning it
into a joke, "Fear and ignorance." This is a different Nuke than we've
seen before. Yes, he probably still thinks Edith Piaf is Mexican, but it's
clear how much he's learned from Crash and Annie. The final beat of
their goodbye is, after Crash bids good luck to him, Nuke's response:
"You too, meat." Nuke walks out the door. Crash just smiles.
    Ebby Calvin "Nuke" LaLoosh is now far from Durham, and is
removed as an obstacle between Crash and Annie. But another obstacle presents itself, one that shouldn't be a surprise but I hoped it was.
Jimmy and Millie have a ballpark wedding—a minor league staple—
before the next game. A little wedding party in the clubhouse and
then Crash is called to the manager's office.

                        SKIP
    This is the toughest job a manager
    has . . . but the organization wants to
    make a change. . . . Now that Nuke's
    gone they wanta bring up some young
    catcher. . . .

```
                    LARRY
Some kid hittin' .300 in Bluefield . . .
probably a bust.


                    SKIP
I put in a word for you with the
organization—told 'em I thought you'd make
a fine minor league manager someday . . .
might be an opening in Visalia next
year. . . .
        (beat)
You've had a helluva year, Crash—you know
how it is.
```

Silence. Crash stands there, nearly nude. He just nods slightly. Without rancor or bitterness, he turns and re-enters the raucous locker room.

That's it. The end of the world starts with "This is the toughest job a manager has. . . ." He did his job too well, but the bitterest of the ironies is that the organization was right. Crash passed his test brilliantly. Nuke LaLoosh was a different player at the end of Crash's tutelage than at the beginning. Crash might indeed make a "fine minor league manager." It's just not what he wants. The organization always wins.

Crash wanders the streets of the boarded-up city of Durham, North Carolina. . . .

Is this the end of Act Two? On page 116? That's pretty late for a second-act curtain. Did the second act end when Nuke was lifted magically out of the story to the big leagues? That was only a few pages earlier, and an act of God shouldn't be the determinant. It needs to be the act of the protagonist or the hero or whomever. Not a phone call.

Does any of this matter? At least Annie and Crash would now be alone together, and that crazy Mexican singer would be playing in the background. This could be a fun scene to write, but it was clear: I didn't have an Act Three.

7

Sometimes You Win,
Sometimes You Lose,
Sometimes It Rains

C rash wanders the streets, stops for a drink, and ends up at Annie's house, where he tells her he's been released and they make love for three and a half pages. It starts with Edith Piaf and ends up with the Dominoes' 1951 version of "Sixty Minute Man," featuring the deep-bass voice of Bill Brown. Both are scripted as music cues, as well as a couple more that didn't make the final cut. There are some obvious storytelling payoffs here—Annie asks Crash to dance again, and this time he doesn't refuse. This time it's Annie who gets tied to the bed while Crash reads Whitman to her (although on the day of shooting we came up with something a lot better). Eating Wheaties, crashing onto the floor, making love on the kitchen table, Crash's ability to undo her garter with a single hand—all are on the page.

In the morning, Crash leaves, because that's what baseball players do. I gave the first draft of the script to a few friends for feedback and they all said, "If Crash doesn't come back, I'm never speaking to you again." I needed my friends, so Crash came back, and they were right. Crash has a private quest that needs to be fulfilled and he deserves to fulfill it, even if he's called it "a dubious honor." In fact, it's not dubious at all; it's a remarkable accomplishment to have hit the most home runs in the history of the minor leagues, and somewhere inside Crash knows this, but can't express it. It may be a symbol of his failure to make it to the Show (for no more than twenty-one days), but there's something glorious about his failure, at least in my mind.

In the meantime, however, after a night of mythic sexual bliss, Annie wakes up to a note from Crash.

> ANNIE (VOICEOVER)
> Crash said he had to get an early start to
> drive to Asheville in the South Atlantic
> League where he heard they might need a
> catcher to finish out the season. . . .
> It's not the first time I went to bed with
> a guy and woke up with a note. . . .

                                          CUT TO:

EXT. GREAT SMOKY MOUNTAINS—DAY
CRASH IN HIS CAR heading for Asheville.

                                          CUT TO:

EXT. ASHEVILLE BASEBALL PARK—DAY
CRASH KNOCKING ON THE BASEBALL OFFICE DOOR
Looking for work.

                                          CUT TO:

INT. ASHEVILLE LOCKER ROOM—DAY
CRASH UNLOADING HIS GEAR into yet another locker.

                                          CUT TO:

INT. ANNIE'S KITCHEN—DAY
ANNIE SCRUBBING HER KITCHEN FLOOR—Down on her
hands and knees, picking up the broken cereal
bowl.

> ANNIE (VOICEOVER)
> The house smelled like Crash for days.
> It was wonderful. The only real cleaning
> I did was on the kitchen floor 'cause who
> likes to walk on spilt cereal?

SHE FINDS A BIT OF A JOINT on the floor as she's
cleaning. She picks it up, sits on the floor under
the table, and lights the tiny joint.

```
The funny thing is, I stopped worrying
about Nuke. Somehow I knew nothing would
stop him. Crash was right—Nuke had a gift.
The world is made for those who aren't
cursed with self-awareness.
```

And then we cut to Nuke in a major league stadium, where he spews clichés like a veteran, which reveals he's been listening to Crash all along and, in a certain way, represents his growing up.

```
                    NUKE
I'm just happy to be here and hope I can
help the ball club. I just wanta give
it my best shot and, good Lord willing,
things'll work out. . . . You gotta play
'em one day at a time, y'know, 'cause
sometimes you win, sometimes you lose, and
sometimes it rains . . . etc. . . .
```

Crash was hired to "mature the kid" and he's done it. Babbling nonsense to the media is a sign of actual growth. Though we haven't seen Crash and Annie smoking weed the night before, it seemed right that she rescues a "bit of a joint" as she sorts it all out.

The last few pages of the script become more reliant on voiceover, much like the beginning of the story. It's Annie's view that shapes the tale and we must return to it. Like Crash, she's not so sure of the things she embraced at the outset. She hasn't abandoned them but she's more relaxed about them, just as Crash is facing the end of his own journey.

Annie is more at peace with her own evolution. In a way, she's embraced change; it's part of who she is. The end of the road for Crash is more traumatic. He's played baseball since he was a child and dreamed of the major leagues; he achieved that goal for twenty-one days and, ever since, he's believed he would get back, but now he knows he won't. His decision to go to Asheville to finish out the season is telling. The Asheville Tourists were a team in the South Atlantic League, but, at the time of the story, were a notch below the Durham Bulls in the Carolina League. He's landed so far from the Show that, given his age, there's not even a road map to calculate how to get back. He's going to Asheville to finish the season but more than that—and only he and Annie can know it—he's determined to get the minor league home-run record. And when he hits it, we cut back to Annie:

```
ANNIE LIES IN BED READING—She suddenly jerks up.

                ANNIE (VOICEOVER)
     I was reading in bed when Crash hit his
     247th home run. I knew the moment it
     happened.

EXT. ASHEVILLE STADIUM—DAY
CRASH UNLOADS A MONSTROUS HOME RUN deep into the
trees. He stands at home plate watching it . . .
like Reggie or the Babe.
```

After some reflection, I changed Annie's voiceover to quote a poem that somehow always stuck with me from my days in college English class, Thomas Gray's "Elegy Written in a Country Churchyard."

```
                ANNIE (VOICEOVER)
     "Full many a gem of purest ray serene,
     The dark unfathomed caves of ocean bear:
     Full many a flower is born to blush unseen,
     And waste its sweetness on the desert air."
```

As I typed it in, I blanked on the poet and for a moment confused the poem with William Cullen Bryant's "To a Waterfowl" and allowed Annie to be confused as well.

                          ANNIE (VOICEOVER)
Thomas Gray . . . or William Cullen
Bryant . . . I don't know, I get 'em mixed
up. . . .

Now that Crash has hit his home run in Asheville and finished
his private quest, the only thing left is for Annie and Crash to get
together. In practical dramatic terms, it didn't feel right that he would
come calling again, knocking on her door, as he had the night he was
released. To flip that, Annie goes to a game so that, when she returns
home, he can be waiting for her.

    It's imperative that on Annie's final trip to the ballpark, it's rain-
ing. In the dugout, as scripted, Skip is now reading Thomas Pynchon
(Annie has an impact on everyone) and Larry is reading *Mayan Wisdom Made Easy,* as he chews and spits tobacco. Eventually, Pynchon
got dumped but the Mayans stayed. The tarp is dragged across the
infield, the game is called off, and Annie heads home.

EXT. ANNIE'S HOUSE—DAY
AS SHE APPROACHES—She stops. Looks up.

P.O.V. CRASH SITTING ON THE PORCH SWING—
Still raining.

CLOSE ON ANNIE—She hesitates and smiles.

                          ANNIE
    Oh, my . . .

ANNIE SITS DOWN on the porch swing next to Crash.

    What happened?

                          CRASH
    I hit my dinger and hung 'em up.

A moment of silence over the significance of quitting.

> ANNIE
> I'm quitting, too. Boys, not baseball.

> CRASH
> There might be an opening for a manager
> in Visalia next spring. You think I could
> make it to the Show as a manager?

> ANNIE
> You'd be great, just great.
>   (rattles quickly)
> 'Cause you understand nonlinear thinking
> even though it seems like a linear game
> 'cause of the lines and the box scores
> an' all—but the fact is that there's a
> spacious "nontime kind of time" to it—

> CRASH
> Annie—

> ANNIE
> What?

> CRASH
> I got a lotta time to hear your theories
> and I wanta hear every damn one of
> 'em . . . but right now I'm tired and
> I don't want to think about baseball
> and I don't wanta think about quantum
> physics. . . . I don't wanta think about
> nothin'. . . .
>   (beat)
> I just wanta be.

                    ANNIE
    I can do that, too.

He rises, takes her hand, they head inside. And as
the rains fall on Durham . . .

                                        CUT TO:

INT. ANNIE'S HOUSE—DAY
THE SHRINE GLOWS—Candles everywhere. Rain pours
down on the windows outside.

                ANNIE (VOICEOVER)
    Walt Whitman once said, "I see great things
    in baseball. It's our game—the American
    game."
        (beat)
    He said, "It will repair our losses and be
    a blessing to us."
        (beat)
    You could look it up.

The music—Dave Frishberg sings "Van Lingle Mungo."

                THE END

    The scene on the porch wrote itself quickly and I figured I'd
rewrite it endlessly, but it remained untouched. I thought Annie's
last line—"I can do that, too"—was a little soft, but it stayed.
The baseball quote from Whitman I'd known for a while; it was
an appropriate way out of the story, and it never changed. Casey
Stengel's famous line, which he used whenever challenged about
one of his occasionally apocryphal stories—"You could look it
up"—was a good complement to Whitman. "Leaves of Grass" meets
Casey Stengel seemed the right balance to the "Church of Baseball"
opening.

At the end of the screenplay (and movie) we do not know what happened to the Durham Bulls, who, up till now, seemed to be having their best season on record. Nuke is in the big leagues, Crash is out of baseball, there is no big game to tell us how to feel. And so, on page 125, the story is finished. There's still no third act.

8

"Can't Anybody Here Play This Game?"

—Casey Stengel

I sent the script to Thom Mount, expecting pages of notes about what the rewrite should entail. I was sure he'd redline many of the scenes that weren't about the three protagonists/heroes, Crash, Annie, and Nuke. Or, since he was a former studio head, I was sure there'd be a complete rethink. *Why Durham? Why a woman? Why the minors? Where's the big game? Why did I ever say yes to this?*

Instead, he said, "I love it." For a writer, these words are never heard. The best you can hope for is a set of editorial notes that aren't incomprehensible. Mount then said, "Let's make it." That's the second-rarest thing a writer ever hears. I told him I had a way to get to Kevin Costner, who was starting to appear on everyone's radar and, as trusted sources told me, could really play ball. There's a box on the back of every actor's 8×11 photo that asks, right after a list of roles played, for "other skills." If this is taken at face value, every actor in Los Angeles can play flamenco guitar, break-dance, speak five languages, perform open-heart surgery, and play at a professional level in every sport. I never believe anything actors put on their résumés. Costner was different.

Kurt Russell was also different—he had played in the minor leagues—but when I initially contacted his agent, I was told he was not available. I'm not sure that was true but it was clear that his reps didn't want him meeting with a first-time director with a minor league baseball tale. I knew Kurt from his role in *The Best of Times*, and we'd hit it off—but I didn't have a way to get in touch with him except through his gatekeepers, and they kept the gate locked.

So, Costner became the leading candidate. I had seen him in *Fandango,* a wonderful little indie by Kevin Reynolds, and in *Silverado,* a Lawrence Kasdan movie that Costner practically stole. He'd just been cut out of Kasdan's *The Big Chill,* but it wasn't for performance reasons; the movie worked better with his character already dead when his friends all gather for a wake that is the heart of the story.

I knew J. J. Harris, Costner's junior agent, a little bit, as she was part of Roger Spottiswoode's agency on *Under Fire.* She took my call, read the script right away, and gave it to Kevin.

The problem was that Columbia Pictures, where Thom Mount had his production deal, hated the script. The news surprised me because the script was getting a strong response, as a piece of writing at least, not necessarily as a piece of commerce. It was especially strange since Columbia was run by the Englishman David Puttnam, who'd made his reputation producing slightly off-center, inexpensive movies that earned great reviews and had done surprisingly strong box office. Movies like Bill Forsyth's *Local Hero* (among other wonderful Forsyth films); *Chariots of Fire,* which broke all the rules and marketing expectations and was a huge hit, not to mention won the Best Picture Oscar; *Midnight Express* (another Oliver Stone script), about an American jailed in Turkey for smuggling drugs; and *The Killing Fields,* Roland Joffé's harrowing tale of the Khmer Rouge's Cambodian genocide. Say what you will, these movies break the studio rules. I asked for fifteen minutes to meet with Puttnam or his right hand, David Picker, to walk them through what I thought the tone of the movie was and why, at a modest budget, it was a good bet. But nobody wanted to meet me. Columbia did promise Mount, however, that we could have the project back in "turnaround," which means the originators of the project could have a limited window of time to set it up elsewhere, thus getting it financed by someone else. They would be reimbursed their modest investment (my script fee was extremely modest) and that would be that.

In the meantime, Harris called to say that Kevin really liked the script and wanted to meet. Almost immediately, Costner and I were having lunch at a small place on Melrose called the Studio Grill. We hit it off and then he said one of the most remarkable things I've ever heard from an actor:

> COSTNER: I like the script. I want to audition for you.
> SHELTON: If you want the part, you got it already.
> COSTNER: No, I want you to see if I can play baseball well enough.
> SHELTON: I said the part is yours.
> COSTNER: You played professionally, I played in high school. I gotta pass the test.

He then ordered a couple of vodkas for both of us. Lover of spirits though I am, I never imbibe at lunch because I'll fall asleep; plus I don't care for vodka. But we downed the drinks and headed to a place on Sepulveda Boulevard in the Valley, a few acres of miniature-golf courses, noisy arcades, and a batting cage where you could pick the speed of the machine and test your skills for a quarter. I brought a pocketful of quarters, but first we played catch in the parking lot. One catch and one throw is all it takes to know if someone can play, and clearly he could. Each of us, it seemed, kept a glove and ball in the trunk of our car for reasons neither of us questioned, though I don't remember ever having used it. While we played catch, people walked past Kevin, not knowing who he was. That was about to change.

In the cage, he had a beautiful right-handed stance and then offered that he could switch-hit and flipped to the other side and had the same form left-handed. I thought immediately that wherever the sun was, he could be lit beautifully. It also occurred to me that if Crash Davis was a switch-hitting catcher, he surely would have had a longer run in the Show than twenty-one days, but that was just me. Kevin was an athlete, and as we left the batting cage, I told him I was going to call the producer and figure out how to move forward.

Thom Mount, who was back and forth to Paris in the middle of all this, producing a Roman Polanski movie, *Frantic*, made a brilliant and proactive move to land Costner. He offered him three times more money than he'd yet made on any movie. The genius of this is that Mount certainly didn't have the money but everyone assumed he was speaking for Columbia Pictures, who technically now owned the script of *Bull Durham* because they funded Mount's development. He never mentioned that Columbia hated the script.

I now discovered that Costner was committed to another movie in the upcoming fall time slot, *Everybody's All-American,* based on a novel by the great sportswriter Frank Deford. The movie was set up at Warner Bros. with director Taylor Hackford, with whom, coincidentally, I had gone to high school. Costner's commitment wasn't finalized and, I was told, he was having creative differences with the people involved. I also soon learned that his senior agent at William Morris, Ed Limato, wanted him to do the Warner Bros. movie and not *Bull Durham.* This bifurcated agency position was about to cause big problems. Kevin, respectfully, did not discuss with me the other film or what the issues were.

Our first problem was that we didn't have a studio to finance or distribute the movie. The other movie did, plus it had a director with a track record of commercial successes with *The Idolmaker* and *An Officer and a Gentleman,* among others. Mount brought a young producing partner, Mark Burg, onto our project from another film he'd just finished, *Can't Buy Me Love,* and Mark helped coordinate a strategy for problem number one.

Our second problem was that Costner's agents were afraid (for damn good reason) that we'd fail to land a studio quickly and that Kevin would lose a movie for the fall. The urgency was exacerbated in mid-summer, when *The Untouchables,* directed by Brian De Palma from a script by David Mamet, opened, with Costner starring opposite Robert De Niro and Sean Connery. It was a big hit—Costner was now hot, and everyone wanted him. To force our hand, William Morris announced that we had thirty days to get *Bull Durham* a studio deal to shoot immediately, or they'd sign Costner to the Warner Bros. movie or something else. The script was sent to every studio, and meetings were set up.

I went back to Durham with Burg. Because we couldn't afford a location manager to scout, we began securing locations. We drove around Durham for a couple of days with a student from Duke.

I pointed to a house for rent near the ballpark and said it would make a good Annie house, and pointed to some abandoned tobacco warehouses across the street from the Durham Athletic Park and said we should rent them as soon as we got the money . . . if we got the money. Essentially, that was the scout.

Back in Los Angeles, time was running out and we were getting nowhere with the studios. We went to Orion Pictures first because I'd had a good experience with them on *Under Fire* and they had a new Costner movie in the can so we figured they liked Kevin. The problem was that they were nervous about releasing the movie, *No Way Out,* a political thriller set in Washington, DC, with Gene Hackman and Sean Young, directed by Roger Donaldson, because it had a double-twist ending that revealed Costner's character was actually a Soviet spy. Orion had sat on the movie for several months and finally assigned it an August 14 release date; in those days, the end of summer, before school starts, was considered a burial ground for movie releases. As it happened, the *No Way Out* release date was also our deadline to find a studio to make our movie.

Orion passed. Mike Medavoy, head of production and partner in the company, said that they already had a baseball movie in preproduction, *Eight Men Out,* to be directed by John Sayles, and another in development, *The Scout,* with Rodney Dangerfield attached. (Years later it would be made with Albert Brooks in the Dangerfield role.) It was hard for us to make a case for a third baseball movie when no other studio wanted even a single one.

MGM was in chaos and not interested in meeting. Ted Turner, who had owned the studio, had sold it to Kirk Kerkorian after holding on to the library. The studio was swimming in debt service and the road out was not with the Durham Bulls.

Universal met with me, but it was immediately clear this was a *polite* meeting. They didn't want to insult Costner's agents. Then Leonard Goldberg, chairman of Twentieth Century–Fox, and rising young executive Scott Rudin responded that they liked the script but didn't like "part of the package." There was never anything more specific. Mostly I was alone at these meetings, as Thom was stuck in

Paris dealing with issues on the Polanski movie, and I didn't carry much weight in the room as a first-time director who'd written two movies that nobody had gone to. Force of personality goes only so far. We sent the script to Tri-Star, a mini-studio split off from Columbia Pictures, and heard nothing back. Then we got a call from Paramount Pictures, saying that Ned Tanen, who ran their motion-picture division, loved the script and he loved Costner and he wanted to meet. This felt real.

Tanen was a throwback studio chief who not only had served in the air force but rode motorcycles and liked fast cars and could throw down a drink with the best of them—at least that was his reputation. We'd never met. He'd also previously run Universal Pictures during one of their greatest streaks, greenlighting movies as diverse as *American Graffiti, Coal Miner's Daughter, Melvin and Howard,* and the mega-hit *E. T.* He had wide-ranging tastes, was a straight shooter, and was—I was told—my kind of guy. With great hope, and time now running out on our thirty-day hold on Costner, I met with Tanen and his team at Paramount in one of those enormous Hollywood studio-chief offices that was just like we imagine. I'll give him this: he was a straight shooter:

> TANEN: I like the script a lot. I like Costner in it a lot. It reminds me of a movie I once made called *Slap Shot*—which was directed by the hottest director in town, George Roy Hill, and starred the biggest name in the business, Paul Newman, and it did lousy business.
> SHELTON: Yeah, but it was a really good movie.
> TANEN: Nobody gives a fuck.

That was the end of the meeting and the last time I ever saw Tanen. I wish I could have made a movie with him because he certainly could cut to the chase, but it never happened. He summarized the movie business in haiku. Nobody cares if the movie is any good—it just has to sell tickets. In the pas de deux of Art and Commerce, Commerce leads, Art follows. Tanen thought of *Slap Shot* as a failure. I thought of it as a success. I would have been a disastrous studio chief, making *Melvin and Howard*s and *Slap Shot*s forever, or at least until I was fired, which wouldn't have taken long. I was also told, but never verified, that Tanen and Mount had crossed swords when they were at Universal. I didn't ask; I moved on.

I called Kevin and told him we'd struck out. He was angry, not at me but at the studios, and he insisted we reset the meetings—this time he'd accompany me and be an outspoken salesman for the project. With a week left in the thirty-day window, we quickly rescheduled the meetings. The studios didn't want to say no to this emerging star, so almost overnight I went back in to meet the moguls, this time with Kevin. Tanen didn't want to meet because his answer wasn't going to change, but as we went around town (I for the second time) it was clear that baseball wouldn't sell, even with Kevin as a passionate and convincing advocate. Years later I was told by allies within the agency and studios—stories that were all confirmed—that Costner's senior agents at William Morris were calling the studios after each meeting to say that Costner was tied to the Warner Bros. film and therefore wasn't free to make ours. Welcome to Hollywood.

We had three days left until our deadline, a Friday. The only studio left in the running was Tri-Star and that was only because we hadn't formally been rejected yet. Now that Kevin would be in the room, they agreed to set a meeting for Thursday, with studio head Jeff Sagansky. In today's corporate studio environment, meetings could never be set for two days hence—more like two weeks or two months—but Costner brought some weight. I figured they weren't interested in the script but they wanted to meet Kevin for future projects. We showed up and pitched like Baptist preachers, and Kevin kept pointing at me saying, "This guy can do it!" Sagansky said he liked the script and was intrigued but there was some concern within the company that baseball didn't travel, which meant, in movie-speak, that there would be little foreign interest in a baseball movie. I said I was aware of that but at our low budget this needed only to be a domestic success. A Tri-Star associate was also in the room and the enthusiasm seemed genuine; nobody blinked when Kevin added, "We have to know by tomorrow or I'm doing another movie." Jeff said he'd call me by noon the next day, and Kevin and I left Tri-Star (which was on the old MGM movie lot) feeling reasonably sanguine. We returned to my temporary office at the Mount Company on the Columbia lot in Burbank, where I had a bottle of something stashed. It was late afternoon.

Over Scotch in plastic cups, Kevin asked, "Why did Orion turn this down?" and I told him that Medavoy said they had too many baseball movies already. Kevin reminded me that his Orion movie *No Way Out* was opening the next day and suggested we call the New York office, specifically Eric Pleskow and Bill Bernstein, two of Orion's executive partners (along with Medavoy). I had good relations with them from *Under Fire* and they'd been generous enough to fly me to Venice for its successful screening. When we reached them, it was close to 7 p.m. their time, and they said they'd be happy to read the script. We said, "But you have to read it tonight," and Kevin explained why. Costner called his New York agents at the Morris office and had them messenger two printed hard copies to Eric and Bill. (These days it's all instantly done electronically, of course, and we were lucky to get this transaction accomplished.) We went home, and I forgot about the Orion call for the night but felt good about the Tri-Star meeting.

The next morning, I arrived fully caffeinated and eagerly awaiting Sagansky's call from Tri-Star. I'd fired up people on Mount's staff that the meeting had gone very well, though there was no reason to get Thom's hopes up in Paris, where he was still stuck on *Frantic*. At eleven-thirty, Sagansky called. "Ron, I'm terribly sorry we have to pass," he said. "We just don't think there's enough foreign sales to justify our commitment." That was it. I began cleaning out the few things in my desk drawer in the temp office, figuring that, without Costner, this movie would never get made, not to mention that we had really run out of time to prep a movie to shoot in the fall anyway.

At noon, 3 p.m. in New York, the phone rang again. Pleskow and Bernstein wanted to make the movie. They asked if it was really true that a deal had to be made that day or we'd lose Costner to Warner Bros., and I said it was. They called Mark Burg to confirm the budget (which was still a bit squirrelly), and Mark reached Mount in Paris. By Monday morning, the movie was greenlit to begin shooting six weeks later.

What I didn't realize for several days was that *No Way Out* had opened that morning to a rave Vincent Canby review in *The New York Times,* and that had greeted Bernstein and Pleskow over breakfast. Any other kind of review and *Bull Durham* might never have been made. Still, I've never heard of a script being submitted to a studio on a Thursday night and having a deal virtually closed by the next day. Especially a project that everyone had passed on . . . twice.

I now had six weeks to hire a crew, cast the movie, and start shooting.

Part Two

Preproduction

9

Building the Toy Train Set

Orson Welles famously said, when he first set foot on the lot at RKO to begin prepping *Citizen Kane,* "This is the biggest electric train set a boy ever had." In the hopes that I would have the chance to build my own toy train set, I had offered a job as my assistant to my former college English professor. Leonard Oakland had a PhD in English and was the man who, twenty years earlier, had inspired me to read. He had also introduced me to foreign films. As luck would have it, he happened to be in Los Angeles (from Spokane, Washington) on a one-year sabbatical from teaching. A director's assistant is a low-paying, thankless job, running errands, typing script revisions well past midnight, driving the director to the set, grabbing a coffee, finding the bar that sells the right Scotch or gin, and listening to a lot of howling at the moon. The main perk is being close to all the bloodshed and fun, with a front-row seat to the sausage making. He took the job, and I planned to pay him the pittance of a salary out of my pocket until the movie was either financed or had died on the vine. Leonard kept notes.

While we'd been shopping the script, Mark Burg had worked up a budget of $4 million "below the line"—which means all the hard costs of shooting and editing the movie. In addition, there was $3.5 million in "above the line" costs, which covered cast, script, director, and producers, and another $1 million for the 10 percent contingency and bond.

The first crucial position to fill was the director of photography. The DP is responsible for not only photographing the film, but also supervising the camera department, with its hierarchical staff of camera operators, focus pullers, various assistants, and trainees. The director and DP work very closely to determine what the film should look like; the creative desires are always at war with the shooting schedule and the demands and limitations of the budget. John Alcott, who had offered to shoot my first movie (and coincidentally had shot *No Way Out*), had recently died of a heart attack at the age of fifty-five while in Cannes. I was nervous about the number of script pages set for night exteriors and how slow that work would be. I had hoped to get Alcott not only for his sheer brilliance, but also because of how efficiently he'd handled the night work on *Under Fire* in remote areas of southern Mexico.

Someone recommended a young DP named Charles Minsky, and we hired him after I screened some of the *Amazing Stories,* a TV series heavy on night exteriors, which he'd shot for Steven Spielberg. Since the budget was tight, he'd have to build a crew out of locals and people from Wilmington, North Carolina, where Dino De Laurentiis had set up a studio. Budget and cast/crew availability drove a lot of decisions, but it also forced us to look past the usual suspects to emerging talent.

Somehow, we found a talented young costume designer out of England, Louise Frogley, who accepted the small salary and the even smaller wardrobe budget. In the interview, she confessed she'd never seen a baseball game and didn't know how they dressed. I told her I'd make sure the ballplayers wore their uniforms correctly and trusted her with everything else. She's now a big star in the costume design world. When Kevin and I went to the costume department in an abandoned tobacco warehouse across from the ballpark, the intention was to see what ideas she had for his wardrobe. I had on a bomber jacket, white dress shirt, jeans, and huaraches on my feet. She decided that's how Crash should dress, and Kevin agreed.

Costuming Tim was trickier. I wanted him to dress like a Travolta wannabe in *Saturday Night Fever,* but it was a delicate balance to get right and not make Nuke look idiotic. After some experimentation, she found the balance. Susan's wardrobe evolved a bit, and when it occasionally started to drift into something a bit excessive, it was pulled back. These are normal parts of the dynamic. Most of Annie's clothes were found in secondhand stores, and there were no "doubles" or backups to replace anything that got torn or stained in production. Frogley got frustrated with the lack of time we had to communicate, but I trusted her to work on her own from the beginning.

I then hired another Brit who'd never seen a baseball game. Bob Leighton, editor of *This Is Spinal Tap* and other films, confessed he knew nothing about the game, but I assured him that I preferred it that way. I wanted an editor to be cutting drama and comic timing and not worry about the baseball—that was my problem. Also, it was commonly believed that *Spinal Tap* had gone from a million feet of often hilarious film that didn't add up to a coherent narrative to a brilliant classic and original mock docudrama (or something), thanks to Leighton's dogged and shrewd editing.

Big-time New York casting director Bonnie Timmermann (who had just cast *Frantic*) was again hired by Mount to immediately begin making actor lists and send the script out to agencies. The urgency was to find Annie and Nuke—especially Annie—but we needed to read actors for all the principal roles. A week later I was to be in Bonnie's office in New York to begin the audition process.

In the meantime, Mount returned from Paris and hired David Lester in the critical position of unit production manager, doubling as line producer. This is a high-pressure position, the person who gets the trains to run on time and is responsible for the thousand details of daily production. The UPM is forever caught in the crosshairs between the director, who always wants more equipment, more time, more everything, and the producer, who's necessarily worried that the director is destined to flip out of control and turn into the raging, money-spending egomaniac of movie mythology. Directors think producers are insensitive bean counters—sometimes they're right. Producers think directors are prima-donna faux artistes—sometimes they're right. Lester had been the UPM on a Francis Ford Coppola movie, *Gardens of Stone,* and James Brooks's *Broadcast News,* a film

set in Washington, DC, where film production was famously difficult. He would go on to line-produce movies such as *In the Line of
Fire* and *The Shawshank Redemption,* so he knew his stuff. David is
a smart, tough little Irish American, and from the day I met him, I
assumed he'd been hired to kick my ass—or at least keep me in line.

I view myself, then and now, as a production-friendly director
and make a point of knowing the budget intimately because, sooner
or later, money's going to have to be moved around, and it's the
director's job to make his case. Studios have a self-destructive and
insane policy that if, during production, one area of the production
is costing less than estimated, it cannot automatically be applied to
another area that has been underestimated. This policy incentivizes
filmmakers to not be frugal. Luckily, the Orion deal did not, strictly
speaking, make *Bull Durham* a studio movie. It was designated a
"negative pickup," which meant that the studio signed papers with
the Mount Company guaranteeing to buy the finished picture at an
agreed-upon cost, at a certain date after production finished, and
then to release the movie theatrically on a guaranteed number of
screens. The producer then takes the paperwork to the bank and bor-
rows the money for production. The good thing about this method is
that a movie can be made a lot less expensively if it doesn't have to be
run through the studio system. The bad thing about it is that there's
no going back to the studio to beg for more money.

A production company can make better deals all around, because
the agent or vendor or location owner knows up front that they're
negotiating with something called "North State Films" (our LLC for
one movie only) and not Orion Pictures . . . or Warner Bros. . . .
or . . . For me, the great thing about negative pickups is that nobody
from the studio is micromanaging the budget on a daily basis.
They're not micromanaging anything else, either, and that's worth
a great deal. Studios have layers and layers of bureaucracy and over-
sight that take energy to engage with—you can get buried in memos
and paperwork, electronic and otherwise. The key to dealing with
that, I was told by a veteran production woman, was to answer every
memo with three of your own—basically to overwhelm the enemy

with paperwork. She said that the amazing thing was that the studio was happy that way. They loved paperwork. They couldn't send and receive enough memos. The production just had to have someone on staff generating more paperwork back than was coming in.

The script had been conceived with production in mind, and as a result, 90 pages of the story (out of 125) took place at three nearly adjacent locations—the ballpark, the locker room (which I assumed we'd have to build as a set), and Annie's house. It had been calculated from the beginning as a way to keep the budget down and, in a certain way, the script had been scouted before it had been written. The thing that kills productions is the endless loading and unloading of trucks full of grip and electrical equipment (not to mention cameras, wardrobe, props, and so forth) as they move the company from location to location. It's a traveling circus, and it costs time and money every time it moves.

I hired Armin Ganz as production designer and sent him to Durham to look around. The production designer oversees the art department and designs the sets, as well as having input into virtually everything the camera will record. He's responsible for set construction and decoration, has a hand in finding locations, and works closely with the director to create a "look" for the film. Ganz had been set decorator on *Tucker* for Francis Ford Coppola, but didn't yet have a production-designer credit other than on a movie directed by Norman Mailer, *Tough Guys Don't Dance*. Armin said that it shouldn't count because Mailer was the least visual director he'd ever met. They shot the movie in scenic Provincetown, and every time Mailer set up a shot, it was aimed at a blank wall. Ganz and the cinematographer, John Bailey, had to keep telling Mailer to turn the camera around and take in the boats and the bay, the reason they'd moved the circus to Provincetown in the first place.

Ganz got to Durham and we immediately had our first small crisis. The Durham Athletic Park, home of the Bulls, was blue and Ganz thought it should be dark green. I agreed with him but couldn't imagine we could do much about that, and I soon got a phone call from David Lester, who was now in Durham.

LESTER: You want to paint the ballpark green?
SHELTON: Armin and I think it's a better color. What'll it cost?
LESTER: I don't know. I never painted a ballpark.

I could hear the producers thinking, "Here comes that egomania-cal faux-artiste first-time director," but in this case, I thought Ganz was right. Ballparks are supposed to be dark green. David Lester wasn't a bean counter, he was a filmmaker, and the next thing I knew, he'd figured out a way to move some money around and paint the ballpark green (but left the gold trim because Armin was convinced that the palette of the show was dark green and tobacco gold). Mark Burg confirmed the decision but said we couldn't possibly afford to repaint it blue when we were done, so we had to hope that the owner of the team, Miles Wolff, would fall in love with our, well, palette. (He wouldn't.)

The bigger problem that couldn't be solved with paint presented itself when Chuck Minsky, our director of photography, stood in the ballpark with David Lester and me in the dark at home plate and we turned on the lights. Minsky couldn't get a reading on his light meter. This was the same light (or lack thereof) in which professional baseball players in the Carolina League faced pitchers every night. We now realized that though we had many nights of work scheduled at the ballpark, it wasn't bright enough to get an exposure reading. All I could think of was a pop fly in Lodi that I never saw, that nobody ever saw, that landed between me and the right fielder before it could be spotted, much less retrieved—and by that time the batter was on second base. Lester announced that Mothers Mag & Aluminum Polish might clean up the lights, and soon a crew was dangling from the grids cleaning off decades of dirt with some compound invented to clean magnesium wheels on cars. Lester was smart about things like that—he was the kind of guy who'd know what Mothers Mag & Aluminum Polish was. We tried again, and this time the needle on the light meter moved, but it was still too dark to expose film. In today's age of digital cameras and lenses that can record images at remarkably low lights, we would have been okay, but film was a different animal.

Throughout this period, I was flying back and forth to L.A. and New York to cast the movie. This sort of chaos is normal while prepping any movie, but what was abnormal was the condensed time period in which it took place. In addition to Nuke and Annie, there were nearly forty other speaking parts to be cast.

10

"I Thought My Body of Work Would Be Enough"

The chief casting urgency was finding Annie Savoy. Annie would have been my age when I wrote the script, and the opening monologue told me all I knew about her. I wanted to find the actress who could show me things I didn't know. That's a principle of casting critical to how I approach the process—I want to be able to hand a part to the actor and tell them, "Up till now, I know more about this character than anyone. Now it's yours—show me all the things I don't know." I want to be surprised by casting. The audition process should one of discovery, not just one of finding a face to match what's in your head.

A couple of years after making *Bull Durham* I wrote the female lead in *White Men Can't Jump* for an "upper-middle-class young woman from Smith or Bennington who runs away with a man she thinks is a rebel-warrior-poet-athlete, but five years later he just looks like a slacker slob." It does not say she should be white, but it's kind of built into the character breakdown. The part went to Rosie Perez, who fit nothing in the character description. Not a line of dialogue was changed for Rosie, and the performance was far from what I had in my head (it was better). In the script, the character description was succinctly summarized when Rosie's character appeared on *Jeopardy!* and I rewrote the off-screen line for the *Jeopardy!* announcer to introduce her as "a former disco queen from Brooklyn, New York." So much for the upper-middle-class (white) woman going to Smith or Bennington.

Auditioning for a part is typically an excruciating exercise for an actor. Pages of dialogue have to be learned and performed in a room with an antsy director, producer, and casting director. It's a most unnatural act. The actor doesn't have a clue what the director is looking for, and yet has to make specific choices about how to play a scene. Play it big? Play it small? Underscore lines? Throw away lines? Is it supposed to be funny? The actor's dilemma is further confused by the fact that often directors don't know what they are looking for until they see it. If actors knew what was really going on behind the curtain, they'd probably look for another profession.

Directors, producers, and casting directors fight and argue about casting more often than they agree, and when that gridlock is negotiated and a piece of agreed-upon principal casting is presented to the studio, inevitably the studio weighs in to shoot down the consensus choice and offer a dreadful idea of their own. The studio has final say. They write the check. The casting process is as political as it is creative. There is lobbying, cajoling, arm-twisting, and horse-trading going on behind the scenes. Producers have secret relationships with favored agents, and have made promises nobody knows about. (Costner, after all, had been promised to Warner Bros. for another movie.) Casting directors have similarly private relationships with talent management companies and wink-and-nod agreements are made to get favored actors in the door and push them to the top of the list. The director, likewise, comes loaded with biases and crazy ideas. Some of the crazy ideas are fresh and original. Most are not. Still, I like the casting part of the process because I get to meet people.

The audition is an athletic exercise. For an actor, it should be about going to the gym to work out, not trying to get a job. Job interviews are pressurized and inauthentic. Wanting a part too badly unleashes pheromones of desperation, and it shows. I want the actor to relax. A coach who orders a pitcher to throw strikes or risk being pulled guarantees the pitcher won't throw strikes. It's the equivalent of a director telling an actor, "Do it better." Think Thurman Munson's mound visits to Goose Gossage.

In that vein, I believe in the small talk before an actor has to read the lines. I want to know where they're from—I might have played ball there or might have an anecdote to loosen them up. A bogus anecdotal story works just as well as something with verisimilitude. The small talk is intended to relax the actor who's terrified, get them to replace the *trying-to-score-a-job* thing with *this might be fun.* The process simply needs to be one of human engagement.

Today, these sessions are always taped, and, even worse, the actor is often asked to "self-tape" and blindly submit his audition. This is a miserable excuse for human engagement, and unfair to the actor. It's also unfair to the director and producers, who aren't getting to interact with a live human being, missing out on the energy, unpredictability, and spontaneity that can be more revealing than the line readings. If it were possible, I would never tape, because that tape gets passed up the food chain to someone at the studio or network who passes instant judgment, having never been in the room to see what's possible. If Rosie Perez had been on tape, she wouldn't have gotten the job.

We started with Annie but mixed Nukes in immediately, and squeezed in as many Skips and Larrys and Jimmys and Millies as possible. I was determined that the bulk of the movie's ballplayers would be cast from real players whom we would find in the Raleigh/Durham area.

Within days, Bonnie Timmermann arranged for me to meet with Thom in her New York office to begin the auditioning process. She called me while I was in Los Angeles to say that she had sent the script to an actress who had recently opened a movie to rave reviews, and that actress was suddenly very hot—in movie terms that translated to suddenly very *bankable*—and that she loved the script and wanted to meet. Bonnie also said, however, that this actress wouldn't audition; she wouldn't read lines for me and the producers. I said that anyone coming in for any part had to read, and that I would prefer to not meet with an actor or actress who didn't want to read the lines. There's a term for this in Hollywood—"offer only"—which means that the actor is of such stature or has such an impressive résumé that they're beyond having to audition and will accept only parts that come with an up-front financial offer. It's a fair position for the actor to take, if they can pull it off. There's enough humiliation built into that profession already, and some great actors are mediocre in auditions, while some mediocre actors are brilliant in them. I told Bonnie not to bring in this "suddenly very hot" actress if she wouldn't read a couple of scenes.

I flew to New York, through Dallas, for some reason, and had my wallet stolen while I was at a pay phone during a connecting-flight delay. So, I landed in New York with no wallet, no ID, no credit cards, no cash. I borrowed some money from somebody and made sure I was always out to dinner with someone who'd pick up the check. This was good preparation for the moviemaking process, as it turned out.

Soon enough, I reported to Bonnie Timmermann's office, where Thom Mount was also waiting, to begin the casting process. It was 9 a.m. Bonnie announced that the first actor of the day would be, in fact, the "suddenly hot" actress, so I naturally assumed she'd consented to read lines from the scenes that had been sent out to all the candidates for Annie. The actress came into the office in a remarkably short skirt and high heels, and we all settled in for the small talk. I congratulated her on the success of her new movie and told her how much I liked it, even though I hadn't seen it. As a lie, this was well within industry standards.

The chitchat was pleasant enough, and after a few minutes:

SHELTON: Well, why don't we play around with the script. I'd
    love to hear you read.
ACTRESS: Oh, I thought you knew I wouldn't read?

We looked at Bonnie, who just shrugged. Caught in the middle, she'd probably done the right thing by bringing the woman in to see if anything good came of it. Now I was caught in the middle.

SHELTON: I'm sorry there's a misunderstanding but I need to
    hear the words.
ACTRESS: But I don't read.
SHELTON: I hope you understand that up until now, I'm the
    only one I've heard say these lines because I say the dia-

logue aloud as I'm writing and I make a crummy Annie Savoy. I'd really love to hear you read the part.

ACTRESS: I said I don't read.

SHELTON: I think Annie is the kind of person who would read to anyone, to everyone, that she'd stop people on the street and read to them just because that's who she is.

At this point, this "suddenly hot" actress shifted to face me, subtly hiking her skirt as she did in an effortlessly choreographed revelation that would in later years become known as the "*Basic Instinct* gambit." And as she did, she offered: "I thought my body of work would be enough."

"And it's a lovely body of work, but I still need to hear you read."

Perhaps that was the only time in my life that the right line came instantly and not three days later.

The meeting was pretty much over.

Happily, it was quickly clear that we were awash in good candidates for Annie. The actresses seemed to like the character on the page and were full of ideas about how to make her their own. The problem wasn't a lack of terrific actresses, but something known as "The List." Every studio, network, or financing entity has one. The List consists of the names of actors or actresses who are acceptable for a lead role because they are either bankable on their own or, in some combination with other co-leads, are bankable enough. Kevin Costner was soon to become such a big star that the co-lead part could be an unknown, but he wasn't there yet. There are usually fewer than a dozen names on The List, and every studio has their own, although most of the names are common to everyone's List. The problem when you're trying to cast the leads in a movie is that The List keeps changing. Names drop on and off The List as films open big or flop, so an actor who might be acceptable last week isn't on The List this week.

First on our list for Nuke was Charlie Sheen, an emerging name who had just starred in *Platoon,* and was getting offers everywhere. He was a real baseball player and seemed a great foil for Costner. He was also committed to Orion's other baseball movie *Eight Men Out.* He said he'd given his word to the production and wouldn't drop out, even though they weren't close to shooting. It was an honorable pass. So the search for Nuke began as the search for Annie widened. We were less than a month from shooting.

I got a call from Martha Luttrell, a big agent at ICM, who suggested Susan Sarandon for Annie. She wasn't on The List, but a director can't share that with an agent because that's a betrayal of confidence with the studio. So, though I'd made a personal pledge that whatever else happened, I would be frank and honest with everyone I dealt with, I was forced to lie in a way that was more ridiculous than telling the "suddenly hot" actress that I'd seen a movie I hadn't (yet) seen. This was a real lie. I told Martha that I didn't think Susan Sarandon was right for the role, though I privately thought she was a great idea. It didn't matter—she wasn't on The List.

We kept meeting very good Annies while we were having trouble finding Nuke. The trickiest thing about Nuke is that he has to be different from Crash (and from Costner) while still appealing to Annie. Ebby Calvin "Nuke" LaLoosh also has to be someone Crash cannot compete with, in the way that Nuke can't compete with Crash. Otherwise, Nuke becomes a junior version of Crash and that's nobody we want to watch nor anyone Annie would want to sleep with. Most of the actors coming in for Nuke were athletes and felt like versions of who Crash might have been fifteen years earlier. Many even looked a little like a younger Costner, which was not their fault but hurt their chances. Nuke needed to be different in every way. It's the whole screen-chemistry thing again, where each principal player in the cast has to occupy separate and unique territory—otherwise there can't be conflict. Or humor, in this case. I met Nukes in New York and Nukes back in Los Angeles, and the casting office made endless lists looking for the right guy. Ironically, Nuke didn't have to be hired from The List—only the leading lady did; he could be an unknown. And we still couldn't find him.

An actor coming off a Warner Bros. hit came in for Nuke. He was the lead, he was all over the trade papers, he was hot. He was also glum. Strangely, I thought, he showed up for the audition in a black T-shirt with a pack of cigarettes tucked into a sleeve on his bicep. It was a James Dean move, or maybe Brando in *The Wild One,* but it was an odd choice for Nuke. He didn't like the idea of small talk and just wanted to jump right in, so we did. He mumbled his lines, never smiled, and affected a twitch. It made me nervous and I did something I rarely do—I stopped the hot actor.

SHELTON: Excuse me, but I can't hear you and you seem to feel that Nuke is rather glum.

HOT ACTOR: He's dark.

SHELTON: Nuke?

HOT ACTOR: I've thought a lot about this. I don't think you know how dark he is.

SHELTON: Nuke is the sun. He lights up every room. I love Nuke.

HOT ACTOR: There's a lot going on deep inside him.

SHELTON: *Nothing* is going on deep inside him. That's the point. He's an innocent, a man-child.

HOT ACTOR: Let me show you some things you might not know about him.

Well, I have to admit, that's exactly what I want actors to do. However, there is a line that can be crossed and this fellow found it quickly. When he finished the first of three scenes, as firmly but gently as possible, I told him, "This is just not going to work. Thank you for coming in."

He pulled out a cigarette and stuck it into his curled lip as he left. I think it was Brando, not Dean.

Back in L.A. we got a call from Orion with a fresh Nuke idea: Anthony Michael Hall. He no longer was the short, lovable character from the John Hughes classics *Sixteen Candles* and *The Breakfast Club,* but he had charm and a little angst and he was now six feet one, we were told, and was an athlete. Besides, he had a movie in the can at Orion called *Johnny Be Good* that the studio said was testing through the roof and was going to be a big hit. This was the first time I'd heard the expression "testing through the roof." It meant that the scores from cards filled out by the audiences after studio preview screenings were so high that everyone was convinced they had a box office smash on their hands. *The cards are never wrong* is a mantra of the movie business.

I thought Hall was an inspired idea and possibly a perfect foil for Costner's world-weary Crash. We enthusiastically endorsed giving Hall the script, and Mark Burg and I flew back to New York a few days later to meet him. The Columbus Bar and Restaurant on Broadway near Eighty-Second Street was the designated place to meet. It was an actors' hangout and comfortable to all. When we arrived, we discovered it was also a hangout for John Gotti, who held court at a corner table with his back to the wall, which was satisfying to see because lore taught that the boss of the Gambino family is supposed to sit in a corner with his back to the wall.

We got a table outside. Hall was late. When he arrived, he was accompanied by six of his friends. After the usual small talk that I put so much stock in, though it was complicated by having eight people involved—his posse had things to say—I offered that it was time to talk about the script. "Oh," he said, "I haven't read it yet." Pauline Kael had said about me in a review (I think it was regarding *Under Fire*), "Shelton is frequently appalled but never shocked." I was somewhere in between at that moment, and said, "We'll meet you back here at six p.m. tomorrow, without your entourage, and you will have finished the script by then." Mark and I got up and left, and went back to the hotel to call his agent, who was both shocked *and* appalled, and promised to get Hall back to the Columbus, fully prepared, promptly by six the following day.

The next day we auditioned some of the other parts while I waited for and looked forward to six o'clock. The part of the manager, "Skip" Riggins, was of concern because coaches and managers in movies have traditionally been portrayed as over-amped screamers or overly earnest Knute Rockne types. I knew that most actors had experienced these archetypes only through movies and theater, not in the daily grind of endless baseball seasons that take the edge off being too amped or earnest. Right away, an actor I'd always admired came through the door and nailed it. J. T. Walsh was the embodiment of the world-weary professional who carried his cynicism with ease. He was great with words, he was centered, he seemed not to give a damn—all perfect for a baseball lifer in the minor leagues. It's common after a first read-through by an actor in an audition that the director will offer an idea or two—known euphemistically as "adjustments"—and then the actor will make another pass, with those adjustments. It's a lousy term for the creative process and should be reserved for chiropractors working on your back, but it's accepted terminology. After Walsh's first line reading I knew he was the guy. I was ready to have a drink with him. He might have left the audition thinking he'd missed out on the part, but I was ready to hire him. I'm sure that casting director Bonnie Timmermann thought this was another case of a first-time director jumping the gun, since there were more actors coming in for the same part. Still, I knew that J. T. Walsh was Skip, the manager of the Durham Bulls.

Shortly after Walsh's quick, perfect audition, Trey Wilson came to read for the same part. Trey was a Texan, most recently seen in the Coen brothers' *Raising Arizona,* and, with his casual western drawl and higher-energy line readings, he was different from Walsh in nearly every way. Except one—a pack of cigarettes was in his pocket. Trey's higher-energy line readings needed, well, an *adjustment,* and I reminded him that the manager's frustration couldn't boil over every day or he'd have a heart attack because the season was so damn long. He ran through the lines again and let the anger simmer but never boil over. He was a talented pro and would be easy to work with but, in my mind, he was in line behind J. T. Walsh.

After a day of auditions, I headed back to the Columbus bar with Burg to meet with Anthony Michael Hall again. This time he showed up with half his posse, which was a hopeful improvement, at least. We sat down and I cut right to the point. "Well, tell me what you thought of the script and the character of Ebby Calvin 'Nuke' LaLoosh." He answered: "I'm only up to page forty. Maybe thirty-five. We can talk about that."

I got up and left the table without saying a word, returned to the old Mayflower Hotel, and called the agent to say I was done with this idea. Mark stayed to try to explain why this was bad form, or maybe to down a couple of drinks. I then called the studio to announce that we had to keep looking.

• • •

Two of the trickier parts to cast were the Bible-thumping relief pitcher, Jimmy (no last name), and Millie (also no last name), the young woman who's been in bed with half the league. He's a virgin, she's far from it, and because they're barely sketched out in the script, it's easy to caricature and make fun of them. If this was a Broadway musical, they'd be called the "B" couple. (Later, they almost were.)

Coming out of the evangelical world and loathing what that had predominantly come to mean—racism, misogyny, homophobia, anti-intellectualism, judgment, anti-science, myopia—I was still concerned that Jimmy be a real young man, comfortable in his beliefs, and not myopic. There wasn't enough space in the story to fill him out, so the actor had to help do that. The first few actors in the room wanted to comment on the character in their interpretation, rather than embody him. They wanted to have fun with him, and my adjustments didn't help at all. Then William O'Leary showed up and played the lines with quiet dignity and simple belief. He wanted to invite everyone to his private chapel and wasn't bothered if he was mocked. In those days, players didn't point to the heavens when they hit a home run or struck out a key hitter, and team chapels and prayer meetings were unheard of—at least on all the teams I played for. O'Leary, who had just gotten good reviews in *Precious Sons* on Broadway with Ed Harris and Judith Ivey, gave a first reading that was unforced and quietly convincing. He smiled, he was charming, and he didn't make fun of this character. I liked his take on it, but then he asked to try something else—he had another angle to explore. His second take was excessive, noisy, showy, and frankly pretty terrible. I said he should stick with the first take. I then asked if he played baseball and he said he did. He was lying. He got the part.

That lie would be fought out in Durham but it was, I would argue, *within industry standards,* at least for an actor. Much later he revealed that he had grown up in the Roman Catholic Church, a seriously committed young lector who later became a born-again baptized Protestant, and finally left it all for the theater. He had attended the Immaculate Conception Catholic Church and School in Highland Park, Illinois, which ultimately provided the space for the Steppenwolf Theatre Company to present their first full season of work, which lends credence to my belief that the Roman Catholic Church and evangelical melodrama are the best training grounds for a life in the theater.

Millie needed to be different from Annie in the way that Nuke had to be different from Crash. But we didn't know who Annie was yet. A young actress beginning to break (be discovered), Laura San Giacomo, gave a strong reading and had a distinct look. She was Italian-American, pretty, with olive skin, and I felt she would stand out in the bywaters of North Carolina. She became the number one contender. More important, she played Millie as innocent but not ignorant. The idea for her character may have been left over from the sixties and seventies, when sexual abandon wasn't tempered by a conservative backlash or, soon enough, the beginning of the AIDS crisis. Sex used to be fun and it didn't kill you—at least that was the conceit. San Giacomo was perfect.

Back to Durham and L.A., where some studio panic was setting in about casting Annie and Nuke, all while Martha Luttrell kept calling to push for Susan Sarandon. I kept saying, "She's just not right for the part." Finally, Martha said, "She's living in Italy with her baby daughter and is willing to fly to New York or L.A. on her own dime to audition." Our company line was that we didn't want her to spend her money if she wasn't being seriously considered. It was all about The List she wasn't on.

Time was becoming a real problem and it was decided that rather than keep commuting to New York for casting, there would be one big day in Los Angeles where we'd try to cast all the remaining parts and bring in any Annies and Nukes we hadn't yet seen. Forty actors were lined up in the hallway on the marathon day, which isn't fair to anybody but was the only way to catch up. There was no opportunity for small talk and barely any to play with line readings. It was memorable anyway, for two reasons. First of all, we found Nuke.

Second, I was privy to one of the worst auditions I've been part of before or since. It was bad, but it was also authentic and original and unconscious. It wasn't an audition at all, but some kind of amped-up revelation of essential character—the id on steroids, or (to be consistent with my own era), the id on uppers. "Greenies" or "beans" were the nicknames for Dexedrine and other speed drugs that were available in every clubhouse when I played, often sitting in bowls next to the lunch meat, mayonnaise, Red Vines licorice, and candy bars—which comprised the training table of the day. I was never a drug guy, but I took them, especially after an eight-hour bus ride before a doubleheader in Bakersfield or El Paso. They weren't even illegal until 2006.

Robert Wuhl, a standup-comic-turned-actor with credits like *The Hollywood Knights* and *Good Morning, Vietnam,* walked in the room talking a hundred miles an hour, and I was sure he'd taken a few greenies before the meeting. He was on his feet, he was sitting down, he jabbered baseball stats and dropped anecdotes and seemed deeply concerned with how I felt about Tim McCarver as a baseball announcer.

Robert's audition for Larry Hockett, the pitching coach and tandem running mate of Skip the manager, as best I can remember it, with apologies to Robert:

ROBERT WUHL
Hey hey great script great script love it
y'know I'm thinking this guy's gotta stay
connected to Skip in case Skip gets called
up called up then he's Skip's guy in the
show am I right an' I wanta ask you what
you think of Tim McCarver even though he's
not a pitching coach of course he's a TV
announcer but he knows pitching coaches is
what I'm saying 'cause he caught Gibson

and all that but do you think he talks too
much 'cause some people love him and some
hate him 'cause he talks so much but he
knows what he's saying but he says it too
much maybe I wonder what's your call? By
the way, is William Bendix the worst movie
baseball player ever and Babe Ruth are you
kidding me? Forty-two-year-old guy playing
an orphan, what a joke, but Tony Perkins
catching a fly ball is a disgrace and is
Bang the Drum Slowly really about baseball
or is it about dying? Whatta you think?

I don't remember getting to a line reading. I don't remember saying anything other than, "I think Tim McCarver talks too much."
Robert just finally finished talking after bouncing off the walls and
he left. Bonnie apologized for bringing him in. I said I wanted to hire
him. She said that was probably the worst audition she'd ever seen.
I agreed. But I still wanted to hire him. I said that I couldn't teach
what he did but I thought I could coach it, or put a lid on it, or steer
it in a direction that made the manager–pitching coach team a kind
of vaudeville act. His nonaudition had me already rethinking the
part. Plus, Robert knew baseball. He got the job.

• • •

Tim Robbins is a very big man, about six feet five, and when he
walked in, the first thing that struck us was that he was different
from Costner in every way. His boyish face, his physicality, an impish
grin: none were things that would get confused with Costner's Crash
Davis. He was being pitched as a new face, a possible *discovery*, a New
York City native holding a theater degree from UCLA, with a film
starring Jodie Foster and John Turturro, *Five Corners,* in the can. I
liked him right away. His reading was simple, and when he feigned
standing on the mound to deliver one of Nuke's voiceover musings

while pitching, he just filled the space and didn't hurry anything. He was a big, imposing pitcher.

He'd also just costarred in *Howard the Duck,* which neither Tim nor his agents bothered to mention, as they shouldn't have (it was a legendary flop). Tim was also cast in *Eight Men Out* but less committed than Sheen had been. He was available and everyone liked him, but I wouldn't make a commitment until I put him in a room with Kevin to see how they played off each other. When they met, it wasn't exactly George and Lennie from *Of Mice and Men,* but their different physicalities, manners, and voices suggested they could play together. Tim was from theater, Kevin had worked in the grip/electrical department at Raleigh Studios across the street from Paramount when he was trying to break in. One guy could talk Brecht. The other could identify a light hanging from a rigging in a soundstage. What was compelling was that it was Nuke who could talk Brecht.

Then Martha Luttrell called again to announce that Susan Sarandon didn't care what anyone thought and was flying herself to Los Angeles in two days and expected to be seen. This was an Annie-like move, which we appreciated, motivated by discovering she wasn't on The Damn List.

A meeting with Susan was arranged, and I asked Kevin to be there, partly out of respect for Susan, partly to see how they worked together, and partly out of desperation that we were shooting in two weeks. Susan flashed into the room looking brilliant, hardly like someone barely off a ten-hour flight. She wore a tube dress with four-inch red and white horizontal stripes that announced her presence with authority. Brassy, funny, physical, and off-book. She didn't need script pages in her hand. She knew the character. She *was* the character. There was nothing precious in her treatment of Annie, nor any apparent concern whether or not she was what I was looking for.

Meeting over, she blew out of the room in a hurry to go somewhere. Kevin and I looked at each other and said, "That's Annie." We sat down with the producers and wondered about the protocols. Should we call the studio and lobby for Susan? A new list? I suggested my usual strategy—let's find a bar. But the phone rang and it was Mike Medavoy, head of production at Orion, who said, "Y'know, I saw Sarandon a couple of weeks ago and she looks great." As Susan had been in Italy for months, clearly Mike didn't see her "a couple of weeks ago." As lies go, it was, well, within industry standards, as mine had been to her agent. Susan, it was later revealed, went straight to Orion Pictures offices on her way to the airport and worked the hallways, dazzling one male exec after another. She can't recall whether she actually found Medavoy, but she confessed it was a shameless (but highly effective) ploy and word spread in the halls of Orion that "Sarandon looks great!" She was on The List in minutes, which explained Medavoy's call.

She flew back to Italy and the small town of San Felice Circeo, where she was living. The next day, while walking through a park by the beach, a neighbor lady said that someone from Los Angeles was trying to reach her on the phone. She called her agent to learn she'd not only been hired, but she was needed for rehearsals immediately. She gathered up Eva, her eighteen-month-old baby, packed her bags, and flew to Durham.

We had a cast.

11

Practice

Two weeks before shooting, the cast came to Durham for rehearsal—as well as to put all the actor ballplayers through a baseball camp that would run throughout filming. The actual manager of the Durham Bulls, Grady Little, was happy to earn a little extra money in the off-season and run these camps. Little, a few years later, worked his way up through the system to earn the job as manager of the Boston Red Sox and the Los Angeles Dodgers, and became infamous for not pulling Pedro Martinez in the seventh game of the 2003 ALCS against the Yankees, who went on to tie the game and then win in extra innings. David Lester also went to the University of North Carolina and Duke to recruit college players to fill out the movie's Bulls team—at fifty dollars a game plus two hot dogs—but the NCAA, in its predictable wisdom, wouldn't allow it. For a college athlete to stand in right field for a pittance in a brutal all-night shoot would destroy his amateurism, it was reasoned.

It fell to Grady Little to round up minor leaguers looking for work. The season had just ended and some might still be hanging around Durham. Little also recruited local players who had finished high school or college. The camp consisted of getting and staying in shape as well as running routine baseball drills—hitting, fielding, throwing—and trying to locate enough legitimate pitchers as we needed. Grady found Jeff Greene, Butch Davis, Paul Devlin, and other minor leaguers and college players happy for the gig. We added Lloyd Williams and Tom Silardi, actors out of L.A. with some baseball experience, to round out the Bulls infield.

Actors trying to play professional athletes tend to get serious in a hurry when they're surrounded by the real thing. I knew that once our cast showed up and found themselves with real minor leaguers and ex-professionals, they would have to get up to speed or be exposed quickly. Athletes never seem to tire of repeating the same actions over and over. They don't whine, they don't bitch, they just repeat the commanded action tirelessly. It's the discipline of muscle memory and brain training that makes the difficult routine, and actors, in my experience, watch that with respect. The flip side of this is that the real athletes invariably marvel at the actors' ability to memorize pages of dialogue on a daily basis.

In L.A., I was lucky to find my Bulls shortstop, "Deke" in the script, when a young comic named Danny Gans walked in the door. He had played some minor league ball and did impressions of celebrities; he seemed the exact right kind of guy to stand at the front of the bus and do Elvis. The shortstop had plenty of lines and some comic moments built in; not only was Gans perfect, like everyone else, he came cheap. He had the same deal most of the regular cast had—twenty-five hundred dollars a week for four weeks; ten grand, total. A few years after the movie came out, he signed a $100 million, ten-year contract with the Rio Hotel and Casino in Las Vegas.

At the end of rehearsal each day, the actors who had roles as players hurried to the Durham Athletic Park to be drilled by Little. The baseball camp quickly sorted out who could play from who *said* they could play. A couple of days into camp, I showed up to see how things were going and a Latino actor/player whom I'd hired out of New York as José, the first baseman, was playing in a scrimmage. A ponytail stuck out of his hat and he was chomping on a small cigar during the game. The ponytail I maybe could have lived with, but when I challenged him about the cigar, he insisted, "It's part of my character." I told him there were rules about smoking *while* you played, although many players snuck drags in the dugout or, more commonly, in the runway to the clubhouse. He was dug in.

PLAYER: You know when you made that speech about knowing
    the characters better than anybody but when you hired an

actor you handed the part to them? Well, this is me bringing me to the part.

SHELTON: Nonetheless, you can't play with a cigar in your
mouth.

PLAYER: What if I don't light it?

SHELTON: Technically, I suppose, that's within the rules. But it
looks stupid.

PLAYER: That's your opinion.

SHELTON: Yes, and my opinion is the only one that really
counts right now.

PLAYER: I think you'll learn to accept it.

SHELTON: Actually, I won't.

PLAYER: Give it a little time.

SHELTON: There is no time. Pack your bags.

I felt lousy firing someone so soon, but he gave me no choice. I
called Bonnie Timmermann in New York and asked her to bring in
some more Latino baseball players. She asked how she would be able
to tell if they could actually play, and I told her to have a bat in the
office and ask them to hold it in their hands for a photo. Two days
later a stack of Polaroids arrived and I liked the way Rick Marzan
held the bat, so he got the part.

Then I saw Billy O'Leary (Jimmy) throwing on the sidelines and
was appalled. I approached him and said he had obviously been lying
to me, which he confessed, but said he could quickly learn. I'm told
I was livid but I don't remember the moment, and I liked him as an
actor, so I just figured we'd never see him throw a ball in the movie.
From that moment forward in my other sports movies, I required an
athletic audition before the script-reading test.

Rehearsals were already under way when J. T. Walsh took a better-
paying job. Trey Wilson was still available and he got the call. Laura
San Giacomo was also now unavailable to play Millie, and again
I turned to the Polaroids and remembered a young actress named
Jenny Robertson, and she got the call. In the predigital days, long
before auditions could be texted or emailed, Polaroids were the coin
of the realm and the only way to remember anybody.

—

Rehearsals were critical; it makes little sense to me that so few movies bother with that anymore. It creates an opportunity for everyone to bring their good and bad ideas to the table. It's a workshop, really, and I'm of the there-are-no-bad-ideas school, which is a lie, of course, but it suggests a point. A cigar in the mouth of the first baseman, for example, was a bad idea. Several years later, I was working on *Cobb* with Tommy Lee Jones, who had been a star pulling left guard for Harvard's football team (All-Ivy League First Team). He was also an active theater student and referred to rehearsal as "practice," as in, "Hey, Coach, we need some practice here." I've thought of it the same way ever since.

Another reason I believe in practice is so I don't get stuck rewriting during production. There's no time, I have little energy left for it, and I've had enough experience on sets to know how much cast and crew loathe getting rewrite pages stuck under their doors at midnight. Cast members who've prepped and learned their lines are suddenly asked at midnight or 5 a.m. to learn a new scene. Invariably, a new prop will have crept into the rewrite and catch the prop department off guard as well, and perhaps the camera department will have rehearsed a scene that now doesn't exist. Maybe even the lights and electrical prerigging is suddenly rendered ineffective.

Each time a rewrite is done, it's given a color. Newly rewritten pages are printed in that color when they're handed out so that cast and crew members can insert the new colored pages into their scripts and easily identify the changes as they evolve. After the white pages that everyone starts with, script pages come out in blue, pink, yellow, green, goldenrod, buff, salmon, cherry, tan, ivory, and then, God forbid, it starts over with double white, double blue, and so forth, always in the same order. To be clear, there will always be minor revisions during the shooting process—a bit of dialogue change here and there—but I try to avoid significant rethinking of a scene unless what's on the page clearly isn't working. In *Bull Durham* that scene was the one in which Annie bursts into Crash's boardinghouse room while he's in his shorts ironing a shirt with a Scotch sitting on the ironing board. I rewrote that endlessly and we rehearsed it endlessly and it never worked—until the day we shot it. But mostly everything got sorted out in rehearsal, and I could hear the rhythms of the actors playing off one another, especially those of Kevin, Susan, and Tim.

There is a driving philosophy here that I still believe in. Learn the lines so well that we can rehearse the behavior and make discoveries while we're practicing. That way I can rewrite during that period—so on the day we shoot, the cast is so ready to go they're like horses at the gate at Santa Anita. Again, the athletic model: you can also *overrehearse,* so it's important to know when to stop and leave some energy and enthusiasm for the game.

The second part to that approach is that, contrary to what I've just said—and contrariness is a director's prerogative—I do believe in improvisation, but only when it makes sense and only if we can first commit the script, as written, to film. The text is the melody and the chord changes and the lyrics and the improvisation is the jazz music built out from that foundation. It's more Betty Carter than Ornette Coleman. During practice, if an actor came up with a line that felt right, I'd put it in the revisions that night and we'd try it out in a couple of days to see if it still worked. (The script supervisor always sits in on rehearsal to take notes, but we hadn't hired one yet and were still looking for a local hire to save travel and per diem.) Sometimes an alternative line comes up in practice that doesn't cause me to change the script, but I remind the script supervisor to make a margin note of the line so that on the shooting day we can try it out. I take pride in the dialogue, but if somebody's got a better line, I'm the first to put it in the script. I'll take good ideas from anywhere.

A man in a bull suit showed up at the local casting office looking for work. He was hired on the spot and I added him to the script. Later, I would have Nuke throw pitches at him, on Crash's orders. When a pitch hit him, as newly scripted, he took his own stunt falls and was given an extra fifty dollars every time he did.

With three days to go before production, there was one last piece of casting I couldn't get a handle on. The role of Teddy Cullinane, the announcer, was more important to me than it might have appeared on the page. His voice would run throughout the show and was critical to suggesting place and, in a way, the timelessness of this life.

Most of the minor league players are from elsewhere; only Annie has a broadly southern accent (though we don't ever learn where she came from). So the onscreen/off-screen voice of the man in the booth had to be very evocative. I wanted the real thing but hadn't found it through local casting. Before I got on my high horse about finding the "real thing," Bonnie Timmermann had suggested the comedy team of Al Franken and Tom Davis. They were funny men but their voices, I feared, would say "comedy" and comment on what was happening around them. I wanted the announcer to be *part* of what was happening. I borrowed the surname Cullinane from Joe Cullinane, the longtime radio broadcaster for the Rochester Red Wings. I occasionally hung out with Joe on road trips when I couldn't find a player interested in visiting the Edgar Allan Poe museum in Richmond, Virginia (for example). He often invited players to accompany him on visits to the mental institutions around Rochester, and sometimes I was the only player willing to go. Many of the patients were die-hard Red Wings fans and he brought them souvenir T-shirts. I always thought that being a professional ballplayer meant you went to Little League clinics and pancake breakfasts, and visited hospitals during the day, in exchange for carousing at night. A kind of spiritual balance could be attained.

About this time, I woke up after midnight with my hotel TV blaring *Late Night with David Letterman.* His guest, whose name I didn't catch, was telling stories and spinning yarns about his adventures as a famous undercover moonshine-revenue agent in North Carolina. He had a thick, rich, authentic drawl—slightly incomprehensible at times—and was an extraordinary storyteller who didn't seem to mind being both famous (a book had just been published about his life) and on national television, even though he was still an active undercover agent. More important, Letterman couldn't get in a word and finally gave up, pushed back in his chair, and let the man talk.

I called Bonnie in New York the next morning and asked her to find out who he was and where he lived. His name was Garland Bunting and he lived ninety minutes from Durham in Scotland Neck, North Carolina. I drove up to meet him that night after he'd returned from New York and had dinner with him and his formidable wife,

Colleen, at an all-you-can-eat buffet for $4.99. Bunting turned out to be one of the greatest talkers I've ever met. He was hired on the spot, though he had to call his daughter to run it all by her. Being in a *Kevin Costner movie* was what legitimized the whole thing. When he learned of my Baptist roots, which I readily volunteered, he began reciting entire chapters in the King James Version of the Bible, with this rolling, rural, deep, and glorious inflection. We became fast friends and over the course of years, I've put him in another movie and even developed a script about him; although I was never able to get it off the ground, it's still on my list.

Garland Bunting became Teddy Cullinane, the Durham Bulls announcer, and when he wasn't on the set, he continued rounding up moonshiners in Halifax County, North Carolina. He explained that I shouldn't worry about his being discovered by dangerous moonshiners, even though he was on TV and soon in a Hollywood movie, because "those kinda fellas don't watch these kinda shows."

Part Three

Production

12

There's a Hat on the Bus

The first goal of a director is to stay on schedule and not get fired.

Toward that goal, some things are in your control and some are not. Bizarrely, studios track what time the first shot of the day is made, as if that carries any importance. Somebody on the set is always standing by to call the head of physical production at the studio at precisely 9:03 a.m. (or whenever) to duly note this accomplishment. It matters not if it is well done or poorly done or if it is an insert shot of feet walking or a complicated master involving all the principal cast in a difficult location with a tricky camera move. It is just a haphazard daily marker that means nothing, but a great deal of weight is attached to it.

What is of more consequence is "making the day," which simply means shooting everything on the daily schedule. First-rate line producers know how to schedule the first few days of the shooting schedule in a way that shows off the movie (usually the movie star) and doesn't risk *not* making the day.

Bull Durham set up as a nonunion movie, and North Carolina was a right-to-work state. This kept the budget down and created some problems later on that had to be negotiated (the crew was a mixture of union people out of Los Angeles and nonunion crew from North Carolina). Crew deals are based on negotiated flat-rate guarantees based on the number of hours worked a day—usually twelve, but occasionally more. If the daily shoot went longer, on a union production there would be an overtime bonus kicking in. We had a twelve-hour flat rate with the crew, which meant I had to wrap it on time every day. That was a goal I would fail to hit, and a rebellion would soon begin brewing that I didn't know about until much later.

That's another thing that good producers do—they keep the director in the dark about certain things. But if they keep the director in the dark about the wrong things, they aren't good producers. I like to know things. Sometimes, the things you want to know, when you know them, you wish you didn't know.

Most films are not shot in chronological order because production schedules are dependent on availability of locations, set construction demands, the need to move the film company to different towns, and so forth. When a "practical set" (a real location, as opposed to something built by the art department) is used, it's necessary to shoot all the scenes using that set in one continuous time period. The costs of going to and from a practical location, continually relighting and redressing the set, would be unrealistic; these practical locations would become impractical. The order of shooting doesn't matter much for the crew, but it can create challenges for the cast, especially the principals. A particularly emotional scene, for instance, might be impossible for the actors to pull off on the first day or even first week of shooting. Every movie deals with this, and film actors know the drill. Even so, if there's a particularly difficult scene, I make sure the actor is comfortable if it happens to come early in the schedule. These issues explain why I insisted the lovemaking scene between Kevin and Susan be scheduled for the end of the shoot, when everyone was familiar and hopefully comfortable with one another.

It was decided to shoot Crash's minor-league-record home run in Asheville, at the Asheville Tourists' gorgeous old ballpark in the mountains, before we started principal photography. Since it was one of the last scenes in the script, we could film it with my directing a second unit and could save money. Second units are a small version of a film production's sprawling first unit; essentially, they are glorified camera units. We didn't need to bring hair, makeup, wardrobe, and lots of other departments, which instead could stay in Durham to keep prepping. Asheville was roughly a three-and-a-half-hour drive due west, the same route I had taken a year earlier when I dictated Annie's monologue into a recorder. The sequence was simple: Costner would look heroic, and the images and color would suggest the movie to come. It was a good scene to show the studio that I knew what I was doing. A first-time director has to think of these things. Everyone is nervous about a rookie, but I was calm and confident. I tend to focus better in crises, and moviemaking is a series of small fires that you try to identify and snuff out before they turn into conflagrations. Every first-time director has certain strengths to rely on and weaknesses they have to address on a fast learning curve. Sitting in editing rooms on two features with Roger Spottiswoode was enormously beneficial to me, and having John Alcott grilling me at 5:30 a.m. outside the camera truck in Chiapas, Mexico, about lenses and shots I planned to make on the *Under Fire* second unit was experience that couldn't be gained in film school. The rest I'd have to figure out.

I was confident about working with actors, for some reason. I liked them, I listened to them, and I didn't mind being tough when called for, which rarely happened. The time spent on playing fields and in locker rooms had been invaluable in watching how teams worked. Any group working together as intimately as an athletic team—or a movie cast—will inevitably have clashes of egos. Conflict is built in, but the old adage *You must treat everyone the same* is horseshit. Mickey Mantle wasn't treated the same way that Phil Linz was, nor should he have been. The boss has to treat everyone fairly, but if the center fielder or the movie star is making ten times more than the manager or the director, well, that becomes part of the dynamic to deal with.

DAY PLAYER: I want another take on that scene.
DIRECTOR: Sorry, we have to move on.
DAY PLAYER: But the star got another take.
DIRECTOR: He's the star.
DAY PLAYER: I can improve on what I've done. I've got a fresh
    idea.

DIRECTOR: Next time put your fresh idea in the first take.
DAY PLAYER: So, you don't really treat everyone the same.
DIRECTOR: I never said I did.

The main thing is to listen to the actors. Even the day player—
but not *after* his scene has been shot and the crew is in another setup.
Actors do know things. Sometimes they're full of shit, sometimes
they're onto something. The director's job is to know the difference,
and to say no to their first nine bad ideas in a way so they feel encouraged to offer the tenth, which could be brilliant and shine light on
the character in a way you never imagined.

My learning curve had to do with the endless education about
the speed of film stocks and lenses, though that was the air the camera department breathed. Chuck Minsky and I were still reviewing
scenes and forming a battle plan when we ran out of prep time, but
there would be weekends to catch up. Actually, there would just be
Sundays—we were shooting six-day weeks to save money.

The only position of importance still unfilled, three days before
shooting, was the script supervisor. Lester had located one with credits on De Laurentiis–produced movies in Wilmington, and sent her
the script in advance. She drove to Durham for an interview. In my
mind, she already had the job—there was no time to look for anyone
else. I got out of the scout van in the backyard of "Annie's house,"
where the crew was gathered, and went off to the side to interview
the woman. First question: "What do you think of the script?"

It seems like an easy question, in fact, the easiest. Can't you lie?
And isn't that—under industry standards—acceptable? She said she'd
been busy and was only halfway through, though she'd had it for a
week and would finish it right away. She liked what she'd read, she
offered. In truth, it doesn't even matter if the script supervisor likes
the script. They could hate the script and still be a great script supervisor (the job consists of sitting next to the director and keeping a
shot-by-shot record of production, later valuable in the editing room
for locating specific takes and notes). The one thing the script supervisor can't do is not read the damn script.

Then she asked the strangest question I'd ever heard from someone trying to get hired: "What kind of snacks do you like?" I said I wasn't a snacker and never went to the craft service table (where snacks are available all day and night). She then offered a short account of the snacking preferences of directors she'd worked with. It was her job, she told me, to keep the director well snacked throughout the day.

I told Lester this wasn't going to work, and the woman was sent back to Wilmington to work with hungrier directors. Burg said he'd located another possibly available supervisor out of L.A. and they'd pay to bring her to Durham if I liked her. He'd already sent her the script as backup.

I called Karen Golden in L.A. and asked for her feature credits. She'd only done two features, but the most recently completed was John Huston's adaptation of James Joyce's great short story "The Dead," from *Dubliners*. The movie hadn't yet been released but as a fan of Huston and the short story, I looked forward to it. Leonard had assigned the story in class when I was nineteen, and it meant nothing to me. Twenty years later I read it and was rattled. I wanted to hire Karen immediately, if only to ask about working with Huston. Then she volunteered that her father used to have season tickets to the Hollywood Stars' Pacific Coast League Triple-A games at Gilmore Field in L.A., and she used to go as a child. I hired her on the spot. "Don't you want to know what I thought of the script?" she asked. "Who cares," I said.

I wanted to hear her stories of Gilmore Field, next to the Farmers Market at Third and Fairfax, where Carlos Bernier once played and Humphrey Bogart reportedly had a box seat and the first baseman was Chuck Connors before he starred in *The Rifleman* on television, a show cocreated by Sam Peckinpah himself. Karen ultimately became one of the highest-priced and most successful script supervisors in the movie business, and I hired her whenever I could. She never brought me a snack.

•   •   •

The Asheville shoot went easily. We showed the studio we had no trouble "making the day" and our first shot was in the can plenty early. Kevin looked like a career baseball player, swinging the bat easily and convincingly, and the sun cooperated and gave us heroic backlight when we needed it. He hit the home run left-handed because the sun was behind him, the very thing that had occurred to me at the Van Nuys Boulevard batting cage when we first dropped a few quarters into the batting-machine slot.

As Costner rounded third on his home run, and shook hands with the third-base coach (New York publicist Bobby Zarem, a friend of his), I noticed for the first time that a billboard next to the third-base foul pole revealed a solid evangelical message. I made sure a long lens shot that followed Costner, now Crash Davis, also revealed the sign and its mandate. The sign reads: MAKE HEAVEN YOUR HOME BASE BY GIVING YOUR LIFE TO JESUS.

Three days later we began the first day of principal photography, which I thought was a triumph, but unbeknownst to me, a fire was being lit that nobody knew about—one that would cause a calamitous problem two weeks down the road. Like most production problems, it didn't have to happen. It existed in someone's head and not in the real world, but then it grew until the very production was in crisis. It involved shooting the bus sequences, which Lester had wisely put at the beginning of the schedule to allow Armin Ganz's art department more time to prep other locations.

My photographic mandate was that the interior of the bus should feel real, not like something we shot on a stage where there are perfect controls for lighting. I had spent enough of my life on these buses to want to evoke a certain grittiness. I wanted the dugouts and other nooks and crannies of a ballpark to not feel like a Hollywood set, to not feel like something on a soundstage.

Minsky and key grip Bob James worked up a rig for the top of the bus that was wrapped in silks to diffuse the light, as well as provide some generator-driven additional lights. The cleverness of this was that the bus could drive in any direction and the light that got through the silks was fairly evenly distributed and the interior of the bus needed only minimal fill light. The rig was made of wood rather than the conventional "speed rail" metal alloy rigging, and it was clamped onto the bus like a big hat. It looked like the raft from Thor Heyerdahl's *Kon-Tiki* had landed on the bus. Orion's studio guy from physical production, who was on set to make sure we made the day, was alarmed at the sight of this strange contraption, and I later learned he immediately began notifying the mothership that something was amiss in Durham. This was on the morning of day one of shooting principal photography.

The *Kon-Tiki* rig worked brilliantly, and the light inside the bus was exactly what I hoped it would be. Shooting in a real bus is a nightmare to begin with, and the old bus we found and dressed with faded Durham Bulls signs and peeling pinups was cramped and full of seats secured with bolts rusted into place. It was difficult to move cast and crew around inside, but the limitations were liberating in a way. The restrictions forced me to shoot only the essential shots—there was no time for overachieving. It was also impossible to turn the cameras around to shoot the reverse direction (with one exception), so everything had to be conceived in one direction, with modest angles off an axis that would cut together. Had I three times the money and the schedule and a fancy soundstage, it wouldn't have looked as good.

But the studio guy, for no known reason, hated the hat on the bus. Which meant someone at the other end of the phone in Century City, where Orion was located, also hated the hat on the bus, because it was his duty to support his boss, whose boots were on the ground. As a result, people in the hallways of the studio began whispering, "Have you heard about the hat on the bus in Durham?" Nobody called the producers or me to ask about it and, worse but emblematic, nobody seemed to notice that the footage was terrific and part of that was because of the hat on the bus. This is how wars start.

Unaware that there was a problem brewing, in the Sheraton office that night as we prepared for day three, I reviewed the shooting schedule with Leonard, who was always nearby. An assistant came in and said, "Crash Davis is on the phone." I figured it was Kevin and said, "Tell Kevin I'll call him back in a few." The assistant said, "No, this man says he really is Crash Davis."

Since discovering that a man named Lawrence "Crash" Davis had played for the Durham Bulls in the late 1940s, I assumed that he was long gone. Nobody stayed in their last stop in the minor leagues—I even gave Annie the line to Nuke before he goes to the show, "When someone leaves Durham, they don't come back." I was alarmed that perhaps the *real* Crash Davis was still around and offended—or litigious about the fact—that I was using his name. But still convinced it was Kevin on the phone, I told the assistant, "Ask him how many doubles he hit in 1948." The assistant came back moments later and said, "Fifty." It was the real Crash Davis. I grabbed the phone and congratulated him on how many doubles he'd hit nearly forty years earlier. He said that his granddaughters had read in the local paper that I was making a movie about him. I assured him it wasn't so, but that I loved his name and wanted to use it for a character Kevin Costner was playing. He said that he'd never heard of Mr. Costner but his daughter and granddaughters liked him a lot. I asked the real Crash Davis if he could come to the set the next day to visit and we could discuss the use of his name. He agreed.

Day three of shooting was the scene in Annie's backyard in which she gives Nuke a pitching lesson by introducing him to chakras and his parietal eye and Fernando Valenzuela, among other things. The art department had built a small pitcher's mound in the backyard, and after a quick rehearsal we were ready to shoot. Nuke stands on the mound, Annie's a couple of feet away, mitt in hand, and we settled in on the first camera position. But when I looked through the lens, Annie couldn't be seen. Tim, at six-five, on top of a twelve-inch pile of dirt, stood so tall that only the top of Susan's head was in the frame. In all our rehearsals I hadn't factored in the possibility that a pitching mound in the backyard would lift Nuke out of the shot. Things were going slowly, the light kept changing, and the only solution was to use a wider lens on the main camera and add a second camera to shoot Annie's close-up at the same time. There wasn't time to shoot Nuke's matching close-up, which meant that, even as we shot, I knew the scene would cut together awkwardly unless it played in a "loose two-shot." In addition to the sun ducking in and out of the clouds, there was an endless stream of low-flying aircraft spewing enough noise to not allow for a complete take. Each time an airplane flew over, our redoubtable sound mixer, Kirk Francis, would shout, "North Carolina—First in Flight!" which is on every license plate in that state. But it wasn't funny. This was our first day to move the company, the studio guy was lurking, and it seemed that maybe we wouldn't make the day. And then the assistant director, Ric Kidney, turned and said, "There's somebody claims he's Crash Davis here to see you."

The real Crash Davis was an elegant southern gentleman with a buttery North Carolina accent and a gracious manner. A Duke graduate, he played in the major leagues for the Philadelphia Athletics, served in the navy, taught at Harvard, and returned to Durham to run the human resources department for Burlington Mills until a recent retirement. He was unlike any major league player I'd ever met. After a short talk—the light was fading—I asked for his permission to use his name for the movie. He said, "Tell me, young man, do I get the girl?" I said yes indeed he did, and if he'd like to meet her, she was standing over there. I pointed to Susan, who came over, matched his charm, and the deal was closed. The real Crash Davis and I became friends, and I gave him a line a few years later in *Cobb*, casting him as Wahoo Sam Crawford.

The sun was low, and we scrambled to fill it in for the final shot, when Nuke prepares to carry Annie off to her bedroom:

```
                    NUKE
    I give up. Let's go inside and make love,
    and fall asleep until it's time to go to
    the ballpark.


                    ANNIE
    Or . . . we could just take that sexual
    energy and kind of hold on to it for a few
    hours and rechannel it into your pitching
    tonight. You're a powerful young thing,
    Ebby Calvin. . . .
```

We knew the light was in and out for the ending of the scene, but Minsky and I were confident that we had shot just enough angles to be able to cut around the problems. We had what we needed but not much more. But we made the day.

• • •

In 1987, when the movie was shot, there was no such thing as video feedback, the system in which a video feed is plugged into the camera(s) so that the director and DP and script supervisor can watch the scene in real time on a screen. If it had existed, we wouldn't have been able to afford it, but because we didn't have it, there was great anticipation (and a little anxiety) waiting for the dailies to come back from the lab. Exposed film stock was shipped overnight to the lab in Los Angeles, where it was quickly processed and sent back so that it could be reviewed on location a day or two later; this was how it had been done for eighty years. The move to digital filmmaking has killed an institution that I embraced—the presentation of dailies each night for the cast and crew, a ritual that brought everyone together in some kind of celebration (hopefully) of the previous day's work. Beer and light food were usually served in a hotel room turned into a projection room, and it was an opportunity for every department to "own" their work. It was great for camaraderie, on one hand, but it also raised the stakes for everyone at the same time. Every department was exposed, but every department could also take credit for and pride in their work.

Some actors chose to go. Some actors refused to go. But all were invited. And so it was, a couple of days later, at the end of dailies, as everyone was getting out of their chairs or climbing off the floor, where cast and crew sprawled with their beer and chips, that Susan entered with Mark Burg. She apologized for being late, but I said it wasn't a problem—we would run the dailies again for her. Then she said, "I heard I look bad in my close-up." I asked, "Who told you that?" She looked sheepish. She didn't want to implicate Burg but he was the only one standing with her.

I consider myself a patient man. Job-like, at times. I also have a temper, though it is rarely accessed. I can count on two hands the times I've gone out of control, and always it's been on the same trigger: Don't lie to me. That's it. I talk to every department head before shooting and make it clear: "If you fuck up, own it. I'm good with that. If you cover your ass with a lie, I'm not good with it."

Burg didn't exactly lie, but he had clearly told Susan she didn't look good in her close-up, which, to me, was just as deadly. It also wasn't true. The scene with the fading light would be easily fixed in the editing room, but that wasn't the point. I discovered at that moment that my connection to the actors was elemental. Part of my comfort zone was mutual trust—and he had violated it. If he didn't like her close-up, he should have come to me.

The rush of adrenal rage came from the earth (fifth floor, Sheraton, actually) up through my feet, calves, thighs, belly, through all chakras (I never quite understood the concept until that moment), on through my throat, and out the top of my head. The entire movie was threatened, at least in my mind. I grabbed Mark by the collar, the throat. His beer flew away. I shoved him to the ground. Chairs crashed. The cast and crew were still there but I didn't care. "How dare you talk to my actors! Don't you ever talk to my fucking actors again!" It got ugly. Crew members were pulling me back, yelling, "Don't kill him!" Leonard said I burst into his office, where he was still working, my hands still on Burg. Terrified, he hurried out.

It was inexcusable, and it was all on me. I'm not sure where the proprietary view of my relationship to the cast came from, but I hope it wasn't parental. *Les Enfants du Paradis?* I don't view directing actors as a militaristic exercise—you don't "handle" actors, you "work with" actors. Maybe I was just protecting that which felt threatened, but it's fair to say I went berserk.

Gene Corr, a close friend I'd hired to direct the second unit, says he tried to intervene but I was crazed, and he'd never seen me lose it like that. He also said he understood that I was trying to protect the movie and, regardless of the excess, it coalesced the cast and crew. We were all in it together.

Kevin and Tim watched silently (in horror, I think), and called me "Cujo" thereafter. They said it was a term of affection. I figured that when the powers that be heard about this, my directing career would be over after four days.

I don't know how the brawl ended, but finally I walked down the hallway to the production office, where Lester was mopping up for the night. He'd missed the melee, and I told him that he'd soon be getting a call from either Thom Mount, who was out of town, or the studio, or the Durham Police. He would be getting reports that I'd assaulted a producer and the reports would be correct. David, unperturbed, just nodded a "got it."

Nothing ever happened. Mark had the good grace to say nothing of the incident, for which I was forever grateful. Three decades later, it should be noted, Burg and I are discussing a new film project.

The scene at "Annie's house," in which her close-up was questioned, was the same sequence in which we had issues with weather, airplanes flying too low, and Nuke being too damn tall on the mound. It cut together beautifully. Susan looked great. And nobody spoke with the actors again, except the director.

•   •   •

The production sound mixer was a cranky and volatile SOB who also became a dear friend, though Kirk Francis was an acquired taste for some. Leonard thought I hired him for his overarching and general moral outrage, which might have some truth in it, but what mattered more was that Francis cared deeply about sound and the tracks he recorded. He had opinions about everything, had the bedside manner of Charles Bukowski, and was probably the most well-read person on the set, not counting Leonard. He was a fly fisherman and a philosopher-curmudgeon who always had a book in his hand and his beloved Aussie shepherd, Dorothy, sitting in a chair next to him. He took Dorothy and a stove in a pickup truck all over the country to film locations. He was also a serious chef, though he prided himself on never buying anything that was advertised, including foodstuffs.

Kirk suggested that we record Annie's entire monologue for the movie while we were based at the practical location for her house. We'd need it for a "guide track" to edit the movie, though we'd later re-record it in postproduction at a proper sound studio in L.A. Kirk, ever the misanthrope, had set up his production recording for Annie's house in an upstairs bedroom in the house next door. This way, he correctly determined, he wouldn't have to talk to anyone. The crew generally thought that was a good thing as well. Cables draped from one house to the other; it looked ridiculous but it seemed a good sociopolitical solution. Kirk was liable to go off about Senator Jesse Helms in front of a local, and, however sympathetic some of us were, it wasn't a good look for the show.

But for the studio guy, a cranky sound mixer who's recording from the neighbor's house looked like another hat on the bus.

13

A Thousand Pigeons

B ob Hoskins, the late, great Cockney actor, always wanted to direct a movie. When he finally got the opportunity, he said it was the worst experience of his life. He described it as "being pecked to death by a thousand pigeons." I don't share that view; I find it a mostly joyful act and the best job in the world. But there are a lot of pigeons out there, waiting.

We began shooting the baseball sequences. They were going slowly, but I thought the footage evoked minor league baseball, so let the action play out naturally. We weren't relying on camera moves to over-sell a moment. It was clear that I'd have to keep the coverage simple and loose without many close-ups or cutting angles. The creative decisions were driven by how time-consuming it was to shoot a game spread out over a few acres.

Minsky's camera operator, Dennis Smith (also a pseudonym), was a big man and put the camera on his shoulder to follow Crash out to the mound for his various confrontations with Nuke. All their conversations on the field were recorded on the hand-held camera in an attempt to create a more intimate feel between the men. A Steadi-cam was out of our price range, but I preferred the camera on the shoulder anyway because it felt more natural. I wanted to stay away from the very long lenses that every movie seemed to be shooting with, and much of the hand-held footage of Crash and Nuke is on a thirty-five-millimeter lens to approximate the human eye.

Tim had to work on his pitching motion, which later received some criticism, though I remain pretty defensive about it. There are a lot of big-league pitchers with hitches and hiccups in their deliveries, and when Tim follows through—my big directive—he's convincing. In retrospect, I offer the pitching deliveries of Dontrelle Willis and Bronson Arroyo and Craig Kimbrel and even the great Clayton Kershaw, whose hesitation tic delivery might not work in a movie but will get him to Cooperstown.

The night games were tediously slow and cold. In an early scene, Millie (Jenny Robertson) is sent behind the plate with the radar gun to time Nuke's wild pitches. Her breath looked like cold smoke coming from her mouth, a dead giveaway for how chilly it was in October. I told her to try not breathing, but that didn't work. Somebody said to keep ice in her mouth for the shot, which she did, and her breath didn't show. It was a trick we'd use again.

Susan's daily arrival at the ballpark began to feel like Annie's arrival. She greeted extras, crew, ballplayers, all with a wave and a smile as if this were her domain and they were welcomed guests. Susan was Annie from the outset, and generous to me as a first-time director. Before shooting, I had been warned by my New York theater acting friends that there were things that a director could safely say to an actor, and things that a director, if he said, would make a fool of himself. I could never remember what I was supposed to say or not, so I kept it simple. The big warning was to speak in action verbs and not say things like "More energy, please," which I never would have thought of anyway because it wouldn't have made sense as a directive to an athlete.

After the first take in one of the first scenes I shot with Susan, I didn't know what to say. I thought it was pretty damn good, actually, but since we were all there and the room was lit, I didn't want to walk away after one take. (Ever since then, I'm happy to walk away if the first take works.) So, I sat in my director's chair trying to think of an action verb until everyone started to look at me, waiting for my wisdom. Finally, Susan recognized my unease.

SARANDON: Well? Anything to say?
SHELTON: I'm thinking, I'm thinking.
SARANDON: It's okay if you can't think of anything to say, hon—I didn't go to film school, either.

I was racking my brain for an action verb. What was an action verb, anyway?

SARANDON: You can just say louder, softer, faster, slower.
SHELTON: Let's try louder, faster.

And she did. The first take was better, however, and is the one in the movie. From that moment on, I began directing with a stopwatch (assigned to the script supervisor), and later read that Billy Wilder used one his whole career. Faster and louder is usually funnier, unless it's Peter Sellers playing Chauncey Gardener in Hal Ashby's *Being There.*

I was pleased with the chemistry among the three leads. Getting Tim to trust himself to fully be Ebby Calvin "Nuke" LaLoosh was evolving quickly. His articulate intelligence and commitment to things that Nuke would be oblivious to needed to be rechanneled into a character who read only comic books. I asked Tim to realize that Nuke read *Sgt. Rock* comics with the same rigor that Tim read Brecht. In any case, Crash, Annie, and Nuke seemed to be all I could have hoped for.

Monday of week two started with a stock market crash and has ever since been known as "Black Monday," October 19, 1987. It turned out to be a Black Monday and a grim week on the production, as well. At first, I heard something I didn't think could be true. It was some fragment of a rumor that someone repeated, then said they shouldn't have said it and maybe they were wrong, but when pieces of a story keep floating around in the air like lint and never quite go away, they seem to gain credibility. The fragments added up to something deeply upsetting, and I had to check it out. What I heard was that Orion didn't like Tim's performance. There was an *unnamed executive* assigned to us, back in L.A., who was still pushing for Anthony Michael Hall, and he wouldn't let go. I asked Mount and Burg and they confirmed it, and shared that there was a wave of anti–Tim Robbins sentiment in the hallways of Orion. My first response was that I could get Kevin and Susan behind me—the studio wouldn't dare touch Tim if they thought Kevin and Susan would rebel. Then I got even angrier, and pulled an Earl Weaver, said they should fire me first. "They're thinking about it" was the answer. This was chilling.

Orion also felt that Susan didn't look good and that the disparity between her and Tim's ages would preclude Annie's ever going to bed with Nuke. The irony was that though it was unknown to me, Tim and Susan were falling in love on the set. In the meantime, I had Bob Leighton edit together the scene in Annie's backyard that had led to the near assault on Burg. The scene worked perfectly and Susan looked fabulous. Chana Ben-Dov, who ran Mount's office out of L.A., presented the "sizzle reel" to the studio and called to say they "don't like anything" and had commented specifically on how dark the dugouts looked. "They look gritty, they look real, they don't look like fucking Hollywood dugouts, they're not over-lit, they're exactly what I want!" I responded.

I didn't know fully what was going on behind the scenes, but I knew I had problems. I just couldn't figure out why. It was later revealed that the studio was leaning hard on Mount to get rid of Robbins—they technically couldn't do it since it was a "negative pickup" production; they financed and distributed the film but had to keep hands off the actual filmmaking process. The hands-off part wasn't working very well.

Somehow Anthony Michael Hall not reading the script over the course of two meetings at the bar where John Gotti was hanging out had made him more attractive to the Unnamed Executive who was stirring the pot with the studio. And Tim's fresh and original performance was resonating with everyone except those writing the checks. And Susan? Nobody could understand how anyone didn't think she looked great.

Matthew Naythons, friend, photojournalist, and consultant on *Under Fire,* arrived as a favor to take some "specials"—a term for specific photographs to be used in publicity. (The production could not afford a stills photographer, someone who's on set every day recording everything.) Matthew had walked into a snake pit.

—

The final scene of the movie—in which Annie comes back from the ballpark in the rain and finds Crash sitting on her porch swing—was originally scheduled for the following week, the third week of shooting. The weather forecast for that week was bright sun, so it would be almost impossible to stage fake rain. In order for rain to be visible on film, it must be backlit, and artificial rain is created by "rain towers," which are nothing more than giant sprinklers mounted twenty feet above the ground. For a rainy-day scene, ideally the rain towers operate on a dark, overcast day in which the sun can't poke through the clouds and light up the wrong side of the fake raindrops; fake rain can be lit artificially. Rain was an important element for the final scene. There could be no game at the ballpark and it seemed an appropriate end to Crash's career, as well as a possible beginning for Annie and him.

Lester came to me now and asked if I'd mind switching some scheduled days around because the next day—Tuesday—was predicted to be darkly overcast all over the region, a perfect day to shoot rain. He had rain towers standing by. I talked to Susan and Kevin and they agreed to be ready for the final scene, which required the actors to flip an emotional toggle switch. The production moved to Annie's house the night before.

Tuesday, the day after Black Monday, broke without a cloud in the sky for a hundred miles. All that could be done was to hang silks and black cloth and everything the grip truck was carrying to block out the sun in limited ways, then narrow the lenses to accommodate. In other words, all the shots had to be smaller. The sun showed through anyway but I hoped not enough to detract from the scene or the desired mood. Because water from the rain towers was crashing down from the eaves, it was difficult to hear the actors; their performances would have to be re-recorded later—a process known as "looping"—but that's the given when filming in such circumstances. Susan and Kevin looked perfect but not self-consciously so, and Minsky deserves the credit. The sun shone brightly from dawn till dark, as we kept pumping water through the rain towers.

I had nothing to say to the actors, other than "Think of the porch swing as a child's swing," at which point Susan curled her feet under her as a little girl might, and Kevin, without prompting, dropped some of Crash's bravado and righteous anger and sought comfort and consolation. Annie and Crash were vulnerable and exposed and ready, however cautiously, for what was next in their lives.

Despite Minsky's saving the day, the studio remained unhappy about everything, including Tim Robbins. Once a corporate mind is made up, all reason and judgment are forfeited. I thought we needed to dig in and fight, which seemed like the only position I was ever taking. Mount told Burg that they had to give something to the studio. A blood sacrifice, in order to hold on to Tim Robbins. In retrospect, I think they would also have fired me if they thought they could get away with it. My original insistence that the contract protect me from being fired until after one week of shooting might have saved me. The studio had heard that I was already tight with the three leads, who would come to my defense. Perhaps that was an unintended consequence of the Cujo incident.

By the time the Wednesday of the second week of shooting had ended, the air was thick with tension and anxiety. I called my agent, Geoff Sanford, who was not only my first and critically important agent, but had become a close friend, colleague, ally, and couch provider when my marriage had crashed. I told him to get on a plane to Durham at once. I didn't know if I was going to be fired, or if it was Robbins, or both of us. I didn't know what was going on and couldn't figure out what the problem was.

Of course, there wasn't a problem. It was all invented by people who have to invent problems in order to prove their value to their employer because then they can suggest a solution to the problem that doesn't exist. Or *something*. I really don't know what the something is but it's palpable and has weight and gravitas and is evil. Man fell from grace in the Garden of Eden and it led to bureaucracy.

It was all about the hat on the bus, which was a brilliant solution to a real problem but was incomprehensible to the observer, who built a nonproblem into a made-up problem with destructive nonsolutions. Alas, I couldn't have another volcanic blowup—that would begin to look like a pattern—but I quickly understood why legendary directors sometimes had legendary tempers. What would John Ford have done?

The next morning, we were on tenterhooks as we shot on the baseball field around home plate. Geoff had arrived and sat in the third-base stands watching. He was the only person there. Just before lunch, I looked over, and Thom Mount was sitting in another spot in the bleachers. He waved me over.

Mount said that Minsky had been fired and was going to be replaced by Bobby Byrne, a longtime director of photography who'd shot a number of movies for him. In fact, Byrne was already here, waiting in the hotel with his crew. I asked why this was happening. He said the studio didn't like Minsky's work. I said that was not possible. His work looked terrific. What I didn't know at that time was that the cameraman was being sacrificed to save Tim Robbins. It was grotesquely unfair. Then Mount said it was my job to give Minsky the news. It wasn't my job, but I did it anyway so at least I could tell him face-to-face that I didn't agree with what was happening. It was ugly and brutal.

I don't remember how we finished the day, but Leonard shared his notes, which say: *Chuck was the consummate professional. He handled himself with style and grace. And when the lunch hour was finished, he smiled and said, "What is the next setup?"* So, he finished the day, something I don't think I would have had the style and grace to do. Leonard's notes add: *Ron seethed, nearly out of control all afternoon.*

The cast and crew were shocked, and when they learned the decision had been made over my head, they seethed, too. Susan said nobody had asked her about the cinematographer—she had no problem with how Minsky had been photographing her. The entire crisis was avoidable.

Bob James, the key grip and a critical team member, would have been perfectly justified in leaving the show, as he was Minsky's guy. The grip department supports the camera department with dollies and dolly tracks, cranes, and scores of rigging schemes that serve both photographic and electrical department needs. A DP and a key grip work closely together and often have long professional relationships. I was always grateful that James chose to stay and finish the production, which was only 20 percent completed at this point. He was now the only person in the extended camera department who knew the show, the schedule, the locations, and the plan. Now I had a new cameraman, with an entirely new crew. (Camera departments are tightly knit teams, often trained by and always devoted to the DP.) In addition, Mount asked me to have dinner with Byrne to introduce him to the show. I didn't want to but I couldn't very well show up to shoot the next day with a director of photography and complete crew who'd never met, who'd rehearsed nothing, had no knowledge of the locations or the plans that Minsky and I had been working on.

So, I met Bobby Byrne for dinner. He was a very sweet guy, very experienced, but when he asked why I had requested him to come on the show, I told him the truth. "I didn't request you. I liked Minsky. I frankly don't know why you're here." Sometimes telling the truth doesn't resonate in the moment. Byrne was stunned. He'd been led to believe I wanted to make a change, and I'm not sure being frank was politically smart. But there it was, out on the table. I then acknowledged that we had to figure out how to move forward quickly and together, regardless of how we got here.

He wanted to know about the look of the film we were developing, and he walked through some of his own credits to see if something resonated. One of the films he mentioned was *Sixteen Candles*. Starring Anthony Michael Hall, I might add. It was going to be a tough trip. I asked Bobby to review everything we shot and, to his credit, he thought it was very good and he said he called Minsky to tell him so.

Geoff Sanford couldn't do anything about the train wreck, but his presence was calming and welcome. Leonard reported that he and Geoff hit it off and ended up in a deep conversation comparing Joseph Conrad's *Nostromo* to *Heart of Darkness*. Sanford much preferred the former because "it gives a fuller, more rounded view of human nature, including the good as well as the dark," according to Leonard. This wasn't normal conversation between a director's agent and his assistant, but it was probably more constructive than adding to the anxiety on the set.

The second weekend, in the middle of all the chaos, my older daughter (who was in college) visited the set with Leonard's daughter (they were friends). This provided a brief respite and some family nourishment and I tried to pretend that everything was going smoothly. I suspect my performance was unconvincing. When they returned to the West Coast, it was back unto the breach.

Another day amid the chaos, we were shooting a baseball scene and one of the players we'd hired was a former University of North Carolina star player, Paul Devlin, who was still taking classes. In the movie, he hits a home run, but between setups, he got into a conversation with Leonard and shared that he was having trouble with a paper he was writing on Restoration comedy for a drama course. Leonard gave him some ideas, reviewed his first draft of the paper, and got him on the right track. I don't know what Leonard told him, but the possibility that while I was raging around the set, he was elucidating William Wycherley's R-rated seventeenth-century comedies was satisfying.

Leonard was my dinner companion most nights. We had a long history—it was twenty-three years earlier that he had exposed me to eighteenth-century English lit, the poetry textbook of John Ciardi, and New Wave cinema, among other things. I exposed him to sports, but they didn't take. I tried contemporary painting and sculpture— David Smith to Hans Hofmann—and they did. We shared movies and didn't always agree, but always talked about them. Many nights we'd retreat to dinner at the Magnolia Grill (there weren't many choices in Durham at that time and it had a hard bar) to review the day's work and the next day's schedule. He said he didn't feel that he had much to offer me, but his presence was critical to me. Plus, he often was in the office during the day and might be aware of little fires starting. But once Minsky was gone, I felt more embattled and dug in even further. On almost anything.

• • •

We'd lost half a day along the way in the middle of the daily shitstorm, and dropping behind schedule guarantees that a general panic will break out in the land. Coming up on the schedule was a split day (half in daylight, half at night) at the ballpark; the evening's sequence would be the players meeting at the mound while Nuke was pitching. To regain the half-day we'd lost, the producers suggested we cut the scene and not shoot it. I fought back hard and said this scene was the reason I wrote the script, a hyperbolic rant, perhaps, but not without truth. The scene captures the part of the game I love and, if it worked, would deromanticize or demythologize some of the tropes that sports movies were built around. I won the argument— maybe somewhere someone was feeling bad about the sacrifice of Minsky (probably wishful thinking on my part) or maybe we were too far into production for anyone to seriously consider replacing Robbins anymore, but it was another fall-on-the-sword moment for me.

There were a couple of hundred extras in the stands—extras were a big expense for us—and the weather was now so cold that, between takes, everyone in the scene or in the bleachers quickly bundled in heavy winter gear.

The scene was simple, and I had one note for the actors: this is about a bunch of men in the workplace and they all have problems to share in front of the elder statesman, Crash Davis, who will help them sort it all out. My only other directive was to play it real—don't reach for laughs.

The last line of the scene was left for Robert Wuhl as Larry, the pitching coach. Robert, as recounted in his audition scene, tends to be very big in his readings, so I always saved his close-ups for the end of the day, when his energy level might be dropping to a level closer to that of the rest of us. His scripted line was simple: "Okay, let's get two!" But between camera setups he asked if he could have a second take and try a new line. I agreed, and throughout the night he ran various lines past me, most of which I approved, while he waited for his close-up, the last shot of the night.

We shot the scripted line and I said, "Okay, Robert, one for you," which followed Crash's summary of what is going on out there.

                    CRASH
Nuke's scared 'cause his eyelids are
jammed and his old man's here. . . . We
need a live rooster to take the curse off
José's glove, and nobody seems to know
what to get Millie or Jimmy for their
wedding present. . . . We're dealing with
a lotta shit.

                    LARRY
Candlesticks always make a nice gift or
you can find out where she's registered and
perhaps a place setting or a silverware
pattern might be nice.
      (beat)
Okay. Let's get two.

I knew it would be in the movie as soon as he delivered it, all with great earnestness. What I didn't know was that I'd have to continue to fight for the scene.

• • •

The studio battles continued, though in slightly diminished form, and the production stayed comfortably under the radar. The press never came to write stories (except a stringer for the *L.A. Times* who came uninvited and trashed us because nobody would speak with him). Durham was inconvenient enough to get to that the studio heads didn't bother to make the usual courtesy visit, and the physical production representative stopped giving us grief because he had already scored his pound of flesh that had begun with the hat on the bus.

We had some typical though avoidable crises in our three days at Mitch's Tavern in Raleigh, the location for all the bar scenes. The first night's scene, in which Crash meets Annie through Max Patkin while Nuke dances up a storm in the background, went smoothly enough until, as the scene was about to wrap up, I was approached by the choreographer who had helped Tim and the others work out their moves. She said that she'd been promised a speaking role in exchange for doing the choreography. She was Paula Abdul, whom, in my naïveté, I was unfamiliar with. A producer, she said, had made the promise. I looked around for Burg, who had wisely slipped outside, where it was snowing, and apologized that I was unaware of the arrangement, but I could probably give her a line as the cocktail waitress, if that would suffice. It wouldn't. She stormed out.

The next night was scheduled for Annie's big three-page monologue, the most important scene in the story for Annie (and Susan). I was angry because the camera department only brought "short-end loads," film magazines with less than the full amount of film they could hold. It seemed they hadn't bothered to read the script and understand that a single take of Annie's monologue would run longer than a four-hundred-foot magazine of film could accommodate. They blamed production for not ordering the film they needed. I didn't care—I just wanted the crisis to stay out of earshot of Susan and Kevin because it was a delicate scene to pull off and I didn't want to take energy away from their work. All night we had to shoot the monologue in two halves—and all night I lied to Susan about the reason. I told her there was a camera malfunction we couldn't fix, not that nobody had brought enough film.

Tension between me and the camera department would continue to the very last shot of the movie.

In the middle of the chaos, on the set at night, I was told that Mike Medavoy was on the phone. Directors don't get nighttime calls on the set from heads of production with good news. I took the call:

VOICE ON PHONE: We don't like Costner at all. He's hurting the picture.

SHELTON: You gotta be kidding.

VOICE ON PHONE: We gotta make a change.

SHELTON: We're half done!

VOICE ON PHONE: We're pulling the plug on Kevin and send-
    ing Kurt Russell down to reshoot everything and start all
    over.

Long pause.

SHELTON: Kurt?

Kurt Russell roared.

The cast and crew loosened up as most of the tension moved from
on the set to behind the scenes. One of our actors, Tom Silardi (the
second baseman), had been bragging about a local high school girl
he was dating. Someone—one rumor said it was Costner, another
said it was Trey Wilson—wanted to shut him up and arranged for
two Durham detectives to pick him up during a night shoot in the
ballpark to "haul him in for questioning because the girl was under-
age." Tom was put in the detective's car screaming his innocence and
I rolled the cameras throughout. When the detectives brought him
back to the set later that night, he was properly chastised and he
didn't go near the high school again—or at least didn't talk about it.
It was the sort of stunt that a minor league baseball team might have
pulled on a player, and I felt the cast and crew were becoming that
kind of team. Two nights later his "arrest" was screened in dailies on
full thirty-five-millimeter film.

• • •

Another colleague from the Bay Area, Robert Hillman, was brought
down to shoot the second unit that Gene Corr was going to direct. A
second unit is comprised of a director and an additional cameraman,
who comes with an assistant, and is given support with production
assistants and whoever can be stolen from the first unit. Because it's
a small, guerrilla unit, it can move quickly to pick up shots that are
tedious and time-consuming for the bigger unit to get. As an alum-
nus of second units, I'm comfortable handing important work to

that tiny department. I sent them to Rocky Mount, North Carolina, where there was an old minor league park, long out of use, to stage a July 4 pregame ceremony and some action. Notable in the action was a double play I wanted turned correctly, and I trusted Gene (a ballplayer-turned-filmmaker) to get it right. When Lester asked why we had to send a unit all the way to Rocky Mount to film a relatively few things, I responded that it was where Thelonious Monk was born. He agreed that was a good reason.

The second unit also filmed Garland Bunting in the booth doing a "live broadcast" as well as recording an away game with homemade sound effects, an homage to early radio broadcasts of baseball games. Second units aren't supposed to be able to record sound, but by this time we were stretching the rules to finish on schedule. Hillman had worked with major cinematographers and had a great sense of lighting, and Gene was an experienced director who had made the feature *Desert Bloom,* with Jon Voight. A second unit, traveling light, has time to search out the perfect location for car drive-bys and to find images that serve the bigger film. Our second unit worked only a couple of weeks but made an enormous contribution. (Years later, Gene and Robert made an Oscar-nominated documentary about screenwriter Waldo Salt.)

We had a nervous day on a sequence that shouldn't have been difficult but none of us had thought about much: the "cash-drop" scene, which now featured a helicopter (not a hot-air balloon) dropping thousands of (fake) dollar bills onto the outfield grass while two hundred Little Leaguers in uniform wait behind a ribbon to race on the field and grab the money. As soon as the chopper was hovering and the kids were lined up, everyone on the crew (from L.A., at least) looked around in horror. The tragic accident on the set of the *Twilight Zone* movie, in which a helicopter crashed on the set, killing star Vic Morrow and two child actors, was only five years in the past and had reverberated deeply in the movie business. What figured to be an enjoyable scene to shoot was anything but. When the chopper flew away, there was an enormous collective sigh of relief.

• • •

The locker room set was built in an abandoned tobacco warehouse across the street from the ballpark and was designed so that each of the four points of the compass revealed a completely different look. We had a large page count to film in the space and it was critical to Armin Ganz and me that each scene we shot there have a different feel, though still be connected to the larger space.

The first scene we shot in the locker room was Ebby Calvin's in-flagrante entrance with Millie. Before anyone shooting a nude scene signed a contract, I walked them through what we were going to do; they had to be comfortable with it before signing on. Nobody had a problem, trust was built from the outset, and I always said that if something became uncomfortable, just speak up and we'd figure out how to solve the issue. I never had a problem working with actors this way, though things have changed greatly in the past decade with the introduction of "sex-scene coaches." The locker room was an effective set except for the day our lights heated up too high and activated the sprinkler system in the middle of a scene. We lost a couple of hours but we made the day.

•   •   •

We drove an hour each way to an old minor league ballpark in Wilson, North Carolina, to shoot the scene in which Crash shows the players how to stage a rainout. The only reason I chose Wilson was that it was the home of the legend about Steve Dalkowski once throwing a fastball through the metal fencing of the backstop screen. When the crew was unloading gear and setting up the Rain Bird sprinklers, I climbed twenty feet up the fence behind home plate and found the spot where Dalko had long ago separated a two-by-four-inch section of wired steel with some ungodly, out-of-control heat. Nobody had bothered fixing it because it could never happen again. The night shoot was blessed by the discovery that the legend seemed to actually be true.

•   •   •

Annie's house was our centrally located "cover set," a term for an interior location that the production can control in case the weather gets bad and the schedule has to be quickly rearranged to move inside. Scheduling always places the various cover sets at the back end of the shoot as a kind of insurance to guarantee we make the day.

The first scene we shot in the house was sequentially in narrative order—Annie brings Crash and Nuke to her house on the first night. We ran through the scene quickly, and just before we started shooting, someone from production showed up with a letter from Thomas Pynchon's attorney asking (threatening?) us to not use his name in a derogatory way. This was bizarre for a number of reasons, not the least of which was how the hell they had gotten a copy of the script. Also, we weren't using his name in a derogatory way at all—it was merely two characters arguing about him and taking different sides. Conceptually, they would each eventually switch their position, swayed by the other, or rather swayed by their growing passion for the other. I thought Pynchon, a man who sent Professor Irwin Corey, the fabulously ridiculous nonsense comic, to accept his National Book Award for him, would enjoy the joke.

Nonetheless, it was decided on the spot to drop the Pynchon reference, and everyone gathered to toss out names of writers that Crash and Annie could argue over. Susan Sontag's name came up, not as the provocative and brilliant essayist she was, but for a novel she'd written, and she became the last-second stand-in for Pynchon. It never felt quite right, but there it was. I dropped the idea that Crash and Annie would discuss Pynchon or Sontag or anyone any further. It was too much bother. This interruption caused us some delay and got us behind schedule for the day.

Susan then had the notion that her speech should contain something about pheromones, so I stopped for a bit longer and she and I figured out a line that would work. We added:

```
                    ANNIE
     It's like pheromones—you get three ants
     together they can't do dick—you get three
```

```
hundred million of 'em, they can build a
cathedral. . . .
```

I'm still not sure exactly what it means but it didn't matter, and it
better set up Ebby Calvin's impatient response:

```
        EBBY CALVIN
So is somebody gonna go to bed with
somebody or what?
```

All of which set up Crash's "what I believe in" speech. As I've said,
the speech always felt a bit self-conscious, a little too much calling
attention to itself. If it works it's because Crash is doing just that—
calling attention to himself after a scene that Annie dominates—but
he's doing it by throwing away the whole speech. At least that's the
intention.

```
        CRASH
I believe in the soul, the cock, the
pussy, the small of a woman's back, the
hanging curveball, high fiber, good Scotch,
that the novels of Susan Sontag are self-
indulgent, overrated crap. . . . I believe
that Lee Harvey Oswald acted alone, I
believe there oughta be a constitutional
amendment outlawing Astroturf and the
designated hitter. I believe in the "sweet
spot," voting every election, soft-core
pornography, chocolate chip cookies,
opening your presents Christmas morning
rather than Christmas Eve, and I believe
in long, slow, deep, soft, wet kisses that
last for three days. . . . G'night.
```

We did two takes, both in a loose shot over Susan's shoulder in
which Kevin walked up into a medium shot. There was no close-up.

I said we were done and moving on. Kevin wanted more. I said there was no time, which there wasn't, but the bigger reason was I thought he'd nailed it with his casual, offhanded delivery. His hands were in his pockets, he didn't wait for her response, he just tossed it out there. This confirmed my earlier preference for first or second takes, before an actor starts analyzing and thinking about what he's doing. This is where practice pays off. The paradigm is also athletic—there's no coaching when the game starts. It's too late for that. I'm often reminded that the great basketball coach John Wooden never got off his chair during a game, never even called a time-out unless persuaded by his assistant coaches. He said his job was done when the whistle blew. That comparison is limited but full of good counsel. Kevin's first take is in the movie.

• • •

The crew, led by Kirk Francis, rebelled against the overtime I was shooting, which violated their flat-rate twelve-hour agreement. Filming stopped for an hour while Lester met with the crew down the right-field line as I was staring at my watch on the infield, waiting and hoping to shoot. Lester restructured the crew deals on the spot. Then the ballplayers threatened to quit because they'd been told they couldn't eat at the catering truck but had to eat whatever hot dogs were left over from the prop cart at the end of the day. Lester got them back on the catering truck.

Throughout, I kept hearing that the production designer was complaining about the costume designer and vice versa, but I had enough set experience to know that this always happens. The art department wants to control everything visual, and the wardrobe department thinks the art department doesn't understand them. I took Armin Ganz and Louise Frogley aside and said, in essence, "I don't want to hear anything more about how much you don't like each other. I like you both. I love the work you're doing. Figure out how to get along." There were more words to it than that, but left unsaid in the air was "Or I'll replace both of you." I thought each of their work was first-rate and I didn't want to lose either of them.

What I learned was a crisis-management strategy that I've used ever since. In shorthand, the approach is athletic. If a baseball manager has a shortstop and second baseman who don't get along, his speech to them is simple: "I don't care if you guys can't stand each other—I only care that you can turn the double play. So start turning the double play or one of you will be gone." Armin and Louise had dinner that night and the problem was solved. In retrospect, Armin could be difficult and I didn't have the time to review every question with Louise, who had great instincts but was on an American film (much less a baseball field) for the first time. Things were freewheeling, to put it mildly, but adjustments were being made daily, as they are on any movie.

One scene didn't work in the first draft and never got better in rehearsals. It's immediately after Annie unsuccessfully tries to seduce Nuke when he comes home from the road trip and is now committed to celibacy as long as he keeps winning. It is, in fact, Annie's idea that he is now fully committed to, with Crash's not-so-subtle support. When Nuke leaves the site of her failed seduction—her kitchen—Annie flips and goes looking for Crash.

She storms into his boardinghouse room, where he's ironing a shirt wearing only his underwear and a T-shirt. It's the only scene I continued to rewrite throughout the shoot, and we kept pushing it to the end of the schedule in the hopes that the muse would descend. The muse didn't, but a late revision the night before we shot seemed a bit closer to what we wanted. Earlier versions had made her too desperate, which she wasn't, and made him too callous, which he wasn't.

Two other things had been bothering me. First, the script never identified what Annie's job was, and surely, she had one. I decided to give her a job that I had when I finished graduate school at the University of Arizona—I taught part-time at Pima Community College outside Tucson, so I gave her the same job at Alamance Community College, just outside Durham. I shared my other concern with Leonard over dinner. Now that we'd already shot the failed seduction scene, we know that Annie is in a seductive short skirt with high heels, the whole presentation. For all her eccentricities, she might look foolish charging up a sidewalk in that outfit, and I wanted Crash to challenge how she was dressed. More important, I wanted to hear what she said.

I asked Leonard if he knew any great quotes from English literature that might be both Annie-esque and appropriate as an answer to Crash's challenge: "Who dresses you? I mean, isn't this a little excessive for the Carolina League?" He quickly came up with a line that immediately went into the rewrite and into the scene:

                    ANNIE
        "The road of excess leads to the palace of
        wisdom"—William Blake.

I added:

                    CRASH
        William Blake?

                    ANNIE
        William Blake!

Leonard went back to the office to type it up and have it formally passed out in salmon or buff or goldenrod or whatever the hell color was now appropriate. The line brought needed levity to the moment without being a laugh, and the next morning on the set Kevin and Susan and I worked our way through the revisions until the scene started working. At the end of a take, Susan unexpectedly shoved the ironing board to the ground, which gave the scene a button and launched us into the critical scene that followed. The next scene, now beautifully set up, was so important and crucial to the movie that we later cut it out in the editing room.

Late in the schedule, my battles lessened, though, according to Leonard's notes, I was angry and still fighting somebody or something all the time. Mount and Lester had the usual push/pull disputes because we were burning through the contingency money and it was clear that there would be nothing left if we went over budget in postproduction. The contingency was about half a million dollars, and the general philosophy is to save some for the editing room if you wind up needing to create a bigger score than planned or, more typically, to buy some expensive iconic songs that aren't budgeted. Mount was doing his job—trying to make sure we didn't run out of money. Lester was doing his job—trying to put every penny onscreen without spending one penny we didn't have.

Ric Kidney, our first assistant director, whose calm demeanor and great experience were a godsend throughout production, was projecting that we would go six to seven days over schedule, and this remained, understandably, a deep concern to Mount. I agreed to cut and tighten a few things and volunteered to pay to bring the second unit back to pick up some shots previously scheduled for the first unit. Usually when a director makes such a gallant play to show his passion, the producer says, "I appreciate your generosity but it won't come out of your pocket." Mount just said, "I appreciate your generosity." It came out of my pocket.

This is a battleground familiar to most moviemakers, but we were acting in the dark because nobody from the studio had ever communicated anything positive about the dailies. The cast and crew liked what we were doing and the nightly gatherings to watch dailies over beer were a rewarding ritual everyone looked forward to. Since I stopped taking swings at producers, these sessions were less dangerous as well as less dramatic.

We were finished shooting the baseball scenes but I'd missed some shots that Kevin and I sorely wanted. Because we'd lost the light, I was also missing a close-up of Annie in the batting-cage scene. Kevin and I called Bill Bernstein in his New York office and begged for one additional shooting day at the end of scheduled production. We could do the extra day in Burlington, North Carolina, which had a minor league ballpark. After some arm-twisting, Bernstein added a day to the schedule.

• • •

The wedding of Jimmy and Millie was a scheduled night scene that required a full stadium, and our meager budget for extras had long since been depleted. Burg recalls that I saw the empty stands and said, "I'll fucking kill you. Where are my extras!" My recollection is that I wouldn't have threatened to kill him, having dodged that bullet earlier, but my anger would have been real. A ballpark wedding in front of empty grandstands would look ridiculous. What it would really look like is that we ran out of money.

Burg promised that if I shot the scene facing the outfield for three to four hours—there were no bleachers out there, thus no need for extras—it would give him time to fill the ballpark. When I turned the cameras around to shoot the reverse angles, the stands would magically be filled, he said. There was not a lot of conviction in his voice.

I began shooting the wedding facing away from the stands toward the outfield fence. It went slowly, as night exteriors often do, and I kept glancing over my shoulder—the stands remained empty. What I didn't know was that Burg shared an apartment in L.A. with a man who was the sound engineer for Pink Floyd, and the group happened to be performing at the University of North Carolina at Chapel Hill that night. At intermission, Burg's friend, James Geddes, went backstage to see David Gilmour, lead guitarist for the band, and made a request. Gilmour got somebody to make an announcement to the crowd along the lines of: "Everyone enjoying the show? Who wants to be part of the *after show*?" Big cheer. "We'll be partying at Durham Athletic Park when the concert's over and there'll be free beer and T-shirts and the band will show up!"

At eleven o'clock that night, when I turned the cameras around, the stands were full and kegs of beer were everywhere. A close-up of the crowd reveals a sea of Pink Floyd T-shirts. It was a brilliant if long-shot piece of producing, and it mattered not—at least for the film—that the band never showed up.

14

Sixty-Minute Man

Production was about finished. Only the sex scene remained. Lovemaking scenes in movies continue to evolve according to the standards of the time, from even prior to the Hays Code in 1934 to today's era of intimacy coordinators, whose job is to protect actors and actresses from uncomfortable situations. The biggest influence on such scenes in the last two decades hasn't been mandated corporate policy but the existence of readily available pornography on everyone's home screens. In some way, it's freed up more creative thinking about how sex is portrayed in movies because there's no added dramatic shock value to seeing nude stars and fake orgasms. Some nudity was fine for our film but a lantern didn't need to be hung on it. My solution was to ensure onscreen sex was fun or funny, as an antidote to the new age of sexual paranoia that was beginning at the end of the 1980s—a new thing called AIDS was starting to be written about, and there was a concomitant re-emergence of STD awareness.

It seemed like nobody was having fun in bed anymore. Adding to that, the sweaty-wrinkled-brow school of onscreen fake sex (even in first-rate movies) always was embarrassing to me. I felt bad for the actors and actresses grimly going through the task of pretending to be in blissful sexual nirvana. I knew that they were surrounded by lights and rigging and a crew and a body makeup team ready to dart in when the lights started melting the body makeup to reveal Grateful Dead or Celtic love knot tattoos where they shouldn't be.

The big lovemaking scene between Kevin and Susan was scheduled for the last two days of production because Annie's house was the perfect default cover set, and because I wanted it to be at the end so that Kevin and Susan would feel comfortable doing lovemaking scenes together, and comfortable with me. There are few things less sexy than shooting a sexy lovemaking scene.

I was also on edge because Mount informed me, hours before we were to begin shooting, that we were out of money and the lovemaking scenes had to be cut. I said we'd spent an hour and a half leading up to these people getting together and it would kill the movie if they didn't. If we ever made it into theaters, the audience would walk out. I insisted we had enough money to finish the last two days, and he and I got into a heated argument about it. The only leverage I had was that Kevin and Susan would object if it were cut. Normally, in such a situation, the director could call the studio and ask them to back him and any cost overages that might be accrued. The risk is that the studio might back the producer and cut the scenes entirely. Given my tenuous relations with Orion, and the fact that I'd already gotten one extra day's shoot, I chose not to call.

The entire sequence was shot as I waited for the plug to be pulled. Thankfully, it never was. Kevin and Susan are generous actors, empathetic to the other player in the scene. Costner hangs around late at night to be the off-screen presence for another actor's scene. Many stars don't; they have their stand-ins do it. Susan is equally sensitive to the other actors, and in such a sustained sequence of sex and thrashing around and nudity, trust is needed by the bathtubful.

There's a story that may be apocryphal but was told to me by a Peckinpah crew member on *Bring Me the Head of Alfredo Garcia*. It's one of those *better than true* stories that illustrate the point and the kind of atmosphere I was trying to avoid. Isela Vega, the beautiful Mexican star, was the leading lady opposite Warren Oates and was scheduled to do a nude scene several days into shooting. Sam chided and teased her as the day approached, warning her that she would have to be totally nude. On the day, Vega walked stark naked to the center of the set first thing in the morning, sat in her chair with a cup of coffee, and waited until they got to her shot. She owned the set. Sam and the other men were embarrassed, and the great Peckinpah directed the sequence respectfully. Or so the story goes.

The camera department and I were still straining to get along. I asked for a tracking shot in low light with a longish lens to start the scene. They weren't sure they could pull it off but they did. We doggedly began, and things improved between us. Maybe we were out of things to fight about but Bobby Byrne and his crew did a beautiful job of the interior lovemaking sequence, which was shot on three floors of the rickety old Victorian house, not an easy place to drag cables and equipment around.

When Crash pulls Annie's dress up, the Jockey brand is highly visible on the waistband of her panties, but we couldn't see it until dailies since we had no video playback. I didn't know Jockey made women's underwear, and I figured we'd have to pay to have the brand name removed because we didn't have a deal with the company. On the other hand, it was a great advertisement and maybe they'd pay us to keep it. It did seem perfect that Annie was wearing the Jockey brand.

The lovemaking was put together, shot by shot, in a workman-like manner, with little camera movement after the opening, save for some small dolly shots. The actors brought life and humor to the party and, though film viewers' memory might suggest otherwise, there's no lingering nudity, only glimpses of flesh here and there in service of the fun Crash and Annie—really Kevin and Susan—are having. The set, as is common practice in shooting such scenes, was "closed" except for critical crew, mostly the camera department. Even so, the process is anything but erotic.

There are only a couple of lines of dialogue in the scene. The first is Annie's "Oh, my" when Crash unsnaps her stocking with one hand, an easy follow-up joke to Nuke's ineptness when she tries to seduce him in the kitchen. The other dialogue occurs when Crash and Annie are taking a sex time-out in the kitchen. Annie's eating a carton of Häagen-Dazs ice cream while Crash downs a bowl of Wheaties. Once again, we had no clearance to use either brand but nobody seemed to care.

```
                    ANNIE
    I think . . . in another lifetime I was
    probably Catherine the Great, or Francis
    of Assisi, I'm not sure which one.


                    CRASH
    How come in former lifetimes, everybody's
    somebody famous. . . . How come nobody
    says they were Joe Schmo?


                    ANNIE
    'Cause it doesn't work like that, you
    fool.
         (stares at him)
    God, you are gorgeous. You wanna dance?
```

They dance a silly, drunken dance—something even I could choreograph—and it pays off the setup in Act One at Mitch's Tavern.

I didn't bother shooting the only other scripted dialogue in the sequence, in which Annie ties Crash to the bedposts and reads Whitman, but Susan, Kevin, and I played around to come up with something that didn't require talking and would keep it light. Out of that rehearsal with the meter running on the day of shooting, what evolved was a slow panning dolly shot across Susan's face and torso until it reveals Crash painting her toenails. Again, it took the curse off taking things too seriously (the toenail painting might have been Kevin's idea). All I knew at the time was that somebody in the prop department had to run out to a drugstore and come back with some nail polish. After one take, it was obvious that the scene worked.

The final shot of scheduled production had Crash and Annie in the bathtub. The only clue to the action in the scripted stage directions was that "two bodies slosh wildly in the dim glow. Water splashes, dowses some candles." Kevin and Susan followed the script while the camera was twenty feet away in another room, shooting through a doorway. Keeping the lens at a distance seemed to avoid violating their privacy, both Crash and Annie's and Kevin and Susan's. When the candles were dowsed, we were done.

If there was a wrap party, I don't remember anything about it, but I do know there was one problem we were stuck with. Miles Wolff, owner of the Bulls, had not fallen in love with the green color we had painted the ballpark and he asked us to repaint it to the blue we had inherited. We didn't have a dime left in the budget to repaint it because Lester had spent everything in the contingency fund to finish production.

We got lucky when some vandals broke into the ballpark, drove two or three vehicles in, and did wheelies all over the wet outfield grass, turning up big circular chunks of sod, rendering the outfield unplayable. As the ballpark was still being rented by the production, it was our responsibility. A claim was quickly filed and honored by the insurance company. As it turned out, there was just enough money in the claim to not only re-sod the outfield but to paint the ballpark blue again.

As it also turned out, I later learned, someone in the production office (not David Lester, probably Mark Burg) had organized the ballpark break-in and destruction of the outfield grass, all with an eye toward filing an insurance claim. That, of course, is a crime. It's also great producing.

We snuck out of town under cover of darkness, triumphant.

Part Four

Postproduction

15

The Third Time You
Make the Movie

It's accepted wisdom that you make a movie three different times. The first movie is in the filmmaker's head and exists as the script unfolds on the page. The second movie happens when production is under way: actors are becoming characters and dramatic action is being exposed to film and the director is dealing with such things as the cinematographer being fired in the middle of a scene. The movie you shoot begins to take on a different life and becomes something other than what was on the page. The third and final movie is created in the editing room.

In *Day for Night,* François Truffaut's wonderful film about moviemaking, the film director says, "Shooting a film is like a stagecoach ride in the Old West. When you start, you are hoping for a pleasant trip, but pretty soon you just hope you'll reach your destination."

The cutting room was on a side street in Hollywood in an old California bungalow owned by Carol Littleton (a world-class editor whose credits include *E.T.* and *The Big Chill,* from which Costner had been famously removed). Movies were being cut on both floors of the old house—it was a way for the director and editors to stay away from the studio.

Ten weeks after the last day of shooting, the "director's cut" must, by contractual obligation, be screened for the studio. This cut is a still-unfinished version of the movie that has temporary music and almost no sound effects and is visually uneven at best—the print from the negative is still just the overnight dailies that the lab processed in a hurry. In the director's cut there will be scenes still being smoothed out, and ones that simply don't work, performances that need fine-tuning, and dialogue that can't be deciphered because planes are flying overhead or rain towers are dumping truckloads of water near the microphones.

The ten weeks never seems enough time to make a movie out of all the footage, and the first step toward the director's cut is called an "assemblage," which is nothing more than having the editor string all the scenes together in order. Because Bob Leighton had been on the set, I was able to view the unfolding assemblage and make early decisions as to what worked and what didn't. That's the first goal in cutting a movie—get rid of everything that doesn't work. Many directors want to see an assemblage that includes everything that was shot. I don't. If it doesn't work, I don't want to be reminded. There will inevitably be a scene that is awkward but contains information critical to the story. Those types of scenes stay in the cut as long as they have to, but the editor and director are always trying to shorten or eliminate them. Immediately, we had a whorehouse problem.

In the script, Crash goes to a local brothel run by a former minor league player who had "put up big numbers" in the minors and never got "a cup of coffee in the Show," the majors. We see Crash playing a little piano and having a drink with his old ballplayer friend. Nuke shows up, announces he's being promoted to the Show, and we see Crash half-drunkenly howl at the moon and finally become so irritating to Nuke that Nuke decks him. The scene is full of things that matter to the story and the character development and the resolution of the Crash-Nuke relationship. But the whorehouse was a terrible idea and I'd known that from the moment we shot it. Leighton and I couldn't get rid of the scene, but it was hurtful to the movie. Rather than try to tighten the scene in order to minimize its overall damage to the movie, we just left it long and awkward and clunky. It was a strategic move that would either pay off down the road or not. The goal was to reshoot the scene in a different location, but the last thing the studio wanted to hear at this point was that I was hunkered down in the editing room planning to spend more of their money.

The other obvious clunk was the death of Max Patkin. The off-camera reveal of a fatal traffic accident didn't resonate at all—we didn't need to screen it with an audience to know that. The local gospel singer had done a gorgeous job with "In the Garden," but the payoff wasn't worth the setup and the setup was weak to begin with. Plus, the real Max Patkin was still alive. (When I wrote the script for a film about Jerry Lee Lewis, I framed it with the conceit that he was dead and playing piano in hell—Lewis didn't like that, either.) Max's funeral hit the cutting-room floor.

While the assemblage was happening, I looked for a composer and Burg looked for a record deal that could provide "source" music, sometimes called "needle drops," which is just a term for dropping in already-recorded popular or familiar music. I had a strong sense of what the source music could be—there were music references throughout the script—but no feeling for what a score would sound like.

My first idea was to get John Fogerty to write the score. His song "Centerfield" had come out a couple of years earlier, but it wasn't the baseball specifics of that as much as the tone and spirit of his overall work that appealed to me. He declined on the basis, I was told, that it was too much work to get done in such a short time. We found a classically trained young composer, Michael Convertino, who'd written some lyrical scores that I felt might support the emotional journey while the roadhouse jukebox source music drove the surface. He began work but his score wouldn't be ready until after the director's cut, which is normal.

The first screenings of an early rough cut of a movie are always in small theaters for friends, usually in the movie business, who are familiar with seeing unfinished work. These are hard screenings to judge because it's a friendly crowd and everyone is on your side—unlike what's lurking a few weeks away. It was easier to hold tightly controlled screenings then than now; in those days there was no chance someone would post a private review on social media or record the movie on a phone.

Comedy is unforgiving but, if you're the filmmaker, at least you know where you stand. People laugh, or they don't. If they don't, is it fixable? Or are you dead even before arrival? Only horror movies share a similarly unforgiving and immediate judgment by the audience. We screened a somewhat-too-long version of the movie for a hundred people and they laughed. This was the first positive reinforcement we'd received since the start of production. One man laughed so loud at everything that I invited him to all subsequent screenings, which he attended. The man turned out to be Tony Seiniger, who ran the company that would be creating the movie's one-sheets (posters) and trailers, and now that he'd seen and liked the movie, he set a meeting to discuss the visuals for the ad campaign.

The next day at Tony's office with Mount, he asked if I had any ideas, and I shared with him that I thought of this as a Western, and Crash was the hired gun—something I'd never mentioned before. I pointed out that it wasn't an accident that he drove a Mustang, and I thought of the rickety old ballparks as corrals in the background. Tony came up with a poster design that everyone liked immediately, with Crash leaning on his bat (almost a rifle), standing in front of the car, with Annie just-provocatively-enough at his side, the ballpark in the background against a sunset. Crash even has a beer in his hand, which provides the right amount of cowboy swagger.

But every screening lays bare problems that need addressing. Even if people are having a good time, the director and editor aren't laughing. They're taking notes and figuring out how to tighten everything.

The process leads too quickly to the delivery date of the director's cut, the first of a series of cold-blooded torture-chamber trials called "test screenings" that determine the fate of your movie and your career. We were still troubled by the scene in the whorehouse, and though Leighton was convinced he could lessen the damage by some ruthless cutting, it still made no sense to me that Crash Davis was hanging out in a brothel. I wanted to reshoot the entire scene in a reimagined location. This would require that the studio not only like the movie but want to spend more money fixing it. This also explains why we'd taken the calculated risk of leaving a long, clumsy version of the whorehouse scene in the assemblage far too long. We gambled that the studio would like the movie, but not the whorehouse.

I screened the movie for Mount, who was very supportive. He said, "Keep doing what you're doing." We'd fought about the budget, the schedule, the firing of the DP, the attempt to eliminate the sex scene (and endless other issues), but by some miracle we'd finished on budget and were staying on it during postproduction. There's no time to rehash old grievances on a movie. More important, Thom's response to both the script and the first cut of the movie couldn't have been better. The next battle lay ahead. As Annie says, "It's wondrous how men get over things." And given the battles with Orion, we still weren't sure what their reaction would be.

The director's cut presentation to the studio was in the empty Orion theater for the head of production, Mike Medavoy. Filmmakers always prefer a full house and a real audience, but every studio is different. Mike wanted to screen it at 10 a.m. for just him and his assistant. Bob Leighton and I attended, and Adam Weiss (whom Bob had brought in as second editor) stayed in the projection booth to make sure the reels were put up in the right order. Yes, it happens.

In defense of Mike, he was born in China and grew up in Chile, before becoming a superagent and then a Hollywood studio head. Baseball and small-town America are not in his DNA. Nonetheless, he had backed scores (now hundreds) of memorable movies. I would not have chosen to present any movie to anyone at 10 a.m. in an empty theater, when, among other things, it's too early to drink. It is, however, better than an afternoon screening where everyone might fall asleep.

The movie played without a laugh or snicker. The room was a morgue. It could have been a Bergman film. Leighton and I kept sneaking a peek at Mike to make sure he was awake. The movie was still long, about two hours and ten minutes, but it felt like a five-hour cut. Afterward, Mike just said, "I'll tell you at three o'clock what I think. Leave a number where I can reach you." When we went to retrieve the film, the projectionist said that Mike wanted to screen it again at 1 p.m. for the whole company, so we asked Adam to stay behind in the projection room. We got the phone number there so we could stay in touch with him.

Leighton and I went to the Formosa Café on Santa Monica Boulevard and started drinking. I was convinced we were dead. Bob, a first-rate editor who'd been through this more than I had, was measured but not falsely optimistic. He told stories about the slow evolution of *This Is Spinal Tap* in the editing process, but it was not cheering. We called Adam from a pay phone next to the bathrooms at the Formosa Café and gave him the phone number for Medavoy to reach us. Sometime midafternoon, the pay phone rang, I answered, and Mike said, "I like it. Come to my office in the morning." I was stunned. It was the first positive thing I'd heard from the studio since we started production.

I respected Mike for withholding his opinion until three hundred people had seen it. Comedy is infectious, and one person laughing triggers another. So does a yawn. But apparently the movie played well for everyone working in the Century City Orion offices. Still, there was the whorehouse.

The next morning Mike asked what I would do to make it better, and I said: "Replace the whorehouse scene with a scene that's almost identical but isn't in a brothel." I'd already rewritten the script and handed it to him—the same scene, with hardly a line of dialogue changed. The new scene was set in a pool hall and Crash was playing pool, not piano. It was approved and quickly scheduled.

I needed to recast the part of Sandy Grimes, the African American ex–minor league star player who now runs a pool hall rather than a brothel, and for whom Crash has the greatest respect. The original actor was a local hire out of North Carolina, and it made no sense to bring him to L.A. for a reshoot. The casting pool was deep in L.A. and I was sure we could upgrade with a new actor. Driving to the editing room, I saw Henry Sanders crossing a street—a fine actor I recognized from Charles Burnett's *Killer of Sheep*. I called his agent and hired him. Henry later asked where I'd seen him and I said, "In the crosswalk at Franklin and La Brea."

The pool hall was in a basement of an old building in a desperate section of downtown L.A., and required no set dressing. It could have been Durham. David Bridges, a British cinematographer, shot the scene beautifully—it felt rich and natural and unlit, kind of like Minsky's footage. The scene easily cut into the flow of the movie, and I got to keep the speech I felt was critical to Crash's reckoning.

As Nuke heads off to the Show, Crash wrestles with his existential question: Was I unlucky? Or not good enough? And does the differ-ence between being good enough and not good enough reduce to such a paper-thin statistic as a single hit per week over a season? It is Crash-like to have figured out such an absurdly reductive stat—it also separates him from everyone around him. There's drunken gal-lows humor in his wisdom.

                              CRASH
        D'you know what the difference between
        hitting .250 and .300 is? It's twenty-five
        hits. Twenty-five hits in five hundred at-
        bats is fifty points, okay? There's six
        months in a season—that's about twenty-
        five weeks. That means if you get just one
        extra flare a week, just one, a gork . . .
        you get a ground ball with eyes, you get
        a dying quail . . . just one more dying
        quail a week . . . and you're in Yankee
        Stadium.

It matters not that anyone other than a baseball player or fan knows exactly what a "flare," "gork," or "ground ball with eyes" actu-ally means (it means a cheap hit, and in my favorite new addition in today's parlance, it's called a "duck snort"); what matters is it means something to the men in the pool hall.

The studio liked the reshoot, but there was another scene they thought was hurting the movie—the meeting at the mound. I was equally appalled and shocked. Once again, the Unnamed Executive stood in the way with a bleat:

UNNAMED EXECUTIVE: The meeting at the mound has to go.
SHELTON: Why? It's funny.
UNNAMED EXECUTIVE: It's not funny.
SHELTON: It's funnier than the cocksucker scene, and that's pretty funny.
UNNAMED EXECUTIVE: That's not funny, either.

SHELTON: The meeting at the mound is the reason I wrote the
    movie.
UNNAMED EXECUTIVE: Don't talk like that. Plus it doesn't
    advance the plot.
SHELTON: There is no plot!

The there-is-no-plot defense didn't resonate. Everyone was now
more nervous than they had been, and it was decided that the first
test-screening audience would decide if the meeting at the mound
stayed or was cut.

The goal now was to get the film into the leanest and most pol-
ished state possible before a series of test screenings in front of real
audiences. The first test screening is more nerve-racking than the
director's cut shown to the studio because if a cold recruited audience
likes the movie, the studio likes it. If the audience hates it, the studio
hates it. Usually the audience response is somewhere in the middle,
neither hot nor cold, neither fully engaged nor disengaged, which is
its own kind of maddening. And the whole damn process—which
admittedly can be helpful and enlightening—reduces all your work
to hard statistics that can determine your fate. Like baseball.

The National Research Group is a film-based statistical analytics company that operates the test screenings and calculates numbers that reflect an audience's response to a film based on cards. The
analysis is full of simple questions that they hand out to viewers after
a screening. They ask the audience to judge the movie—"excellent,"
"very good," "good," "fair," "poor"—as well as rate the likability
of the essential characters and performances. The audience is then
asked if they would "recommend" or "definitely recommend" the
movie—there's a chasm of interpretation between the two categories.
If "definitely" is in front of "recommend," it can mean millions of
dollars more in the marketing campaign. Elsewhere on the cards, the
audience is asked to rate their favorite five scenes, top to bottom, as
well as their least favorite five scenes. The problem with the latter
question is that an audience might invariably reveal its loathing for
any scene in which, for example, the beloved dog dies, even though
it might be the scene that brings them to tears and causes hankies to

be pulled out and guarantees the audience will *definitely recommend* the movie and it'll be a big weeper hit. No dogs died in our movie, so I thought we were safe.

There are target numbers that predict success and failure; NRG and the studios hold on to these as Old Testament truths. The problem for the filmmaker is not the research screening process, it's how the data is interpreted. Studios tend to think that the numbers are set in stone from the first screening onward, while filmmakers always believe they can continue to improve the movie and raise the numbers.

One thing is certain at the first test screening: the filmmaker will learn two things completely unanticipated. The first revelation is that something in the movie that you are deeply concerned isn't working is actually working very well and won't be a problem at all. For example, in *Bull Durham*, the inside-baseball shoptalk, the vulgarity, the nudity, the fact that there's not the big game that everyone might expect—there were plenty of things we were worried about. The audience had no problem with any of it.

The second thing the first screening will reveal is that something you think is working brilliantly is actually a big problem.

16

Kill Your Darlings

To everyone involved in making the movie, Annie's midday monologue that explained her background seemed like the most important scene in the script, the one critical character revelation that the movie could not live without. Well, everyone was wrong. Including me. It didn't survive.

Page ninety ends the previous scene where Annie bursts into Crash's boardinghouse room while he's ironing a shirt. He's in his underwear, a glass of Scotch on the ironing board. Annie launches into a tirade without orchestration or self-awareness. She's frustrated, angry, confused, and . . . here's the scene:

                          ANNIE
        This is the damnedest season I've ever
        seen—I mean, the Durham Bulls can't lose
        and I can't get laid!

She slams the ironing board to the ground.

                                          CUT TO:
        INT. MITCH'S TAVERN—DAY
        ANNIE AND CRASH SIT IN THE CORNER of the empty
        bar.

                          CRASH
        Why baseball?

                    ANNIE
I never saw my mother. I was raised in
the Baptist Church—got dipped in the
water when I was five—born again before
kindergarten. By the time I was ten I knew
it was bullshit and at fifteen I ran away
from home . . .

SHE SMILES at the painful memories.

                    ANNIE (cont'd)
. . . got married, he ran away. Married
again, *I* ran away. I crashed and burned a
few times. I tried twenty-five religions in
eight years and all of them worked. The
week I decided to make peace with my papa,
he died.
        (beat)
I bought a car for two hundred dollars and
drove to Florida to bury him.
        (beat)
And after we'd sung some hymns in some
wretched funeral home, I went outside and
something happened. . . .

Her tone becomes wistful, nostalgic.

                    ANNIE (cont'd)
The smell of cut grass overwhelmed me and
I heard a noise—
        (makes the sound)
—tok, tok, tok—and some men shouting . . .
then tok, tok, tok . . .

Crash smiles. He knows.

                    ANNIE (cont'd)
I crossed the street—it was the New York
Yankees' spring-training field—tok, tok,
tok was the sound of a ball hitting a bat—
and I sat in the bleachers to think about
my papa . . .
        (beat)
And I saw him.

                    CRASH
Who?

                    ANNIE
Thurman Munson.
        (beat)
He was covered with dirt and he was fighting
with everybody—it was beautiful.
        (beat)
And he called the ump a cocksucker and got
thrown out of the game even though it was
an exhibition!
        (beat)
So I stayed in the bleachers all spring
and gradually came to understand what's so
great about baseball.

                    CRASH
What's so great about baseball?

                    ANNIE
If you know where home plate is, then you
know where first base is, and second, and
everything else—'cause they're always in
the same place in relation to home.
        (beat)

Don't you see? If you know where home
plate is, you know where everything else
in the universe is!

Silence.

                    CRASH
I don't know if I'd go that far.

                    ANNIE
It's true, it's true!
        (beat)
At least it used to be true. It ain't
possible that baseball's not enough
anymore, is it, Crash?

                    CRASH
It's possible.

                    ANNIE
No.

                    CRASH
Are you gonna be waking up next to twenty-
year-old ballplayers when you're sixty?

                    ANNIE
Well, I used to think that wouldn't be the
worst thing in the world to look forward
to. Lately I'm not so sure.

                    CRASH
Why not?

                    ANNIE
Whatta ya mean "Why not"? Are you gonna
play forever?

Before Crash can answer—

SUDDENLY A VOICE interrupts. They turn to see:
MILLIE EXCITEDLY DRAGS JIMMY into the nearly empty
bar. She leads him by the hand.

                    MILLIE
    Annie, Annie! There she is—we've been
    looking all over for ya! Hi, Crash!

MILLIE LEADS JIMMY right to their table. As they
hold hands, Jimmy stands there shyly.

                    MILLIE
    Well, tell 'em, honey.

                    JIMMY
        (nervously)
    We're getting married.

MILLIE STICKS OUT HER LEFT HAND to display a huge
ring.

                    ANNIE
    Omigod, honey, I'm so happy for you.

                    MILLIE
    He's a virgin.

Jimmy squirms defensively.

                           JIMMY

Well, yeah . . .
          (to Annie and Crash)
I guess that probably seems pretty corny
to people like you.

                           ANNIE

Oh, Jimmy, honey, I think it sounds
wonderful!

                           MILLIE

Annie, will you be the bridesmaid?

                                         CUT TO:

EXT. DURHAM STADIUM—LATER—NIGHT
GAME IN PROGRESS—Nuke on the mound.

Okay, so there it is as scripted, and word for word how it was
shot. It was the critical scene we used in auditioning actresses for
Annie. I can't remember the other scenes we auditioned with but
they likely included one of Annie's "flashy" moments, where she
struts and strides and lays out her worldview, and certainly there
was a scene where she interacts with Nuke and Crash. But this was
really a monologue, almost a stage piece. Crash is there as the straight
man, just asking the questions that the audience might want to ask,
ultimately including himself in the revelation when they each consider the existential question of whether it's possible that baseball isn't
enough anymore.

Actresses seemed to love it. They all came in to audition with
some story about the search for a parent or the void after a personal loss that couldn't be filled or—and this is what unexpectedly
connected—the contemplation that something no longer works in
their lives and the thought of change is frightening. That unstated
thing, it seemed, is that they were actresses in the unforgiving world
of movies, where there are few good parts for a woman of forty while

the men get the leads regardless of age. In addition, of course, the decisions affecting their work were being made by men. So not only was there a part they could embrace, but Annie's journey reflected their own. "Is it possible that acting isn't enough anymore?" was the question that, to me, resonated in the subtext in the room.

Annie was at the heart of the tale, and she was fun. She had the punch lines, she determined her own set of rules, including in the bedroom, and, best of all, she never apologized for anything. If Annie was forty in 1987, when the movie was shot, then she would have been in her twenties in the late sixties and early seventies. In other words, she was a contemporary of mine and a composite of many women, some of them imagined. There was a flight attendant in Rochester who singled out a player each season, and a graduate student in Stockton who circled a college guy every year. I'd also heard stories of a woman who had box seats behind the home dugout for a Double-A team and functioned as a kind of Earth Mother/lover/guardian of the home team. I don't know how true any of the stories were, but it didn't matter. Any forty-year-old in 1987 had lived through the social and civil unrest of the sixties, a time when Eastern philosophy and religion were popularized in the West by people like Alan Watts. The Beatles introduced a wider world to Ravi Shankar, and the whole concept of "world music" began breaking down domestic barriers. Institutions were upended in the social free-for-all. The civil rights movement, Vietnam, birth control pills, UFOs, the moon landing, assassinations, acid—all were going on at the same time and all would have resonance with Annie.

On a kind of parallel track, a number of American institutions chugged along through these years, often oblivious to the sociopolitical chaos around them. Sports were conservative, often with a large *C*. Watching a high school football game or attending a professional NFL game, one felt that not much was changing in the world. Unions were frowned upon in professional sports (until the Baseball Players Association blew up the sports world in 1972) and a kind of divide began to form. Sports stood for competition, and to the political left, competition was an evil symbol of capitalism's exploitive nature. How could you be *for* competitive sports and *against* the war in Vietnam? I was asked the question often when I played. Somehow militarism was equated with competing on a sports field, and being against the war was a sign of pacifism at best or being a communist symp at worst. This absurd cultural divide evolved nonsensically on both sides but the polarization gradually gave way to a more powerful national urgency, the desire to end the war in Vietnam, which ultimately transcended political partisanship.

A handful of critical events shook the sports world out of its myopic cocoon. John Carlos and Tommie Smith's protest at the 1968 Olympics rattled the status quo, followed by the terrorist murders of the Israeli delegation at the Munich Olympics in 1972. Social unrest and political protest invaded the staid world of baseball when the fledgling Major League Baseball Players Association, inspired by Curt Flood's refusal to be traded against his will, challenged the reserve clause that subjected a player to remain under contract to the original team he signed with for his whole career. Owners cried foul, insisting that this would ruin baseball, but history shows it might have saved the game. The other hero of this challenge was Marvin Miller, a labor economist from the Bronx who represented the Players Association and quickly became much despised by ownership and the baseball establishment; Miller was inducted into baseball's Hall of Fame in 2020.

Baseball players began sporting facial hair and Afros, and in 1970, Jim Bouton's seminal book, *Ball Four,* blew up the nostalgic baseball tropes and became an instant classic—though not in the locker room. (As a point of reference, *Ball Four* made *Bull Durham* possible, with its anti-heroic revelations about what really goes on with a baseball team.) By the mid-1970s we were out of Vietnam but the legacy was still with us, along with the sobering reality that many of our heroes were dead—from the Kennedys and MLK by assassins' bullets to the drug-and-booze-addled bodies of Joplin, Hendrix, and Morrison. All this is part of Annie's DNA, and mine, and that of anyone of a certain age who lived through those times and came out the other side intact, even if some of their friends didn't.

While writing the script, I knew that somewhere the question of how Annie found her way to baseball had to be addressed. I didn't know where or when it would occur but it seemed essential to ground her amid all her eccentricities (she would object to that description) or else the audience might write her off as some wacky chick, or worse, an unhinged loony. When I finished the first pass of the scene in which Annie bursts angrily into Crash's room to protest that he is keeping Nuke out of her bed with his strange ideas, Crash responds that the ideas really are hers—and she knows it. The masks come off and it's revealed how desperately they want each other. But we're also reminded that they still can't get out of their own way. Being in your own way is a more formidable obstacle than someone else being there—and they know that, too. I hoped the audience would also know it.

The scene ends with her line "This is the damnedest season I've ever seen—I mean, the Durham Bulls can't lose and I can't get laid!" The line is intended to be funny, but I hoped it would not provoke a big laugh as much as a nervous one. In the shooting, Susan shoved the ironing board to the floor and plopped down in a chair, burying her head in her hands. This was neither scripted nor staged—it just happened, and it felt right. When I'd finished writing the scene, it felt like the perfect time to stop the forward movement in the script (if there was any) and give Annie a chance to share her heart with the only man with whom she's ever wanted to share. He's also the only *man* who's ever showed up to play for the team. The rest are boys.

It seemed clear that the narrative should return to the scene of their meeting at Mitch's Tavern. I hoped that an audience was really wanting to know "Why baseball?" so Crash opens the scene with that question. It's about as on the nose a line as could be imagined at this point, but sometimes it's okay to just ask the obvious question.

Annie launches in immediately and goes right to the heart of her backstory—lost parents, drifting, failed marriages, spiritual experimentation—and by now we know that there was probably experimentation everywhere in her life. Annie doesn't need prompting; she's been waiting for this moment, and so was Susan. I knew we had a terrific scene and that the audience would understand her journey to baseball and how it fit into her ontology.

The scene edited smoothly and seemed the perfect conclusion to the heated melodrama in Crash's boardinghouse. The friendly screenings had gone well, though the movie seemed to slow down slightly in the second half. We'd already lost the payoffs for the ice skaters, Max's funeral, and Deke the shortstop singing the national anthem before a game. Everything else was essential, especially Annie's monologue, since everyone loved it.

Our first official test screening was in February at a theater in Costa Mesa in Orange County, a traditional spot for this. Studio execs, the NRG team, and my editing crew were all present, and the movie played wonderfully except, Leighton and I thought, it seemed to slow down during Annie's speech. The focus group run by NRG didn't reveal much, but the scores off the cards were disappointing. In the sacrosanct "top two categories," meaning "excellent" and "very good," the studios want to score 85 percent or higher. We lodged only a 58 percent, with just 14 percent saying the movie was "excellent." This was depressing and disturbing.

Annie's monologue scene wasn't mentioned in anyone's list of favorite or least favorite scenes, but there was that inescapable feeling that somehow the air leaked out of the balloon here, even though the movie quickly pumps the air back. Bob and I discussed losing the entire scene but there were many protests from associates at the studio, in the marketing department, and just fans of Susan's performance. One pragmatic reason, it was argued, was that the scene ends before Crash and Annie can reconcile because Jimmy and Millie arrive to announce their engagement. As it's only a few pages until they get married on the pitcher's mound at the ballpark, it seemed this was a plot point that couldn't be cut.

We trimmed the scene considerably for our second test screening in March, which was at the Cary Grant Theater on the old MGM lot. Again, the audience laughed where they were supposed to and even in some places where I would have settled for smiles. Again, the numbers were soft. Though marginally better, they were a C grade by NRG and studio standards. The top two categories went up only 3 percent from the first screening. We were distraught and confused. Why was everyone laughing at a movie they didn't like?

We cut the scene entirely and had a small, private screening without the studio's knowledge. The movie sailed. Nobody cared about the plot point of Jimmy and Millie's engagement. Nobody seemed to miss Annie's backstory except me (and later, Susan).

How could audiences relate to her when her unique journey was unknown and unexplained? The answer was simple—they didn't care about what they didn't know. It has been said that a movie is like a hot-air balloon carrying a basket full of narrative information and it's necessary to start throwing the cargo overboard until the balloon takes off. I like that metaphor—but Annie's monologue? The most important scene in the movie? The revelation that leads to the reckoning? Gone, and nobody cared! The hot-air balloon took off and never stopped. There would be one more bizarre test screening to further confuse everyone but, luckily, it would be too late to do anything about it.

So, what did I learn? Other directors, over drinks, all have similar tales. It's always your favorite scene you have to lose. Somehow it gets in the way—it's saying what you've already said or doesn't need saying at all. But there had to be something more, and over the years I've formed a view that seems to stick. The scene is intimate in a way that nothing else has been in the movie up to that point. Annie talks about her loss and her endless search for some kind of meaning and comfort—surely these aren't things she's ever shared with Millie or, God forbid, Nuke. They're probably things she's never shared before in her self-invented role as high priestess of baseball. She reveals that she's had to keep inventing a system that works for her. Baseball is the latest one and has probably lasted longer than the others. When she asks Crash if it's possible that baseball isn't enough anymore, she's not only questioning her own system, she inadvertently reveals that Crash is questioning his own, because he answers, "It's possible."

Each of them is at a crossroads they don't want to face, and it's the presence of the other that provokes the dilemma, or at least the revelation of the dilemma.

But there's something else unspoken going on. In many ways, Annie's system builds in the glories of having a young lover for five months every year, then tutoring him to move on to higher ground, bigger cities, more success. What she doesn't and cannot say is that it is a system that guarantees she'll never have a real and complex, mature relationship. Singing the praises of the young men is a defense mechanism, though an enjoyable one for her. Until now. The Nukes of the world all will go away at season's end, she'll return to her teaching at the junior college, then in spring it all starts again. She's had two failed marriages. It's too risky to try another serious relationship, so she's filled the space with the rituals and poetry of baseball and young lovers. Then Crash comes along and he, too, is fighting to keep alive what he's had and what he loves. Like her, he knows he can't keep playing the young man's game, but he has no idea how to stop doing it. He can't make the leap to a real relationship because he's lived a life of one-night stands. This scene was intended to reveal, without quite saying it, that their life crises are very much alike.

When I said that the scene was too intimate for the story at this point, it's because there were too many other issues to resolve. What do we do with Nuke, who's practically become their son? This is a scene that should and would only happen after Crash and Annie have made love—the revelations are too much. And that's why the air went out of the balloon. The movie was over emotionally at that point, but not narratively, and that lesson's been stuck in my brain as I've written every script since—the importance of revealing the right emotional information in exactly the right place.

I miss the scene. But the movie's better without it.

And for the record, the audiences in Costa Mesa and at the Cary Grant Theater and at every subsequent test screening agreed on their favorite scene in the movie—the meeting at the mound.

17

Those Baptist
Whorehouse Chords

Mediocre test scores had not dampened the enthusiasm of Charles Glenn, Orion's executive vice president in charge of marketing (and former head of worldwide marketing at both Paramount and Universal), who had become an outspoken advocate of the movie from the director's cut onward. In concert with Orion's head of distribution, Joel Resnick; the head of PR, Gale Brounstein; and the advertising division run by Tina Tanen (Ned Tanen's niece) and Mike Kaiser, Glenn declared that we would open in early June and go up against all the big action movies. This is known as "counterprogramming," offering an alternative to everything else in the marketplace. It was the first time I'd ever heard that term, and I thought the strategy was crazy. It was also the first time since filming began that the movie had support from anyone at the studio. There were big-budget movies coming out, and animated features, and all manner of action shoot-'em-ups. I didn't want to go up against any of them, especially with our mediocre test results. But Glenn was insistent. The studio needed something in the early-summer slot, and we were it. Glenn revealed that he had a soft spot for baseball—his uncle Joe had been backup catcher for the New York Yankees—but I hoped a sentimental family connection wasn't driving a suicidal film-release plan.

I was convinced that we needed one more screening when the film was completely finished—with final music, a balanced and color-corrected print from the lab, the music score, all the replaced dialogue and sound effects—to prove to the studio that the test numbers were aberrant, and that the experience audiences seemed to be having in the theater wasn't reflected in the numbers. Medavoy agreed to this, and it energized the editing room to finish the movie.

The music score always presents the same problem. As the movie keeps changing, music cues have to keep changing. Beautiful cues are written to scenes that will ultimately be cut out of the movie, or that are drastically shortened, which renders a cue unusable. The composer is endlessly caught between wanting to finish and wanting to wait until the picture cuts are finalized. The built-in problem is that a picture isn't "locked" (the final picture cut) until so late in the game that there's no time to build a new score. So the composer is forever starting and stopping and reconceiving, as per the director's wishes or—God forbid—somebody's wishes at the studio. Trying to protect the music, the director often doesn't want to reveal the score until the very end because even if it's perfect, there will be somebody at the studio who wants to add more strings, or hire a hot pop songwriter to write a title song. Once in a great while they'll be right about the strings and the pop song, but not often. More likely they'll simply be fixated on whatever is the new incarnation of the hat on the bus. Good test scores are the director's ultimate protection, but we didn't have them. After all, there were people at the studio who still felt that nobody would believe Susan's Annie would end up in bed with Tim's Nuke.

Michael Convertino kept turning in gorgeous music cues. They were *too* gorgeous. I kept replacing them with needle drops. He was delivering on precisely what he was hired to do: create a rich, nuanced underscore that was emotional and, perhaps, slightly melancholic. He did just that, but the movie now seemed happier when it lived in the roadhouses. Piaf would provide the nuanced melancholia; I needed Dave Alvin and the Blasters. And so, through no fault of his own, much of Michael's score hit the cutting-room floor.

I called an old friend and terrific keyboard player, Wayne Peet, and asked if he could deliver a handful of cues for the baseball park's B3 organ, including the national anthem and all sorts of fill-in material. He asked, "You want the cheesy vibe?" I said, "Yes, lots of cheesy vibe." He recorded in his garage studio that night. We laid it into the picture the next day and it never changed.

A music cue for the road trip, the bus winding through the Carolina hills, kept baffling us, and it should have been simple. Every needle drop called too much attention to itself, lyrics seemed too specific, and Convertino's cue was too haunting. Burg knew Jeff "Skunk" Baxter from somewhere—Skunk was a guitarist with Steely Dan and the Doobie Brothers, among others—and we called him to lay out what we wanted. We sent him a clip of the movie and asked if he could do something in twenty-four hours. The next night at midnight, Burg and I drove up to his house in the Hollywood Hills. Baxter played what he'd written and recorded. It was perfect, so we bought it on the spot and it was in the movie the next morning. He was paid in cash.

During the "loop group" session, in which actors come in as a team to supply voices and lines for all the background characters onscreen, a woman named Antoinette Forsyth stood out for her rich Carolina accent. She was the real deal, and I had her record all the ballpark-announcer voiceovers, though I'd never heard a female ballpark announcer before. She added a flavor and a color and an authenticity to the minor league evocation, even though there was nothing authentic about it.

Susan came in and we re-recorded all the voiceovers from "I believe in the Church of Baseball" through the final "You could look it up." We tossed it out and used the original "temporary" recording she'd done in a room next door to Annie's house in Durham. On location, she was dialed into the character more than she could reinvent months later, while she was playing another character in another movie. Kirk Francis's "scratch track" recording was high enough quality to be used in the final mix.

Making the movie was becoming fun again. The studio was leaving us alone (only because there was no time left to do otherwise), and everyone was focused on the April screening of the finished film. The studio decided, with my support, to book this final test screening out of town. Los Angeles is a tough place to test-screen because the audience is skewed and opinionated in advance. It's a company town and many in the audience are in the movie business, or have a sister-in-law who works at Paramount or a parent who got fired by Universal or, in some other way, show up with an agenda. It's certain that half the audience members have a screenplay they can't sell and come to the theater believing they're getting a raw deal and that the undiscovered, dog-eared, potential-Oscar-winning screed in their glove compartment is better than what they're about to see. Orion chose Palo Alto for the big April screening.

Capitol Records agreed to a soundtrack deal very late in the process, thanks to Burg's hustling, and we scrambled to find songs from their catalog that served the movie. In less than a week, with the help of music supervisor Danny Bramson, we added the Fabulous Thunderbirds, the Smithereens, Dave Alvin and the Blasters, George Thorogood, and other bands of that ilk. Bennie Wallace provided "All Night Dance" with Stevie Ray Vaughan and Dr. John, and wrote a short, funky song for the end of the picture that replaced what was in the script, Dave Frishberg's "Van Lingle Mungo." Frishberg's song is on my list of immortals, but it was too melancholic—the lyrics are the names of major league players from his youth, nothing else. Burg somehow landed a new Joe Cocker release, "A Woman Loves a Man," over the end credits. John Fogerty's "Centerfield" wasn't in the Capitol catalog but we bought it anyway and had to move around what limited money remained in the budget in order to buy the Edith Piaf songs, which were hugely expensive. When I signed off on the final cost of the movie, I believe we were ten cents under budget.

In the cutting room, we couldn't settle on a cue for the sequence in which Crash shows his teammates how to flood the field and then surprises them by leading them on a glorious, childlike, mud-splashing run around the bases. Convertino's cue featured an intricate weaving of almost birdlike flutes. Once again, it was too beautiful. Leighton found a lesser-known Los Lobos song, "I Got Loaded," and it fit the scene perfectly. The song's syncopated East L.A. Latin rhythms and the lyrics laid over the syncopated Rain Bird sprinklers celebrated a night of drinking. I broke Michael's heart when I replaced his cue.

Music for the title sequence was elusive because it couldn't interfere with Annie's opening monologue and walk through the leafy neighborhoods to the ballpark. Acoustic instrumentation fought against her speech, and a synthesized underscore just kind of sat there, inert. We brought in Shirley Scott, legendary jazz/bop organist, for a session. Without a plan or a structure, the title sequence was played for her a couple of times, and then she was asked to improvise something that played counterpoint to Annie's speech. Scott was considered nonpareil on the Hammond B3 organ, which linked the ballpark's cheesy vibe to the Church's holy one, and we just got out of her way. One or two takes, and the title sequence was finished.

Only a handful of small music cues remained and we managed to get Dr. John (a.k.a. Mac Rebennack) to a recording studio in L.A. We needed to record him singing and playing "Try a Little Tenderness," as well as record the Bennie Wallace song, and I had an idea for coaxing him to improvise some piano cues. The session was late at night—not an unusual request by some musicians—and after Mac recorded "Tenderness," Bonnie Raitt showed up unannounced, but quite welcome, and they laid down a duet of the song. Whatever version they did is buried in a vault somewhere, but it was memorable.

Finally, we set a TV monitor on a piano, cued up three scenes, and as Mac sat down, I stood over his shoulder:

DR. JOHN: When ya want me to play?
SHELTON: I'll tap you on the shoulder when the right images come up on the monitor. When I tap you again you can just kind of fade it out.
DR. JOHN: Awright, but whatta ya want me to play?
SHELTON: Play some of those Baptist whorehouse chords you always do.
DR. JOHN: Oh yeah. I gotta lotta dem.

18

The Numbers Never Lie

The final production issue on any film is the sound mix, which we did just prior to the big Palo Alto screening. Our budget dictated that it be short and simple, and because of that it was a very effective mix. Mixing engineers and sound technicians are so skilled and the equipment is so advanced that the craft of sound mixing has become a highly sophisticated art. Sometimes it becomes too sophisticated. A mix consists of the balancing of twenty-four separate tracks of sound effects, dialogue (production and reconstituted), music (source and score), Foley (the recording of footsteps, glass breaking, balls hitting bats, and so forth)—and the process can produce a result too subtle and nuanced for its own good.

That is, much of the brilliant work can't ever be heard except in a state-of-the-art theater with state-of-the-art equipment. And then, often, only if you're sitting in, say, Row 10, Seat 6. In addition, a theater full of five hundred people soaks up even more sound, and the mix gets lost further in the crowd. The mix for *Bull Durham* is lean, but the audience can hear everything that matters—the lady PA announcer, the ballpark organ, the ball hitting the bat, the chatter of Robert Wuhl in the dugout. For the scale of this movie, but certainly not for mega-action films, less was more.

With enthusiasm and anticipation, we all flew to Palo Alto. The theater was near Stanford University, and the crowd recruited by NRG was highly educated, professional, well read. The picture looked good and the footage by our four different cinematographers—Minsky, Byrne, Bridges, and the extensive second-unit work of Hillman— all timed out and processed well in the lab to create a consistent look. The bus-interior sequences were precisely what I wanted, and it was hard to imagine anyone had ever protested the look inside the dugouts.

Susan Sarandon looked glorious, as we always thought she did. Audiences had been falling in love with Tim Robbins's Nuke, who embodied an earnest dignity as he emerged from the fog of youth. And Costner? He was the movie star many in the movie business thought he could become. But he was much more than that. He was a terrific actor, and played Crash Davis with humor, intensity, vulnerability, and just the right touch of keeping the lid on his simmering, righteous anger. Robert Wuhl's Larry Hockett was stealing scenes, as I hoped he might when he first came in for the godawful audition. The supporting cast was perfectly balanced, in my mind.

The screening played like a dream. Never had any previous audience responded so expressively and enthusiastically to every line, every tiny throwaway, every obscure reference. Even William Blake got a laugh. It's hard to find audiences who see humor in an argument about a pre-Romantic eighteenth-century British Christian poet hostile to the Church of England. The laughter was often so loud it smothered follow-up lines, which is a great problem for a comedy to have. They loved Nuke, adored Annie, and fell for Crash. I wanted to bottle this audience and take them with me forever.

Then the fucking scores came in. We were back at 58 percent. I wanted to kill the same audience whom moments ago I wanted to put on payroll. I stood with Medavoy as Orion management, including the Unnamed Executive, huddled separately in the lobby. The NRG summary stats calculated from the cards were bewildering— only 16 percent of the audience put the movie in the "excellent" column, and 42 percent thought it was "very good." This was another C grade, and the movie was completed—there was nothing more to fix. Our scores had actually gone down from the previous screening. Suddenly the June release was in jeopardy. Studios have been known to pull movies from their scheduled release dates and postpone them, sometimes indefinitely, or shovel them into the "straight to video" bin. But why were people laughing and where did the spontaneous applause come from? The notes said the movie was paced too slowly and was too long. Too fucking long? The running time was one hour, forty-four minutes, plus end credits. Hadn't they seen *Berlin Alexanderplatz,* for crissakes? Fassbinder released his fifteen-hour masterpiece in two seven-and-a-half-hour screenings—and there aren't a lot of laughs. Did NRG run numbers on Fassbinder? Genius or not, how did he play in Palo Alto?

I was suicidal. Medavoy was merely perplexed. I thought the studio might suggest bringing in another cameraman and shooting some new scenes, as yet unwritten and unconceived, and bring in another actor whose recent movie was "testing through the roof." Or someone would want me to put back the whorehouse scene or Max's funeral or change the whole story to football.

We'd just had a perfect screening and things never looked bleaker. Medavoy didn't even bother conferring with his team, but looked up from the cards and said, "I don't understand these numbers but I know what I saw and heard in that room. We're holding the dates and going out on June seventeenth, as scheduled." I loved Mike for that, and forgave much of the needless grief his studio had caused the production. His experience inside the theater outweighed the statistical analysis.

But where did the low numbers come from and why? I took away a lesson from Palo Alto that has since been proven many times over. The more highly educated the crowd, the more severely critical will be its analysis. Even—maybe especially—when the movie-watching experience is good. It's a mistake to hand a pen and paper to professionals with multiple degrees and ask them to critique their experience. There seems to be a built-in expectation that the brain should overrule the heart, that the left side of the brain must dictate what the right side of the brain just processed—even when it contradicts that experience. The note cards were legible, neatly written, and expressed their critique in absurd detail compared to those of more working-class crowds, which tend to be of the thumbs-up, thumbs-down variety. In the heartland of emerging Silicon Valley—high-tech, the venture-capital center of the nation, with Stanford and all its tentacles of research—the audience had to deny its experience. What I thought of was: *All I want is your reaction, not your fucking self-conscious notes.*

It wasn't so much anger at the anal nature of the response, but frustration over trying to understand the disconnect. Still, NRG said from the beginning that the numbers don't change much from the first screening to the last. I still refused to believe it, even if it was true.

We had promised to have a big premiere in Durham to raise money for the Durham Performing Arts Center, to be held in the enormous, ornate, once-gilded-but-now-run-down theater in town. In spite of it all, I had a fondness for the boarded-up town. A few cast members were there, as were Durham VIPs, the performing-arts crowd, some ballplayers from the movie, and the press.

The film projection wasn't very good, the screen was dark, the sound muddled, but everyone seemed to have a good time. I sat in the extreme upper balcony, not to see how the movie played, but to just watch the spectacle in this old movie palace. When the lights came up at the end of the show, I noticed a small sign on the wall that was faded but legible. It read: COLOREDS ONLY. Clearly it was no longer enforced, but nobody had bothered to cover it up.

The usual party followed, drinks flowed, some money had been raised for a good cause. Robert Wuhl and Billy O'Leary were there, and we had a few cocktails too many. The city seemed grateful for the whole thing and we went to sleep at the hotel late that night, well pleased.

The next morning, we awoke to a scathing review in the local paper.

• • •

Undaunted and out of options, we returned to L.A. for a screening at the Academy of Motion Pictures in lieu of a local premiere, which was fine with me. The Academy respects movies and moviemakers, and projections in the Academy theater are always flawless. There's no red carpet and inane interviews ("What's it like to work with Kevin Costner?") and there's no party, just some chicken-on-a-stick and cheap wine in the lobby. Perfect.

When the film started to screen, I went down the street to the Kate Mantilini restaurant for a few drinks before returning to watch the last five minutes. I didn't need to see the whole thing anymore. I took a seat in the back corner of the theater and was delighted that there was much unforced applause at the end. As the lights came up and I rose, so did a man sitting several rows in front of me. It was the Unnamed Executive. He spotted me and said, grudgingly, "Good job." He then added, because it was his nature, "It still would have been better with Anthony Michael Hall."

The final ritual before the movie opened was the press junket, an industry tradition wherein the various studios whose movies are opening soon invite the press to town for a series of screenings and interviews with the stars (and the director—but it's the stars' interviews that they come for). Orion chose to hold the junket at the Century Plaza, a fancy hotel in Century City near their offices. They held a penthouse suite for the director to stay in for both days (it was the suite where U.S. presidents often stayed), and when I took one look at it I said they should fly Max Patkin out to be part of the press junket and he should stay in the suite. Max was quickly flown out from King of Prussia, Pennsylvania, and was so slack-jawed over his accommodations that he flew his brother out overnight to share the suite. This gave me great pleasure.

The movie was going to open on twelve hundred screens on June 17, in direct competition with *Red Heat* with Arnold Schwarzenegger and *The Great Outdoors* with John Candy and Dan Aykroyd, among others. The bigger threats to suck up all the business were the many expensive summer movies that had just opened or were about to. They included *Big, Die Hard, Coming to America, Cocktail, Midnight Run, Rambo III, Poltergeist III,* and *Who Framed Roger Rabbit.* From our viewpoint, we were jumping into the pool with Tom Hanks, Bruce Willis, Eddie Murphy, Schwarzenegger,

Tom Cruise, Robert De Niro, Sylvester Stallone, and a movie where Bugs Bunny could only earn a cameo. Despite our poor testing scores and the singularly bad review in Durham, we knew that the movie played well in front of an audience, and spirits rose throughout the week as good national reviews started drifting in.

Local newspaper reviews remained terrific on the day we opened, with an occasional naysayer who thought the whole exercise was vulgar. Orion's marketing department remained true believers throughout the uphill climb, and it paid off. The campaign was aimed at minor league outlets and sports media that were normally ignored. I'm not sure how the family-friendly promotional ethic of the minor leagues fit the R rating that the movie deserved, but somehow it worked.

The night we opened, a bunch of us drove around to a variety of theaters all over Los Angeles to stick our heads in the back for a few minutes, just to see how it was playing. A comedy is easy to judge—the audience either laughs or doesn't. And how loud? And why did the 7:00 crowd laugh louder than the 9:30 crowd? And why did some audiences laugh at the smallest lines and nuances and others only at the most surefire moments? Would Nuke's opening scene with his pants around his ankles cause people to walk out? The walkouts were few, though each stuck like a knife. The urge to corral the walkouts in the lobby and reason with them had to be resisted.

On its opening weekend, the movie grossed a touch over $5 million, which put it in fifth place but not far behind the number one new movie, *Red Heat*. The shocker was that the grosses went up for the second weekend, and the third. That's extremely rare. By the end of the fourth week, *Bull Durham* had earned close to $30 million domestically and was on its way to chugging along all summer. The movie stayed in release for twenty-eight weeks and grossed a bit over $50 million in the United States, the equivalent of about $120 million today. The main thing wasn't the money—it was that I knew I would work again.

The reviews were terrific—except for the guy in Durham—but

two particular responses stuck with me then and now. First, a message on my phone from Bill Kirkpatrick, a tough pitcher and teammate from the minors I hadn't talked to in years. The message was simple: "Shelly. Willy K. Great fuckin' flick. Bye." I had the guys on the bus. The other review happened when I was having dinner at the Imperial Gardens on Sunset, a Japanese restaurant in the building that was once Preston Sturges's Players restaurant. A finger tapped my shoulder and said there was a man who wanted to meet me. I was led (the tapping finger turned out to belong to Stanley Donen) to the table of his friend and dinner companion Billy Wilder. The brilliant director just said, "Great picture, kid." That was the only occasion I ever met him other than the time, a few years later, when he made a wild, sweeping, utterly illegal left turn on Wilshire Boulevard and almost hit me.

Anybody who loves baseball must also love, to some degree, the numbers that the game generates. Everything is reduced to a statistical record or probability. In the era of sabermetrics and analytics, the search for truth in numbers has never been greater. It might even be argued baseball analytics are out of control. But they never lie.

I'm still not sure about the sabermetrics of movies, however, and so I called one of the most experienced film-screening research men in the movie business, a man who worked with NRG, among others, and asked him to retrieve the test screening numbers for *Bull Durham,* my source for this book.

> TEST SCREENING EXPERT: I'm very surprised how low your numbers were.
>
> SHELTON: As bad as I remember.
>
> TEST SCREENING EXPERT: Only sixteen percent of the audience would "definitely recommend" the movie.
>
> SHELTON: And yet the movie was a hit, so the numbers were wrong.
>
> TEST SCREENING EXPERT: The numbers are never wrong.
>
> SHELTON: How do you explain the movie's success?

TEST SCREENING EXPERT: You had great marketing.

SHELTON: How does that explain the grosses going up for two consecutive weeks after the opening?

TEST SCREENING EXPERT: You had great word of mouth.

SHELTON: From the sixteen percent?

It doesn't matter. The research can still tell you a lot, but sometimes the numbers do lie.

19

Why Baseball?

The movie had exorcised whatever issues I had with walking away from baseball, and I became a fan again. Articles began appearing that discussed the movie from a Christian perspective, in one case, and an Oedipal one in another—Nuke as Oedipus and Annie as Jocasta. I didn't see that coming. But it raises the question that Crash asked Annie in Mitch's Tavern in the scene no longer in the movie. *Why baseball?*

Boxing has traditionally inspired the best writing of any sport. The attraction to the sport seems clear—boxing is primal and universal. Two nearly naked men try to beat each other up. The rules are simple. But baseball also has attracted writers, intellectuals, and statistical analysts in a shared fervor that seems bigger than the fact that everyone played Little League. Why baseball? The rules aren't simple and are endlessly fought over, and the slightest revision of a rule causes outrage and uproar. It's easier to amend the U.S. Constitution.

The infield-fly rule is a poetry killer, but somehow Walt Whitman found his way to the game, not to mention poets from Rolfe Humphries to Donald Hall to Marianne Moore. Halberstam, Updike, Talese, Cramer—the best American writers all wrote about our national pastime, even if it was no longer so. Baseball even has a part to play in Scott Fitzgerald's masterpiece, *The Great Gatsby.* Roger Angell is the dean of baseball writers and Roger Kahn wrote a masterwork, *The Boys of Summer,* though Kahn loathed Jim Bouton's great *Ball Four.* The late Stephen Jay Gould, Harvard evolutionary biologist, sabremetrician, and baseball fan, had an original take on the game. He was also a defender of Bill Buckner and allowed me to meet him in his office once when I made a documentary in defense of the great hitter. It was the only way I ever could have gotten onto the Harvard campus.

But my interest in baseball isn't analytical, romantic, or even patriotic. I like the game—it's nuanced and difficult and physical— but it has an appealing vulgarity, an earthiness, and I've never quite understood the excessive lyrical prose that grows out of it. I've never understood the sentimentality it seems to inspire. Annie reminds us that baseball may be full of magic and deep truths, but it's still a job.

It's a game built around conversation, dependent on the verbal, ripe for storytelling. Baseball may be the only game where players on opposing teams exchange casual conversation between plays that at one moment are dormant but quickly explode at speeds in excess of one hundred miles per hour, only to quickly slow back down so that conversation can continue. The shortstop chats with the runner on second base—his opponent—because they want to resolve an argument in the dugout about where the local college girls hang out. Opposing players share this information as a professional courtesy. When a player asks another on the opposite team, "How's it going?" he isn't referring to the man's personal life, marriage, kids—he's referring to how he's hitting or pitching.

The game goes late into the night. There's no clock—that's the big one, of course; every other sport has one. And we play tomorrow and tomorrow and tomorrow. Professional football plays 17 games now. Baseball plays 162. Baseball is not like life, as people love to say, but it has rhythms that linger.

What do I remember from playing the game?

As an eleven-year old I remember pitching to Jerry Georges with a 2–0 lead and a 3-2 count with the bases loaded in the last inning of the Midget League Championship in Laguna Park. Jerry hit a lazy fly ball to the left fielder, Henry Favro, who dropped it. Three runs scored and we lost. I remember Sal Aparicio, our third baseman, chasing Henry out of the park on his bike. I remember the next day the paper said that Jerry Georges doubled in three runs to win the game. It was a goddamn error, not a double. Who wrote that?

I remember my family never again shopped at Kittler Hardware on Milpas Street, which Henry's parents owned. I remember ten years later Jerry, by then a U.S. Marine, stepped on a land mine in Quang Tri Province, Vietnam, and didn't come home.

I remember a high school playoff game where the catcher for Notre Dame High School, our opponent, hit a line drive so hard that when I jumped for it, the ball hit in the webbing of my glove and ripped it into left field. I remember we lost, 3–0, and that the catcher, Greg Goossen, was drafted number one by the New York Mets. He was later the subject of a famous observation by Casey Stengel when, at spring training, Goossen was hitting line drives all over the park. A sportswriter asked Stengel what he thought of his young phenom, and Stengel said, "Well, he's only twenty but in ten years he has a chance to be thirty."

I remember misplaying a ground ball at shortstop in a college playoff game that cost us a chance to advance. I should have charged harder, or laid back a bit more. It wasn't that tough of a play.

I remember the tipped pitch in El Paso I should have swung at. It's still hanging there like a big juicy piece of fruit from a tree, waiting to be plucked. A few years ago, I flew to El Paso to watch a boxing match between Angel Manfredy and Diego Corrales. I had money on Manfredy, and predictably, he got knocked out in the third round. But I went looking for the old ballpark, where I expected that hanging curveball to still be there, still hanging, lit up like a neon piñata, waiting for my return. The ballpark had been leveled and then rebuilt in a "better" neighborhood, someone said.

We remember our failures and our losses. Why that is so is something I'll probably never understand, which makes it something to write about. It also makes it ripe for humor. Tennessee Williams's log line of *Bull Durham* might have been: "Aging warrior athlete (unlucky or delusional) meets aging English teacher who has worshipped everything in her lifetime and is now fixated on a young man half her age (explaining to herself that she's giving him life wisdom when in fact it's just about sex)"—sounds like a tragedy set in the New Orleans backwaters surrounding old Pelican Stadium. I went for the laughs.

Perhaps *Bull Durham* has resonated all these years because it is about loving something more than it loves you back. It's about reckoning. It's about loss. It's about men at work, trying to survive in the remote outposts of their chosen profession. It's also about the women they fall for, and who fall for them. It cannot be dismissed that it's also about the joy of playing a game for a living. It's about team and connections and risk and reward. It's about hitting the mascot with a fastball just because you want to, it's about running and jumping and sliding around in the mud, it's about interminable bus rides with a bunch of guys who are as lost as you are, and feeling lucky you're on that bus.

It's romantic, and it's supposed to be funny, and despite what most fans of the movie say, it is also about baseball.

Afterword

Six months after *Bull Durham* left the theaters, finishing its U.S. run (the studios were right—it never did much foreign business), I was in Louisiana, prepping my next movie, *Blaze,* when the screenplay was nominated for an Oscar. I flew to L.A. with Armin Ganz, who was now working on *Blaze* and was up for an Oscar as well, for set decoration on *Tucker.* The screenplay for *Bull Durham* was heavily favored, having won most of the other awards, but when the limo ordered by the studio failed to show up (I blamed the Unnamed Executive), I figured it wasn't my night. After managing to make it to the Shrine Auditorium for the ceremony, which opened with the infamous Rob-Lowe-dancing-with-Snow-White sequence, I tore up my speech. The problem with the Original Screenplay category is that it comes up right away, and when your name isn't called, you really do want to get out of there, but the whole show is in front of you. The award went to *Rain Man.*

Armin and I ended up at the Governors Ball, which was known, I discovered, as the "losers' party"—the winners were at Spago or some fancy place in Beverly Hills. On the 6 a.m. flight back the next day, Armin (who also hadn't won), leaned over and said, "That's a long way to go for a piece of fucking chicken." When we got back to Louisiana, we learned that Trey Wilson, on the eve of flying to New Orleans to star in the Coen brothers' new movie, *Miller's Crossing,* had died suddenly of a cerebral hemorrhage. He was forty.

The movie was credited with sparking a renaissance of the minor leagues, and for many years attendance rose, new ballparks were built, and towns and cities across the country embraced team nicknames indigenous to the region. The Albuquerque Isotopes, Amarillo Sod Poodles, and Lansing Lugnuts are among the scores of nongeneric team names that burst onto the baseball scene. Alas, MLB owners are cutting back on their investment in the minors and over forty franchises have recently been eliminated; once again, the organization doesn't understand.

I wrote and published an essay about Steve Dalkowski shortly after the movie opened, and started laying plans for another baseball movie—this one about a pitcher for the Yankees who ends up in the Latin American leagues. It's still not made.

While I was writing this book, both Steve Dalkowski and Joe Altobelli died, within a year of each other. Joe came to the stadium in Rochester in 2017, when I was graciously ushered into the Rochester Red Wings Hall of Fame (I had more hits after leaving Rochester, a sportswriter accurately reported). Joe was in a wheelchair and soon in a rest home, but I was glad to see him. I was honored with a bobblehead doll, which genuinely moved me. I have two boxes of them in my garage and was recently told, by someone who tracks these things, "It's holding steady on eBay." I'm not entirely sure what that means.

Since *Bull Durham* was made, Mark Burg has become a very successful TV and movie producer, Charles Minsky has a built a long résumé as a DP, and Anthony Michael Hall has more than one hundred TV and movie credits, one of which includes playing Whitey Ford in *61**, a movie about Mantle and Maris chasing Babe Ruth's home-run record.

Thom Mount continues to develop and produce independent films and streaming television and to build companies outside the entertainment business. We remain in touch about things related to *Bull Durham.*

Bob Leighton became one of Hollywood's top editors. It didn't matter that he'd never been to a baseball game.

David Lester, whom I always felt had been hired to ride herd on me, became a friend, colleague, and my go-to line producer. He wasn't just a man moving equipment and juggling schedules. He was a filmmaker.

In recent years, I was approached by Broadway producers Jack Viertel, Laura Stanczyk, and Rick Steiner to develop *Bull Durham* as a musical. It was gratifying and inspiring to work with Broadway talent and the process was very different from moviemaking. But the same story issues were there to be resolved. The trick in writing the musical book was simply that structurally and by precedent, the first two acts of a movie screenplay become the first act of a musical book. The third act of the movie becomes the second and final act of the musical. As noted, however, the movie doesn't have a third act; this created some narrative obstacles to which we devoted a number of theater workshops to address. We solved the structural book problems after numerous live cast labs, and an out-of-town run in Atlanta, and we all got significantly smashed the night Steiner announced we were fully financed. Susan Werner's original and raucous roadhouse score provided a perfect musical reinvention of the movie for the stage, and we had Marc Bruni to direct, coming straight off his hit show about Carole King, *Beautiful.* Shortly thereafter, when discussions with theaters were under way, lead producing partner Rick Steiner died unexpectedly, shortly after heart surgery. His passing was a great personal loss to all of us who worked with him. With his death, the show lost a significant financial commitment, and before things could be put back together, the pandemic hit. The show is currently in purgatory, or the bullpen.

There was talk of a movie sequel but it never happened, which was fine with me, though I did work out a setup for how to revisit these people. It wouldn't have worked, however, because the tale was told, the fable ended. In order to create a new set of tensions, Crash and Annie would have to be separated, and that's a lousy way to get sympathy from the audience at the beginning of a story.

For the record, and so it never needs further discussion, the sequel plot outline went something like this: Crash and Annie couldn't figure out how to make their lives work together as he's always on the road as a minor league manager and she is anything but a tagalong support system, so they go their separate ways. Of course, the torch still burns in each of them for the other. Annie ends up teaching at the Sorbonne University in Paris as a PhD and world-renowned expert on Edith Piaf. Annie's specialty? Her writings about Piaf's one great love, French boxing champion Marcel Cerdan, who died in a plane crash flying to New York for a championship fight. Annie falls for a major French director and thinks she's in love with him, but . . . she returns for a year to teach at Duke University. Durham has become a Triple-A baseball town, so that instead of being the doorway to oblivion, it's now the doorway to the Show. Crash is promoted from an obscure minor league town to Durham, which now represents something very different for him—hope rather than despair. In the meantime, Larry Hockett has given up on his dream to become a major league pitching coach and is now a scout, scouring the hinterlands to discover talent. This has led him to Venezuela, where he finds Nuke LaLoosh trying to learn a knuckleball at the age of thirty-five (Crash's age in the original movie). Nuke, we learn, had an up-and-down big league career with flashes of brilliance but, without the mentorship of an Annie or a Crash, he crashed and burned. But he's determined to get back to the Show, and if Venezuela is the way back, so be it. Larry is so impressed, and happy to find Nuke, that he convinces his major league boss to give Nuke another chance. Nuke signs a contract and is assigned, of course, to the AAA Durham team—where Crash has just taken over as manager and Annie, not suspecting any of this, has landed in town. Soon, everyone's paths will cross and, as Yogi said, "It's déjà vu all over again." And then the French director shows up to visit his great love, Annie. Like I say, it's too late for all this. The story's over.

Kevin Costner and I made another sports movie (co-written with John Norville) eight years later—*Tin Cup*—which was very successful critically and commercially. His performance in that movie, his portrayal of Roy "Tin Cup" McAvoy, is a comic gem and underrated—most comedic performances are under-recognized. The character could be seen as Nuke at forty, which would mean Kevin has played both Crash and Nuke.

I became the godfather to Tim and Susan's firstborn, Jack Henry, and stay in touch with both, though they're not together anymore. The godfather ceremony was in the Hollywood Hills and was memorable. I was one of three anointed godfathers—the others were Robert Altman and Gore Vidal—and none of us was up to the task, which was, we were told during the ceremony, to "nourish the spiritual growth of the child." The ceremony was half Roman Catholic and half Druid, but mostly the latter.

Tim, besides writing, acting, and directing, has been active in a program putting theater in California state prisons, working with men doing life without parole. Susan works all the time and texted recently that we should do another movie together. I'm all for that. And Kevin and I continue to circle projects to do together, occasionally playing golf or having breakfast to bat ideas around.

Sometime after *Bull Durham* was released, a process server showed up in my office to deliver a lawsuit to me. I was accused of having stolen the idea for *Bull Durham* from another writer, the man whose chief credit was *Herbie, the Love Bug*, a Disney movie about a talking Volkswagen. Absurd as this sounds, it was a primer in the legal system for me. Although this writer's script was never submitted to Orion Pictures, and it was registered (copyrighted) with the Writers Guild well after my script was financed by Orion, the lawsuit was allowed to play out slowly. I was forced to hire a pricey attorney, who, finally, over the course of eighteen months, got the charges dismissed. It became clear why it is often cheaper to settle spurious lawsuits than to fight them. Pablo Picasso is frequently quoted as having said, "Good artists borrow, great artists steal." But they don't steal from *Herbie, the Love Bug*.

Orion Pictures, despite a strong run of successful movies, was forced to close its doors in the early nineties. I was told that the reason was they could never overcome the debt-service issues caused by starting a studio from scratch—but I'm not an expert on this subject. Despite my battles with them, it was a good place to work, and I still do business with Mike Medavoy, whom I consider a friend. He denies he ever wanted to fire me, and admits he was wrong about Tim Robbins. MGM purchased Orion Pictures in 1997, and with the purchase came Orion's entire catalog of nearly four hundred movies, including *Bull Durham.* Two years ago, the MGM television division decided to develop a TV series based on my movie. Without me.

Thus far, their efforts have come to nothing, and my representatives regularly raise hell with the TV people there, in the hopes that the threat of public embarrassment might dissuade them. This is not a business where people embarrass easily. There is a reason people who make movies walk around angry.

White Men Can't Jump, which I wrote, directed, and coproduced four years after *Bull Durham* and was a bigger commercial success, is being remade by a writer-producer I don't know. I called my agents to protest. They confessed that not only was it true, but they had packaged the remake idea and represented the filmmaker. Welcome to the movie business. It may be betrayal, but it's betrayal within *industry standards.*

I went online to look up what happened to the Unnamed Executive since his days at Orion Pictures. He went on to have a number of vice-president-of-production titles at various companies, started a couple of his own, and seems to have thrived. He is now the CEO of something.

I sometimes get the impression that because of my movies, people think I'm obsessed with sports in general, or baseball in particular. I'm not obsessed in any way. The sounds of sports may be just the thing that can take our minds off the serious, existential crises we're facing, or can give us common cause to join together and recognize our mutual needs. Then again, it could just be the latest sounds of Nero fiddling.

A couple of years after the movie came out, I was in the lobby of a hotel in New York when I realized that the man standing in an overcoat with scarf, next to his neatly dressed wife, was Mickey Mantle. Luggage sat next to them, and the doorman was clearly keeping them informed about the impending arrival of their town car. Mantle looked old, like the men in the photos of Sitting Bull and the Great Plains Indian chiefs. He was short, fit, still powerfully built. He and his wife stood in silence. I started to go up and engage him because I'd been told by numerous people that he'd been on a talk show when the movie came out, and when asked what he thought of it, he said, "It's sad because the man in the movie hit so many home runs and never got a chance in the big leagues." Mantle thought *Bull Durham* was sad; that struck me and moved me in a way I didn't expect. Yes, we all know that humor is based on pain and it's a cathartic response to all human suffering. I wanted to talk with him, maybe invite him for a drink somewhere, though I'd heard he was cutting back. Like staring at Eddie Mathews as he smoked and sweated in the Durham Bulls dugout before I ever wrote the screenplay, I couldn't do it. I just stayed back and watched as finally the town car arrived and he and his wife climbed in and drove away.

A Note About the Author

Ron Shelton wrote and directed *Bull Durham*, which *Sports Illustrated* called the best sports movie of all time. He won the Best Original Screenplay award from the Writers Guild of America and the Best Screenplay award from the New York Film Critics Circle, the National Society of Film Critics, and the Los Angeles Film Critics Association, as well as being nominated for an Academy Award for Best Original Screenplay. *Bull Durham* launched a writing-directing career that includes *White Men Can't Jump, Blaze, Cobb,* and *Tin Cup*. He also directed "Jordan Rides the Bus," a documentary about Michael Jordan's year in the minor leagues, for ESPN's *30 for 30* series. He is currently working on a television project called *Wicked, Kansas,* a post–Civil War Western. A former professional baseball player, he holds degrees from Westmont College and the University of Arizona. He currently lives in Los Angeles with his family.